D1474332

# THE
# LAND WAR
# IN IRELAND

# THE
# LAND WAR
# IN IRELAND

## Famine, philanthropy
## and moonlighting

Laurence M. Geary

CORK **c**u**p** UNIVERSITY PRESS

First published in 2023 by
Cork University Press
Boole Library
University College Cork
Cork T12 ND89
Ireland

Library of Congress Control Number: 2023932109
Distribution in the USA Longleaf Services, Chapel Hill, NC, USA.

British Library Cataloguing in Publication Data
A CIP catalogue record for this book is available from the British
Library.

ISBN 9781782055525
Printed by BZ Graf in Poland
Design and typesetting by Alison Burns at Studio 10 Design, Cork
Cover image: 'The Little Green Fields' by Gerard Dillon, © Gerard
Dillon Estate. Photo © National Gallery of Ireland

www.corkuniversitypress.com

# CONTENTS

*To Sheelagh McCormack*

# List of Figures and Maps

# LIST OF ABBREVIATIONS

| | |
|---|---|
| DDA | Dublin Diocesan Archives |
| DMP | Dublin Metropolitan Police |
| ER | East Riding, Cork |
| HC | House of Commons |
| HC Deb | Hansard's Parliamentary Debates |
| IG | Inspector General |
| INL | Irish National League |
| IRB | Irish Republican Brotherhood |
| JP | Justice of the Peace |
| LGB | Local Government Board for Ireland |
| MP | Member of Parliament |
| NAI | National Archives of Ireland, Dublin |
| NAI, CBS | Crime Branch Special Papers |
| NAI, CO | Colonial Office Papers |
| NAI, CRF | Criminal Reference Files |
| NAI, CSORP | Chief Secretary's Office, Registered Papers |
| NAI, GPB/PEN | General Prisons Board, Penal Files |
| NLI | National Library of Ireland, Dublin |
| PPP Act | Protection of Person and Property (Ireland) Act, 1881 |
| RIC | Royal Irish Constabulary |
| WHO | World Health Organization |
| WR | West Riding, Cork |

# Acknowledgements

My primary debt is to Ciara Breathnach for her careful reading of the text; her apposite and astute comments and suggestions saved me from numerous solecisms. I am solely responsible for any remaining errors or blemishes.

I wish to acknowledge the archival and library staff of the following institutions: University College Cork; the National Library of Ireland; the National Archives of Ireland, particularly Brian Donnelly; Dublin City Library & Archive; Noelle Dowling, Dublin Diocesan Archives, Holy Cross College, Dublin; Bryan Whelan, RCB Library, Church of Ireland, Dublin; Niamh O'Brien, National Gallery of Ireland; Scotia Ashley and Emily Witt, National Library of Australia, Canberra; Aedín Ní Bhróithe Clements, Irish Studies Librarian and Curator of Irish Studies Collections, University of Notre Dame, Indiana, USA.

Maeve Barry, Brian Casey, Maura Cronin, John Crowley, Emily Mark Fitzgerald, James Harte, Stephanie James, Catherine Jennings and Mike Murphy have facilitated this project in various ways, and I am grateful for their assistance.

A version of Chapter 2, entitled 'The Australasian Response to the Irish Crisis, 1879-80', appeared in Oliver MacDonagh and W.F. Mandle (eds), *Irish-Australian Studies: Papers delivered at the fifth Irish-Australian conference* (Canberra: ANU Press, 1989), pp. 99-126.

I acknowledge and am grateful for permission to reproduce © material from:

*Ireland's New Worlds: Immigrants, politics and society in the United States and Australia, 1815-1922* by Malcolm Campbell. Reprinted by permission of the University of Wisconsin Press. © 2008 by the Board of Regents of the University of Wisconsin System. All rights reserved.

*A Greater Ireland: The Land League and transatlantic nationalism in Gilded Age America* by Ely M. Janis. Reprinted by permission of the University of Wisconsin Press. © 2015 by the Board of Regents of the University of Wisconsin System. All rights reserved.

Maura Cronin, *Agrarian Protest in Ireland, 1750–1960*, Studies in Irish Economic and Social History, vol. 11. Reprinted by permission of Irish Economic and Social History Society. © 2012.

I wish to thank the editorial board of Cork University Press for supporting this project, and particularly to acknowledge the professionalism and expertise of publications director Mike Collins and editor Maria O'Donovan.

My remaining debts are to Sheelagh McCormack for her forbearance and unremitting encouragement and to Brian Geary for filial and technological support.

**Laurence Geary**
Ballyvaughan, County Clare
June 2022

# INTRODUCTION

This book is primarily concerned with perceived lacunae in the historiography of the Land War in late nineteenth-century Ireland, particularly deficiencies or omissions relating to the themes of the title: famine, philanthropy, and Moonlighting or Whiteboyism – the generic nomenclature that the Irish administration and the Irish people generally applied to the agrarianism of secret societies.[1] Despite their apparent randomness, the topics were linked by cause and effect, which enabled coherence in the volume's structure and narrative. The recurrence of famine in Ireland in the final quarter of the nineteenth century, with memories of the traumatic Great Famine of the 1840s still fresh, prompted reactions that were the inverse of one another, and social class was the key to unlocking these conflicting or opposing forces. The humanitarian response to the famine that afflicted the country in 1879–80 was essentially the prerogative of the wealthier sectors of society, individuals with sufficient time and resources to engage with and support the relief effort. The other reaction to the severe food and clothing shortages came from 'below' and was more inchoate, a protest on behalf of the disadvantaged and distressed by those who occupied the same broad social stratum and whose economic circumstances were only marginally better. Their concern for the welfare of the starving and the vulnerable, those whom the land and its produce had temporarily failed, was not so much the antithesis of altruism and beneficence, as a different, more rudimentary way of expressing it.

This attempt to redress historical and historiographical hiatuses in the Land War drama is collated in a series of linked analytical essays rather than structured as a continuous narrative. The book's opening chapter introduces the famine that threatened and subsequently scarred Ireland's Atlantic seaboard counties in the late 1870s and early 1880s, focusing particularly on the fever epidemic that the famine unleashed; the substandard, unhealthy living and social conditions in the west of Ireland that food and clothing shortages exposed; and the political implications of the famine for successive Conservative and Liberal governments and for the burgeoning Irish nationalist opposition under youthful and progressive leadership.[2] The chapters that follow develop the famine theme – from occurrence to remedial interventions – concentrating on the role of civic and religious famine relief agencies, and the local and international humanitarian response to appeals for assistance – in effect, the processes by which famine consciousness and consciences were awakened, purses opened, and food and clothing garnered and distributed among the hungry, the needy and the sick. The 1879–80 famine inspired and encouraged benevolence among the diasporic Irish and the charitable worldwide, but it also provoked a more primal reaction, and the book's two closing chapters are devoted to the activities and machinations of secret societies. The first of these is a case study featuring the incongruously named Royal Irish Republic, a neo-Fenian combination centred on Millstreet in north-west Cork which was treacherously undone by its insouciant second-in-command, Daniel Connell. The volume's concluding essay links history and literature, positing a connection between agrarian secret society activity during the Land War years and the Kerry playwright George Fitzmaurice's overlooked and seldom performed 1914 drama *The Moonlighter*.

Land, its ownership and occupancy, in both the legal and moral sense, is regarded by historians and other scholars as one of Ireland's key political and social dynamics, a defining feature of the country's history in the early modern and modern periods.[3] The centenary in 1979 of the Irish National Land League – usually known by its diminutive form, the Land League – and the commencement of the Land War, stimulated scholarship and debate on Irish land questions, and generated several classics of Irish historiography. Young or emerging scholars from a variety of academic disciplines and backgrounds, many of whom were not Irish or were based in overseas academies, infused discussion and text with energy and direction and challenged orthodox analyses – the traditional narratives and nationalist interpretations that held sway until the final third of the twentieth century.[4]

In an engaging survey of Ireland's land questions during the long nineteenth century, Gearóid Ó Tuathaigh describes the Land League and the Land War as 'the most formidable, popular social movement in modern Irish history'.[5] The Land War, whether confined to its first and most intense phase between 1879 and 1882 – the classic Land League period – or defined more broadly as the recurring episodes of agrarian agitation that extended into the opening decades of the twentieth century, continues to hold a seemingly ineluctable appeal for scholars, as Ó Tuathaigh implies. This interest and focus broadened the parameters of inquiry and explication, from a simple nationalist narrative decrying predatory landlordism to increasingly sophisticated and wide-ranging analyses. Historians of various hues and persuasions, political and social scientists and other scholars have provided theoretical frameworks and perspectives on different aspects of land ownership and the landlord–tenant relationship in Ireland, including the dynamics of agrarian unrest; mass mobilisation and modernity; the nexus between agrarianism and politics; and the origins of the Land War itself, which was not a war in any conventional sense, but a socio-economic revolution that dislodged the centuries-old system of landlordism in Ireland and resulted in the transference of ownership to the occupying tenant farmers. The Land War derived much of its momentum from the evolving political landscape of the late nineteenth and early twentieth centuries, particularly the confluence of constitutional and republican ideologies in the New Departure policy of the late 1870s, and the emergence of that new dynamic, Parnellism – the political force and aura emanating from the charismatic Charles Stewart Parnell.[6]

Academic questing and questioning over the past fifty years and more may have provided scholars of the post-Famine Irish land system with fresh insights and interpretations, but their fossicking and sifting did not seriously challenge or supplant the standard chronology and template of the Land War itself. The consensus among traditionalists and revisionists alike is that post-Famine Ireland experienced rapid economic and social change, and farmers, despite occasional turbulence, enjoyed a quarter century of improvement and stability, a period in which agriculture flourished, production and prices increased significantly, and rent inflation was moderate. Agricultural prosperity was largely responsible for substantial amelioration in living standards and in the quality of Irish rural life, notably in housing, diet, education, communications and transport. In the late 1870s, however, the country encountered a series of internal and external shocks that threatened to arrest post-Famine economic and social progress. Beginning in 1877, recurring seasons of unusually wet and cold weather precipitated a disastrous collapse in agricultural production and prices in both the tillage and livestock sectors, while a corresponding depression in Britain, agricultural competition from the United States and Canada, a shortage of money and credit at home, and curtailed emigration – the country's traditional pressure-defusing mechanism – exacerbated the situation. This compound of local and international difficulties engendered famine and associated life-threatening diseases, confronted Irish farmers and agricultural labourers, particularly along the Atlantic seaboard and hinterland, with the loss of traditional livelihoods, threatened them with bankruptcy and eviction, and shaped the environment for the agrarian and political radicalism that emerged at the end of the decade.[7]

The Land War that agricultural recession and a downturn in economic activity ignited in late nineteenth-century Ireland was always more than an instinctive reaction to adverse economic conditions. The leading advocates of the agitation made no secret of the fact that their actions had a political as well as an agrarian dimension, that their ultimate objective was Irish self-government – the establishment of a home rule parliament in Dublin or an independent republic, depending on the political ideologies and perspectives of the various participants – and that land agitation was a key dynamic in bringing their political ambition to fruition, an indication and a reminder of the strong link historically between land and nationalism in Ireland.

The north-west, west and south-west, Ireland's Atlantic coastal regions, which were characterised by tiny landholdings and insecurity of tenure, and where vulnerable tenants and agricultural labourers eked out a living by means of subsistence farming, fishing and seasonal work in the more prosperous parts of Ireland and in Britain, were challenged by the socio-economic crisis of the late 1870s earlier and more fundamentally than the more fertile and better-resourced midlands, east and south of the country. County Mayo in the north-west became the epicentre of Ireland's communal response to its economic and social difficulties, the birthplace and heartbeat of an agrarian agitation that found expression, structure and coordination in the National Land League of Mayo, which Michael Davitt, a Fenian on ticket of leave from an English prison, established in mid-August 1879, and converted two months later, on 21 October, into the Irish National Land League, with Charles Stewart Parnell as president. The organisation's immediate aim was to secure rent reductions for tenant farmers and to prevent evictions; its ultimate ambition was tenant proprietorship, to convert the occupiers into owners of their holdings. According to historian Paul Bew, the Land League incorporated 'open agrarian agitation, parliamentary action, and revolutionary conspiracy', and was thus 'a genuinely novel political form'.[8]

There was a discernible class element to the agrarian advocacy and protest that ensued, and social class as a dynamic was one of the topics that featured prominently in earlier scholarly debates on the Land War.[9] The Land League and its objectives appealed primarily to middling and strong farmers in the more prosperous and resilient parts of the country, individuals who had most to gain from a successful campaign against landlordism. The participation of middle-class farmers in the unfolding struggle for land demonstrated that they were more concerned with protecting and advancing their own interests than in resolving the plight of those who were more exposed, insecure and disadvantaged than themselves. The subsistence farmers of the west and non-inheriting farmers' sons and agricultural labourers throughout the country, whose prospects in Ireland were limited even at the best of times, were drawn to a more primitive type of protest, an agrarianism that expressed its opposition to landlords, land grabbers, exploitative farmers and evictions through the intimidation and violence of traditional oath-bound secretive societies, whose redresser activities and methodologies were generically, and often indiscriminately, classified as Ribbonism or Whiteboyism. The disjunction between the two types of associative response to Ireland's economic and social difficulties in the late 1870s – the Land League and its advocacy of moral force and constitutional processes, and the pervasive agrarian lawlessness prompted and orchestrated by clandestine organisations – was not rigid or irreconcilable, and overlapping membership and loyalties often made it difficult to demarcate between the different protesting forces at local level.

Over the past decade several significant scholarly works have enhanced our knowledge and understanding of the dynamics and structures of secret societies, at local, regional and national level, extending even to these organisations' international reach and dimensions.[10] Margaret Kelleher and Breandán Mac Suibhne, in their studies of the Maamtrasna murders on the Mayo–Galway borderlands in August 1882 and Ribbonism in west Donegal respectively, reveal the complexities of relationships and life generally in post-Famine rural Ireland – family feuds, animosities among neighbours, and trade disputes, often trivial in origin and nature, but with enduring legacies. These cleavages and dissensions were entangled with abstract concepts of pride and status and with the deadly reality of power and possession, and were prompted, among other agencies, by competition for land and grazing rights, rivalries between small farmers, disputes among their larger brethren, and exploitation of the poor and vulnerable by the rural and urban bourgeoisie, who were often linked by blood, commerce and credit.[11] Kelleher contends that the notoriety and enduring potency of the Maamtrasna murders derives from 'their origin in deep animosity among neighbours, fuelled by familial feuds, and ending in a series of brutal killings'. The murders are explicable less by predatory landlordism, she maintains, than by rivalries between small farmers whose economic circumstances were improving – although the extent of any such amelioration is debatable – and by intimidation exerted by an emerging strong farmer class against those who were weaker than themselves.[12]

The vulnerable in Irish society, those exposed to the oppression and opportunism of the wealthier classes, were most susceptible to socio-economic exigencies, including the recurring famines that were such a destructive and destabilising feature of nineteenth-century Ireland. Famine was multi-dimensional, however, and encouraged beneficent as well as malevolent or negative impulses and responses, and the generosity of strangers was an ennobling feature of both the Great Famine of the 1840s, with credit redounding particularly to the Society of Friends or Quakers for their humanitarian intervention, and the famine of

1879–80, which featured more diverse aid agencies and increasingly sophisticated collection and distribution networks. The reality and traumatic memory of the Great Famine – the most catastrophic and defining event in Ireland's layered and turbulent history – remained a vital presence a generation later, as the frequency of references to it in various sources attest. The enormity of the suffering and loss experienced during that calamity – mass death from starvation and disease and further haemorrhagic population depletion through continuing emigration – was seared on the memory of survivors and their descendants scattered throughout the anglophone world and beyond. The collective Irish memory of the 1840s Famine, whether innate or transmitted, whether forged by personal experience or inheritance, infused and informed the immediacy and generosity of the response to famine's reappearance in Ireland in the late 1870s.

The two famines differed fundamentally from one another – in duration and scale and in demographic and social impact. The Great Famine persisted for several years and resulted in profound population loss, more than 3 million people – 35 per cent of the estimated pre-Famine tally of 8.5 million – to death and emigration in the decade 1845-55; the later famine lasted less than a year and had an infinitesimally smaller number of deaths, hundreds, possibly a few thousand, although no accurate computation exists of those who died or emigrated because of the 1879-80 famine. Ironically, the latter's relative containment owed much to the disruption, dislocation and death caused by its predecessor, to the Great Famine's virtual extirpation of the entire underclass of Ireland's poorest and most vulnerable people, and the amalgamation of their tiny uneconomic and redundant landholdings into more commercially viable farming operations. Ireland in the final third of the nineteenth century was not the depleted and demoralised entity of the 1840s and '50s. Its people had benefited and learned from the economic and social progress and the modernising influences that followed in the Great Famine's wake. The political environment, which had been exposed to revolutionary and constitutional influences and developments, was also different, and an expanded, better-educated electorate was more alive to the possibilities of further economic, social and political change.

# PART 1
# FAMINE

*The condition of the west [of Ireland] is daily becoming worse. The people have neither food nor clothes, nor credit to buy them, nor work to earn them ... Pale, thin, and bloodless, silent and without a smile, their condition is absolutely without hope ... Private charity is unable to cope with the state of things, and the responsibility of the government will be heavy indeed unless it sanctions some substantial measures of relief.*

Mitchell Henry, Home Rule MP for County Galway, Kylemore Castle, Connemara, to the lord lieutenant of Ireland, 13 December 1879, *Dublin Evening Mail*, 20 December 1879, p. 4

CHAPTER 1

# 'Little Short of Death by Slow Starvation':[1] The 1879–80 famine in Ireland

I never got such a shock before or since. The people [of Derryvoreda, Recess, County Galway] were living skeletons, their faces like parchment. They were scarcely able to crawl. Even the few pigs and fowls were hardly able to stand, and as far as I could see there was not a house with any food in it. It was appalling.

> Henry Robinson, *Memories: Wise and otherwise* (London and New York: Cassell, 1923), pp. 9–10

The people are poor and miserable, half starved, overwhelmed with debt on every side.

> Reverend John Murphy, PP Schull, County Cork, *Cork Examiner*, 7 February 1880, Murphy to the editor, 5 February, p. 4

## Introduction

In an address to the Irish Conference of Historians at University College Dublin in May 1995, Paul Bew argued for the incorporation of the Marian apparition at Knock, County Mayo, on 21 August 1879, in the narrative of the Irish Land War. According to Bew, one of the pioneers of Land War revisionism, 'two simultaneous developments of great importance' occurred in Mayo in summer 1879 – 'the outbreak of the decisive phase of the Irish Land War and the appearance of the most celebrated of all Irish Marian apparitions', a binary captured in the crisp expressive title of Bew's conference presentation: 'A Vision to the Dispossessed', though he did acknowledge that the phrase was originally Sheridan Gilley's.[2] The reputed Marian apparition at a hitherto obscure and unremarkable Mayo village sparked religious excitement and joy, but it also provoked speculation and controversy that continue to the present. Among the more esoteric contributions to the debate was the dietary historian E. Margaret Crawford's suggestion that the witnesses to the Knock apparition, as many as twenty, were suffering from hallucinations induced by the vitamin deficiency disease pellagra, whose symptoms are dermatitis, diarrhoea and dementia.[3] James S. Donnelly, Jr, a historian of Irish land questions and Mariology among other scholarly accomplishments, responded sceptically to the pellagra explanation for the visionary experience of the attendant Mayo peasants, dismissing Crawford's speculation as 'a famous footnote',[4] and Donnelly's reservations were shared by others, among them sociologist Eugene Hynes in his more recent analysis of the Knock phenomenon.[5] Pellagra is often linked to prolonged and excessive consumption of maize, more commonly known as Indian meal in Ireland, where it was generally associated with food shortages and famine, most notably the Great Famine of the 1840s. Potatoes, which were the staple food of the Irish peasantry throughout the nineteenth century, were in short supply in Mayo and elsewhere in Ireland in August 1879, but maize or Indian meal had not yet become the standard substitute food, and hence Donnelly's misgivings regarding Crawford's pellagra thesis.

The reference to pellagra and Indian meal is a reminder, nonetheless, that one of the factors that prompted both the Land League and the Land War was a famine and accompanying diseases throughout much of the western half of Ireland in the late 1870s. Famine has been variously defined, but, as the editors of a recently published volume of documentary source material on the history of Irish famines remind us, many of the more sophisticated and specific definitions are largely inapplicable to historical Irish famines because of deficiencies in the country's records. However, in a 2012 assessment of famine risk, the World Health Organization (WHO) offered a general definition of famine that appears particularly relevant to the 1879–80 famine in Ireland, which at its most intense left a substantial minority of the Irish population dependent on philanthropy and private charity for survival.

The WHO posited three defining characteristics of famine: a failure in the food supply; a marked increase in death and disease; and the need for an emergency response. Based on these criteria, the WHO concluded that 'famines can be recognised as a regional failure of food production or supply, sufficient to cause a marked increase in disease and mortality due to severe lack of nutrition and necessitating emergency intervention, usually at an international level'.[6]

## A cloud of impending famine

As in similar crises in the past, the weather played a key role in the 1879–80 famine in Ireland. A cold and wet autumn in 1879 – the third successive year in which such conditions prevailed – disrupted the turf, grain and potato harvests. The Local Government Board for Ireland (hereinafter LGB) reported that the 1879 potato crop was 'deficient in quantity, inferior in quality and affected by blight', and that it amounted to no more than half an average crop.[7] Production had fallen from 4.2 million tons in 1876 to 1.1 million in 1879, with western counties disproportionately affected. All root and grain crops and livestock production suffered during these inclement years. Agricultural prices plummeted, their collapse exacerbated by a general restriction of credit on the part of banks, money lenders and shopkeepers. Agricultural competition from America and Canada and contracting labour markets in Ireland and Britain compounded the situation. The subsistence tenant farmers and agricultural labourers of the western part of Ireland were particularly exposed to these changes and were severely affected.[8]

Information and ideology are integral to the formulation of government policy and its response to social and economic crises. Following the disappointingly poor harvest in late summer and autumn 1879, the LGB instructed its inspectors to investigate the consequences for the peasantry in the worst-affected parts of the country. This was neither an objective nor scientific exercise. While the board and its inspectors may have been sympathetic to the plight of the hungry and suffering poor, they viewed Irish distress and its relief through the prism of the Poor Law, and were constrained and influenced by that institution's principles, precedents and practices, complicated further by individual inspectors' idiosyncrasies and prejudices. W.J. Hamilton, for instance, who brought a muscular Christianity to his analysis of the prevailing distress, advocated individual responsibility, self-sufficiency, mutuality, thrift, frugality and temperance.[9] For most of the peasantry, however, such virtues were commonplace, from necessity, rather than by choice or preference. Hamilton's colleague, Algernon Bourke, captured the prevailing reality in a sympathetic assessment of Ennistymon Poor Law union in County Clare in January 1880:

> A father standing idle at his door, a woman with her children crouching round the dying embers of a meagre fire, a stalwart lad loitering by the way, poor hunger-stricken children wandering with aimless purpose on the road, driven out, it would appear, by the inhospitality of their homes. These are the scenes which force themselves upon us, and which speak to those who will observe with an eloquence which carries with it the convictions of the truth.[10]

The effects of food shortages were compounded by deficiencies in clothing, fuel and hygiene. A report from Westport Poor Law union in County Mayo in mid-October 1879 noted that turf was 'inferior, wet, scarce and dear',[11] and similar deficiencies in other parts of the country compelled the poor to burn less-efficient alternatives: furze at Crookhaven in west Cork, for instance; heather or brushwood in Corofin union, County Clare; furze and sticks in Scariff union in the same county; bushes and heather in the west Kerry parish of Dunquin.[12]

For the western peasantry the loss of income resulting from the collapse of the kelp industry proved hugely detrimental. Henry Robinson, recently appointed to the Poor Law inspectorate, attributed the industry's contraction in part to the widespread dishonest practice of mixing sand with the harvested seaweed to increase the product's weight, a ruse that encouraged purchasers to seek an alternative base for the manufacture of iodine. According to Robinson, the negative consequences were most severely felt in the parish of Rosmuc in Connemara, where, he observed, the extreme poverty that prevailed was 'a lamentable illustration of how people can live with no visible means of subsistence'. Robinson noted that the straitened circumstances of the peasantry in the west of Ireland were exacerbated by a reduction in seasonal earnings for harvest work in England and Scotland and in remittances from relatives in America,[13] all of which had implications for security of tenure and for personal and communal health and well-being.

In Cork Poor Law union, low prices for butter, one of the county's staple industries, created financial difficulties for farmers, which prompted banks and merchants to withdraw credit facilities, thereby limiting farmers' ability to employ labourers.[14] Many farmers were heavily indebted to shopkeepers and money lenders, who charged exorbitant interest rates. One LGB inspector discovered that shopkeepers in counties Galway, Mayo, Roscommon and Westmeath charged 25 per cent interest for twelve months' credit on a bag of Indian meal, while the rate imposed by money lenders, or gombeen men, was 'beyond the limits of calculation'.[15] In mid-November 1879 the LGB concluded from these and similar reports that the entire province of Connacht, the West Riding of Cork, and counties Donegal, Clare and Kerry were in 'an exceptionally distressed condition'.[16]

The situation deteriorated alarmingly with the onset of winter. Early in January 1880 Laurence Gillooly, Catholic bishop of Elphin, stated that distress prevailed throughout County Roscommon. 'The majority of our peasantry have neither money nor credit,' he wrote, 'and a large proportion of them not even the necessaries of life', an observation that could have applied to most of the western half of Ireland at the time. Gillooly claimed that landlords were exploiting the situation to evict impecunious tenants, observing, in a reference that linked the current crisis to the Great Famine of the previous generation: 'A conviction prevails amongst the peasantry in every part of the destitute districts that now, as in 1847, the landlords are anxious to force them into the workhouse in order to level their cabins and free themselves from further liability for their support.'[17]

Further north, at Glencolumbkille, County Donegal, labourers and small farmers were reduced to eating 'black seaweed'; at Dungloe, according to the parish priest, they were 'on the very verge of famine'.

Michael Logue, bishop of Raphoe, stated that in at least ten of Donegal's twenty-five Catholic parishes, 'the condition of the people could not be much worse, short of absolute famine'. A 'state of starvation' prevailed at Ardcarne and Tumna, County Roscommon, while a dearth of food, fuel, clothing and credit was reported from Kilgarvan, County Mayo, where some 200 families had been forced to pawn their clothes, leaving their children virtually naked. An inundation of similar accounts from all parts of the country testified to the wretchedness of the poor and the ubiquity of distress.[18]

The Mansion House relief committee in Dublin, one of several national and overseas public relief organisations that emerged in response to the food, fuel and clothing crises, captured the circumstances of the western peasantry: 'Over nearly the whole western half of the island hung a cloud of impending famine; along the sea-coast, famine was actually at its work, slowly wasting the strength of the people to the point of pestilence and death.' The committee noted that in many western districts, the wretched people, 'reduced to a meal a day of turnips, shell-fish, or seaweed, had already sunk into the torpor which is the second stage of starvation'.[19]

William O'Brien, special correspondent of Ireland's leading nationalist newspaper the *Freeman's Journal*, and later a nationalist MP and one of Charles Stewart Parnell's principal lieutenants, substantiated the committee's sober assessment in a series of reports on conditions in the west of Ireland in early January 1880. He encountered broken-spirited men, women and children squatting in darkness around the turf ashes in their cabins,

> or ravening their horrid mess of seaweed or periwinkles; their potatoes gone since Christmas; nothing to sow, nothing to fish with; nothing to pawn; children without a rag of underclothing; sick men and women without a drop of milk or tea to wet their lips with; hollow cheeks, lustreless eyes and broken hearts.[20]

O'Brien captured several features of social crisis in this vivid and dramatic passage, all of them reminiscent of the traumatic Great Famine barely a generation removed: a starving peasantry, stripped of resources, entitlement and hope, their meagre possessions already pawned, their physical and emotional state on open display.

British and American journalists conveyed similar heart-rending accounts to an expatriate Irish and international readership, which helped to publicise the famine plight of the Irish peasantry in the winter and spring of 1879–80 and to promote relief efforts. The special correspondent of the London *Standard* described swarms of individuals at Caherciveen, County Kerry, in late January 1880, 'squatting in rows along the kerbstones, crouching in dozens at the corners, sitting on doorsteps, waiting and watching for food the livelong day'. The people were devoid of energy and initiative, their spirit crushed, and, the writer concluded, humanity shrank 'startled and appalled from the contemplation of such abject misery'. In a subsequent report, the *Standard* correspondent noted that islanders off the Mayo and Galway coast were slowly starving to death, their powerfully built frames 'worn and emaciated'.[21]

The influential American journalist James Redpath, who visited Ireland in February 1880 as the special correspondent of the *New York Tribune*, was an admirer of Parnell and a supporter of the Land League, and his reports, which were coloured no doubt by his political views, were visceral and emotive, reminiscent of famine narratives from the 1840s. According to Redpath, novelists and travellers had described the Irish as 'a light-hearted and rollicking people – full of fun and quick in repartee – equally ready to dance or to fight', but he did not find them so. In the west of Ireland, he wrote, every cabin had been stripped of its gaiety and joy, the occupants 'sad and despondent ... care-worn, broken-hearted, and shrouded in gloom'. The peasantry, 'old men and boys, old women and girls, young men and maidens – all of them, without a solitary exception – were grave or haggard, and every household looked as if the plague of the first-born had smitten them that hour'. Famine had tamed the children's 'restless spirits', Redpath reported; they crouched around 'the bit of peat-fire without uttering a word', uninterested in the stranger who entered their 'desolate cabin'.[22]

## Famine's shadow

Famine and subsistence crises were recurring features of Irish life and had been for centuries. As ever, they were accompanied by the fevers and fluxes that had disfigured, displaced, terrified and killed countless thousands in the past. Fever was endemic in Ireland and flared up periodically into nationwide epidemics, most dramatically and destructively during the Great Famine of the mid- and late 1840s when starvation, fever and a plethora of other diseases combined to claim more than one million Irish lives. The pathogens that cause fever are transmitted from one host to another by body lice, and head lice to a lesser extent. Lice, whose sole food is human blood, exist at a specific body temperature and when this rises or falls, as in the case of feverish or dead victims, lice leave for new hosts with normal temperatures, and in this way fever spreads. Famines and subsistence crises created the ideal social conditions for the generation and diffusion of louse-borne and other epidemic infections.[23]

In the 1879–80 famine the earliest reports of disease emerged from the south of the country. An epidemic of fever and measles on Cape Clear, off the west Cork coast, in October and November 1879 claimed at least sixteen lives, and similar outbreaks were reported from Castletown Berehaven in the following January.[24] On 7 February 1880 an LGB inspector, W.A. Power, informed his superiors in Dublin that there were twenty-three cases of fever in the Castletown Berehaven workhouse hospital, which increased to more than forty during the month.[25] In mid-March there were reports of fever on Hare Island, off Baltimore, west Cork, which had a population of more than 300. According to T. Brodie, an LGB inspector who visited the island, twenty-nine cases of fever had been detected, with one fatality, a twenty-nine-year-old male. Most of the fever cases were children under twelve years of age, their condition diagnosed as simple continued fever, with no evidence of typhus, typhoid or relapsing fever, the infections normally associated with famines and subsistence crises. Brodie attributed the current epidemic to overcrowding in the poorly ventilated dwellings of the island's residents rather than to economic depression or to potato and other crop failures.[26] Brodie's reductive analysis, his minimising of the situation, reflected the government's reluctance to assume responsibility for the relief of distress in Ireland. The official stance was that periodic disease outbreaks, particularly fever, were linked to the peasants' normal economic and social environment, their customary living conditions and circumstances, rather than to exceptional or exigent distress, which would have necessitated direct government intervention and the provision of emergency relief.

The disease epicentre shifted from south-west Munster to various parts of Connacht in January 1880 and intensified as the spring and summer progressed. On 19 January the medical officer at Kilglass, County Sligo, recorded that there were ten fever-stricken families in one townland and he attributed the presence of fever to cold, hunger and deficient clothing.[27] In May fever was detected in up to sixty households on Gorumna island, County Galway, and 105 individuals at Kilmaine, County Mayo, were similarly affected.[28] In the following month the secretary of the Charlestown, County Mayo relief committee reported the prevalence throughout the district of a most dangerous type of 'famine fever', which, he stated, was spreading from the lower to the higher social classes and had already claimed several lives. In a reference to a phenomenon that had long currency in Ireland – the popular dread of communicable diseases – the writer observed that the relief committee's work was comparatively easy while they had hunger alone to deal with, but the onset of disease had created fear and distrust among the people and complicated the committee's task.[29]

Between 28 June and 16 July 1880, the *Freeman's Journal* published a series of articles on 'The Famine Fever in the West', reflecting on the speed at which disease was spreading among 'the utterly destitute population'. The newspaper's special correspondent wrote that the people of the locality were 'living in an atmosphere of fever'. It was the poor who were affected, 'the most miserable of the poor – the most destitute of the destitute of a destitute country'. Doctor Phillips, medical officer of the Charlestown district for the previous twenty-eight years, informed the reporter that he had never previously encountered such 'a deplorable state of affairs'. The prevailing fever, an unusually malignant form of typhus, was linked to destitution, he said, and was therefore 'famine fever in the true sense of the word'. The special correspondent discounted the suggestion by some medical practitioners that the current epidemic was not famine fever, and he referred specifically to Dr Thomas Wrigley Grimshaw, the Registrar General of Births, Marriages and Deaths in Ireland, and a member of the duchess of Marlborough's famine relief committee, which rendered him suspicious in nationalist circles, as one of those medical professionals who were 'manipulating

Fig. 1.1: C.W. Cole, 'A Gorumna Interior' [1880], C.W. Cole Sketchbook, National Library of Ireland, PD 2196 TX15. IMAGE COURTESY OF THE NLI

C.W. Cole was part of a royal naval relief mission, under the command of the duke of Edinburgh, which distributed food and clothing along the Atlantic coast and offshore islands in spring 1880, details of which will be examined in Chapter 5. This sketch shows members of the relief party inside an impoverished one-room cabin on Gorumna island, County Galway. One of the visitors, a female, props up an ailing, attenuated young girl while another offers her a drink; a third, sitting on a stool near the entrance, records the scene in a notebook. The helpless, distraught parents and a suppliant sibling look on; a baby, unaware of the drama, lies in a cradle. The family cat, equally oblivious, cleans itself, a hen crosses the earthen floor, a pot boils on the fire, and inquisitive islanders crowd around the open door. Cole's signature appears at the bottom of the sketch beneath the emblematic legend 'The Embers of Life'.

Fig. 1.2: C.W. Cole, 'Hut, Gorumna' [1880], National Library of Ireland, PD 2002 TX18.
IMAGE COURTESY OF THE NLI

Cole depicts a family, their faces expressionless, squatting around a bed in their simple dwelling on Gorumna island. A dog sits at the foot of the bed near a cradle. There is a washing line overhead and two birds, poultry presumably, perch on a shelf at the rear. Both sketches depict the pervasive poverty among the western peasantry, their basic living conditions and arrangements, the absence of domestic comforts.

the technicalities of their craft'.[30] These references reflected a continuing and contentious debate on the causation and diffusion of fever in Ireland between supporters and opponents of the theory that famine and fever were cause and effect, a medical debate that took on a decidedly political cast in the charged atmosphere of 1879–80.

The village of Faheens, some miles from Swinford in County Mayo, encapsulated the misery and destitution of the west. The *Freeman's* correspondent, despite his conventional protestation of the inadequacy of language to describe the barrenness of the location and the primitiveness of the people's living conditions, likened the village to 'a place where a lot of stones had fallen out of the sky and had got into indiscriminate heaps, into which human beings burrowed holes, clapped bundles of withered heather on top and came and lived'. He concluded with the striking oxymoron that the village of Faheens was 'the perfection of the miserable'. The correspondent claimed that the people of Swinford and Charlestown districts had subsisted for the last six months on watery Indian meal supplied by charitable organisations, which they bulked with boiled green cabbage, a compound that pigs would ordinarily reject without the addition of potatoes.[31] On this and similar compelling evidence, the *Freeman's* correspondent indicted the government for its tardy and inadequate response to the food and fever crisis in the west, levelling particular criticism at the country's chief secretary, W.E. Forster.

The reporter also captured the people's dread of contagion, which manifested itself in their refusal to enter a cabin where fever existed – though they were prepared to leave food and water for the victims near the front door – and in their unwillingness to tend the sick, ferry them to hospital, or remove and bury the dead,[32] a repetition of the human responses witnessed on a far greater scale during the Great Famine and in earlier crises. The *Freeman's* reporter suggested that the western people's 'terror' of contracting fever was prompted by their powerlessness to combat the disease, and by their religious beliefs, which he linked to the delirium associated with typhus fever. He explained that while the people feared death without the consolation of religion, they also believed that it was unchristian to die 'a raving maniac', which, he observed, was not 'a very surprising fear amongst a people so intensely religious'.[33]

F.J. McCormack, bishop of Achonry, adopted the tone and some of the content of the special correspondent's reports in a public letter to T.W. Croke, archbishop of Cashel, on 5 July 1880. McCormack stated that many parishes in his diocese were in a dreadful condition because of the prolonged period of severe destitution and the outbreak of fever in 'hungry July', and he criticised the cold disregard of the official response. According to McCormack, the local Sisters of Charity had been compelled to coffin the remains of a fever patient, because of the fearful refusal of others to do so, and the sisters had to carry the coffin onto the street. In Charlestown, fear of contracting disease and a lack of resources devolved responsibility for nursing fever-stricken individuals almost entirely upon the parish priest. The bishop directed his criticism at several targets: 'the cruel composure of official indifference', the inactivity of the LGB, the inadequacy of medical and nursing staff, the paucity of ambulances, and the absence of financial support, 'so liberally promised by the chief secretary, to save the lives of the people',[34] though clearly not so readily forthcoming.

There were many observers for whom the evolving situation was a stark and painful reminder of the Great Famine which had devastated the country within living memory. On 27 January 1880 one such commentator, the parish priest of Addergoole, County Mayo, noted: 'We have the bitter scenes of '47 re-enacted, and the year of grace, 1880, calling back as a spectre from the tomb, where we had hoped it was buried forever, the ghostly memories of the famine years.'[35] He returned to this theme at a meeting of the local relief committee in May. Following the adoption of a resolution which referred to the alarming distress and hunger that prevailed among the people, the clergyman claimed that unless they received constant and generous assistance for three months, the famine scenes of 1847 and '48 would be renewed in the parish 'in their worst aspects'.[36]

The escalating agrarian and political situation in Mayo and other parts of Connacht in the winter and spring of 1879–80, fuelled by hunger, disease, the disinclination of landlords to sanction rent abatements, and the tardiness and inadequacy of the government's response to the crisis, generated extensive newspaper coverage in Ireland, Britain and further afield.[37] The ensuing publicity prompted numerous parliamentary questions, which produced a guarded response, then and later, from W.E. Forster, newly installed as Ireland's chief secretary following the Liberals' success in the United Kingdom's April 1880 general election. Early in the following month Forster received a large and influential deputation, his first since his appointment, from the Mansion House relief committee, led by the lord mayor of Dublin, which demanded a more interventionist response from the government. R.C. Trench, Anglican archbishop of Dublin, informed the chief secretary that the committee's work was, by definition, temporary and transient, and the ultimate responsibility for the terrible distress that existed throughout the country rested with the government, 'the representative of the nation'. The deputation's pleas and supporting testimony were encapsulated in a telegram which the lord mayor had just received from Dean MacManus, parish priest of Clifden in Connemara: 'Unless promptly relieved, many deaths from starvation are inevitable. Scenes like '47 will result.' The reference to the Great Famine resonated with Forster, recalling his own contribution to famine relief in Ireland in 1847. In his response to the deputation, the chief secretary acknowl-edged that it was the government's duty to relieve 'extreme distress' and 'prevent starvation', but he insisted that responsibility for those who were suffering from anything less than actual starvation devolved on pri-vate charity rather than on the public purse. He referred specifically to small farmers, claiming that they abhorred the Poor Law as a mechanism of relief and ought to be assisted by private charity, and he concluded his lamentable defence of government policy by observing that 'there would be an end of all rule' if the government deviated from its normal practice and accommodated people of this class.[38]

This was the same W.E. Forster who had been an energetic member of the Society of Friends' noble relief effort in the west of Ireland in 1847, an individual who had empathised and sympathised with the suffering and starving poor during the Great Famine. In Dublin, on 27 January 1847, Forster summarised a distressing week-long fact-finding mission in Mayo and Galway as follows:

When we entered a village our first question was, how many deaths? 'The hunger is upon us', was everywhere the cry, and involuntarily we found ourselves regarding this hunger as we should an epidemic, looking upon starvation as a disease. In fact, as we went along, our wonder was not that the people died, but that they lived, and I have no doubt whatever that in any other country the mortality would have been far greater, that many lives have been prolonged, perhaps saved, by the long apprenticeship to want in which the Irish peasant has been trained, and by that lovely, touching charity which prompts him to share his scanty meal with his starving neighbour. But the springs of this charity must rapidly be dried up. Like a scourge of locusts, 'the hunger' daily sweeps over fresh districts, eating up all before it. One class after another is falling into the same abyss of ruin. There is now but little difference between the small farmer and the squatter. We heard in Galway of little tradesmen secretly begging for soup. The priest cannot get his dues, nor the landlord his rent. The highest and the lowest in the land are forced into sympathy by this all-mastering visitation.[39]

A generation later, as chief secretary for Ireland during another – admittedly less severe – famine, Forster danced on the head of the proverbial pin in his attempts to distinguish scales of distress, to differentiate extreme hunger and deprivation from starvation.

The government's strategy was to minimise the severity and effects of the crisis and to claim that the existing relief mechanisms were adequate to meet current difficulties. In mid-April 1880 the LGB insisted that ample provision had been made for the destitute in Ireland through Poor Law legislation, the Relief of Distress (Ireland) Act, 1880, and the liberality of private relief agencies. The board acknowledged that there had been much suffering and exceptional distress in many parts of the country, but denied that privation had reached starvation level anywhere, and was particularly emphatic in rejecting claims that food shortages had been directly responsible for deaths.[40]

Chief Secretary Forster's dissimulation, his resort to semantics rather than action, captured the essence of successive Tory and Liberal governments' relief policies during the 1879–80 famine, encapsulating, as it did, a core principle of the Poor Law – the defining difference between poverty and pauperism – and the question of eligibility. Common humanity and government responsibility predicated the prevention of starvation, but policy and ideology dictated the preservation of the relief system's integrity, rules and guiding principles. As Virginia Crossman, the leading historian of the Irish Poor Law, notes: 'If mere distress was to be relieved the labour market and the economy would be weakened, and the Poor Law undermined. It was only by limiting emergency relief to the prevention of starvation that the government could protect the wider interests of the country.'[41] These ideological concerns were reflected in the disinclination of Disraeli's Conservative government to engage with the evolving crisis in 1879, its grudging and tardy response to food shortages and hunger-related disease outbreaks, and it was not until the beginning of the following year that emergency measures for the relief of distress in Ireland were introduced.[42]

Humanitarian agencies attempted to fill the welfare vacuum created by the reluctance of the Conservative and subsequently the Liberal government to feed those immediately above starvation level, to provide for individuals who occupied that elastic indefinable stratum between chronic hunger and starvation. The first relief initiative was launched under the aegis of the duchess of Marlborough, the energetic and formidable wife of the lord lieutenant of Ireland, who, in mid-December 1879, fearing the imminence of 'a famine of food and fuel', resorted to the columns of the London *Times* to appeal to 'English benevolence' for the relief of Irish distress.[43] Her plea for assistance was prompted by a genuine humanitarian concern, augmented by uxorial sensitivity to the political possibilities and credit accruing from such an intervention.[44]

Independently, the lord mayor of Dublin convened a public assembly at the Mansion House in response to the deteriorating situation in the western half of Ireland. The initial meeting on Christmas Eve 1879 was adjourned until the beginning of January when it was resolved to inaugurate the Dublin Mansion House relief committee and to launch a public appeal for subscriptions. The newly installed lord mayor, Edmund Dwyer Gray, Home Rule MP for Tipperary and proprietor of the nationalist *Freeman's Journal*, was voted to the chair, and the committee included the Catholic and Anglican archbishops and bishops of Ireland, the moderator of the General Assembly of the Presbyterian Church in Ireland, as well as politicians, educationists, members of the judiciary and other civic leaders. The Mansion House committee prided itself on being a genuinely philanthropic, non-sectarian and apolitical body whose sole function was the relief of distress in Ireland, without distinction of creed or party.[45] The committee intended that its fund would complement rather than compete with the duchess of Marlborough's. Given her political and social connections, it was conceded that she would have access to sources of charity, particularly in England, that would have been denied to a purely Irish committee, whereas the latter, representing various shades of political and religious opinion, would have a greater appeal for the expatriate Irish, particularly in the United States and Australasia.[46] These were the two most significant voluntary relief agencies established to combat famine in Ireland in 1879–80, though there were other philanthropic initiatives, as we shall see in a later chapter.

The intensifying famine and fever crisis in the first half of 1880, along with critical reportage and public commentary, prompted medical inquiries into the so-called famine or destitution diseases in Connacht. In early July 1880 the LGB appointed two temporary medical inspectors, C.J. Nixon and Stewart Woodhouse, to investigate fever outbreaks in counties Mayo, Sligo, Roscommon, Galway and Limerick. Doctor Nixon, who was attached to the Mater Misericordiae hospital in Dublin, was assigned to Swinford Poor Law union in County Mayo, where, it was reported, fever was prevalent and dangerous.[47] In an editorial response that kept the political pressure firmly on the government, the *Freeman's Journal* claimed that the current condition of the western people was 'so scandalous as to be a disgrace to any Christian society and any civilised government in the last quarter of the nineteenth century'.[48]

Swinford Poor Law union had a population of some 54,000 and was divided into five dispensary districts: Foxford, Kilkelly, Kiltimagh, Lowpark and Swinford. The incidence of fever, particularly typhus, had been increasing in the union since 1878. The registrar general's returns showed that forty-seven deaths from fever occurred in the union in the three years 1875–7 and eighty-four in the following two years. A further thirty-seven fever deaths were registered between 1 January and 31 July 1880. Nixon reported that Swinford was one of the country's poorer unions, its residents chronically destitute and plunged into crisis with any deterioration in their normal state of poverty. He claimed that an insufficiency of food or an over-reliance on a single item such as Indian meal was a predisposing cause of fever because it reduced the individual's resistance to infection, and that the immediate or exciting cause was contagion, facilitated by the neglect of personal and domestic hygiene and overcrowding in poorly ventilated homes. Nixon reported that once typhus and other contagious diseases were generated, the habits and prejudices of the people, coupled with their extreme poverty and unsanitary living conditions, contributed to the diffusion of these diseases. In times of distress people pawned their clothing and bedding to procure food, and it was normal for five or six family members to sleep together in the same bed for warmth. Nixon noted that the poor were reluctant to send for the dispensary doctor, usually delaying until the illness became difficult and painful. Furthermore, they were unwilling to attend hospital, and their inability to isolate the infected within their single-room cabins spread disease.[49] Nixon's colleague, Dr Woodhouse, blamed social pressures and considerations for the peasantry's reluctance to seek medical assistance; they were conscious, he observed, that 'a "catching disorder" implied social discredit'.[50] None of the features identified by Nixon and corroborated by Woodhouse were new; they could have emerged from any similar socio-medical inquiry into the living conditions and standards of the Irish peasantry in any of the over-populated decades leading up to the Great Famine of the 1840s.

Nixon visited Faheens on 8 July 1880, more than a week after the special correspondent of the *Freeman's Journal*, and he added substance to the journalist's colour. Faheens was a small village, consisting of forty-two, mostly single-room, cabins, which accommodated forty-six families, 188 individuals in total. Living conditions were 'extremely wretched', with most of the cabins housing cattle and pigs as well as their human occupants. Open drains that ran through the centre of the cabins carried off the sewage, and the exteriors featured stagnant pools which contained all sorts of offensive matter.[51] There was no sewerage of any kind in the village, no road within a mile of it, and the food of the people consisted almost exclusively of Indian meal, consumed without milk. In the neighbouring village of Kilkelly, there were eight inches of manure in a one-room cabin occupied by seven individuals. The woman of the house refused to clean it out, explaining that if she did there would be no manure to fertilise the family's crops. Similarly, the sewer that was linked with the effluvia-filled pond at the front of the cabin was deliberately blocked up with a large stone, presumably for the same purpose of preserving the content for use as fertiliser.

In Ballintadder village, where evictions were pending, Nixon encountered a family who had been ill with typhoid fever for some weeks. Their cabin was 'extremely offensive', an 'almost overpowering' odour emanating from the interior. At the time of his visit, the small single-room cabin housed a mother and her two children, each of whom was ill with fever, and the sub-tenants included poultry, three cows, three cats and a large dog. In an adjoining house three boys lay ill, two suffering from typhoid or enteric fever, the other from dysentery. The drinking water of both families, which was dark and muddy and with a greasy scum on the surface, was drawn from a pit enclosed by a stone wall, into which flowed the drainage of the field in which it was situated. In the townland of Baroe, the case of an eight-year-old boy suffering from typhus fever had not been reported to the local dispensary doctor, and when Nixon sent for the ambulance to remove the patient to hospital, the boy's mother refused permission. Nixon concluded that fever patients and their families were reluctant to enter the Swinford Poor Law union fever hospital,[52] an antipathy to fever or isolation hospitals that was common among Ireland's poor and had been for generations.

The diseases that prevailed during the epidemic in the Swinford union were typhus, typhoid, dysentery and diarrhoea. Nixon examined nineteen cases of typhoid fever and twenty-one of dysentery and diarrhoea and attributed all of them to an infected water supply and to the people's diet, which, he said, consisted almost exclusively of inadequately cooked Indian meal, often consumed without milk. The typhus outbreak in the union appears to have commenced at the beginning of March 1880, and over the next five months ninety-six individuals were admitted to the Swinford fever hospital from the union and the workhouse, 75 per cent of these admissions coming from the Lowpark and Swinford dispensary districts. Eighty-four of the ninety-six admissions were infected with typhus, and the remainder with typhoid. Thirteen of the typhus patients died, though all the typhoid sufferers survived. In the Swinford union, 179 cases of fever were reported in the two-month period 1 June to 31 July (the period for which Nixon claims he had the most accurate information); 140 of these were typhus, and there were nineteen deaths among this cohort, a mortality rate of about 13.5 per cent.[53]

Emaciation was common to most of the hospitalised typhus patients and was particularly pronounced among children. Nixon commented on the peculiar body odour of the sick, which was very pungent in some cases. He claimed that it was *sui generis* or distinctive to each patient and he attributed it to the people's diet and their indifference to personal cleanliness rather than to the effects of disease per se.[54] Many medical professionals had commented similarly during the Great Famine, referring to the peculiar mousy smell which clung to the clothes and bodies of the poor, the starving and the sick.[55]

Nixon concluded his gloomy analysis with an implicit reference to the evolving Land War and the aims of the Land League: 'I cannot help doubting if those who speak of rooting the people in the soil ... are personally cognisant of the social misery and helplessness of the inhabitants of the rural districts of that part of the west of Ireland which I visited during my recent inspections.'[56] In an editorial response to Nixon's findings, the British medical weekly the *Lancet* commented:

> It is difficult to realise a state of existence which at the best is barely distinguishable from a condition of chronic starvation, and circumstances of housing and habits of domestic life which are revolting in their disregard of what we look for amidst a civilised community. The endemicity of typhus and enteric fever in the district, as described by Dr Nixon, is the normal result of such conditions.[57]

So long as sub-standard unhygienic living conditions prevailed in Ireland, particularly in the poverty-stricken west, periodic outbreaks of fever and other communicable diseases were inevitable and so were their consequences – impoverishment, social distress, death. The political implications of these socio-economic conditions were already manifesting themselves in the agrarianism and social anarchy that featured in many parts of the country, issues that will be addressed in later chapters of this work.

Many of Nixon's observations and findings were corroborated by a second medical inquiry, which was instigated by the Mansion House relief committee and proceeded at much the same time as Nixon's. At the end of June 1880 the committee sent the prominent physician and cultural nationalist Dr George Sigerson to Connacht to investigate the origins and character of the prevailing epidemic. Sigerson was dean of the faculty of science at the Catholic University in Dublin, an individual of 'high scientific and professional reputation', in the committee's estimation. He was accompanied as assistant commissioner by Dr Joseph E. Kenny, visiting physician to the North Dublin Poor Law union, and well known in Dublin medical and political circles – Kenny was Parnell's medical advisor and political ally and was subsequently elected to the House of Commons.[58] Sigerson and Kenny's inquiry had an ideological and political dimension that was absent, or at least different, from Nixon's, and their remit, both temporally and geographically, was much broader than his.

The Mansion House committee launched its medical inquiry following the publicity given to famine diseases in the west, particularly typhus fever, in early summer 1880, and to claims by some medical professionals that typhus and famine fever were distinct diseases, from which they inferred that the prevailing epidemic was not the consequence of food shortages and exceptional destitution, as argued by nationalist politicians and their supporters, but attributable to poor sanitation and the unhealthy condition of the people's dwellings, and as such was a recurring feature of Irish life and did not require extraordinary government intervention.[59]

Sigerson and Kenny spent five weeks in July and August 1880 travelling through Mayo and Galway, and Sligo to a lesser extent, and they submitted several reports to the Mansion House committee in Dublin on the conditions they encountered, which the committee disseminated widely – in the press, in pamphlet form, and among government agencies.[60] The medical investigators' findings were unambiguous: destitution and deprivation were widespread; the prevailing disease was maculated, that is spotted, typhus, which, they claimed, depended 'most particularly on deficient nutrition' and had been 'peculiarly associated with great distress periods in Ireland'.[61] Sigerson and Kenny were technically incorrect in attributing the fever outbreak to deficiencies in the food supply – there is no direct nutritional connection in the complex relationship between famine and fever – but accurate in their general analysis that destitution, deprivation and periods of exceptional distress, particularly Ireland's recurring famines, were responsible. It was the social conditions and social dislocation arising from famine rather than the shortage of food itself that was responsible for generating and diffusing fever.

The medical investigators referred on several occasions to the unreliability of the official returns relating to communicable diseases, claiming that incidence and mortality were each under-reported and under-represented in the general statistics. Sigerson and Kenny attributed these deficiencies in the official record to deliberate concealment by the families of afflicted individuals, who feared social isolation and segregation. Midway through their inquiry, they noted:

> Wherever we pass, we find, as a rule, that many more cases of destitution-diseases exist than have come under the cognisance of officials ... Families, stricken with fever, are very reluctant to make the fact known, because all intercourse with their neighbours would be immediately stopped. They would be regarded as plague-stricken, and their houses avoided by all.

Based on their experiences in the Ballina and Killala districts of County Mayo, they concluded: 'Official statistics relating to disease lack a solid foundation ... many cases of destitution-disease do exist which are not on the official register.'[62] Their claim suggests that excess mortality arising from starvation and associated diseases during the 1879–80 famine, while modest, was greater than that recorded in official sources, although it is not possible to establish definitively the numbers who died.

Sigerson and Kenny described the Mayo village of Rathlacan as 'a museum of assorted fevers'. They encountered typhus, typhoid and relapsing fever in various houses in the village, in addition to 'a specimen of dysenteric diarrhoea', and yet, they noted, only one family had been reported sick to the medical officer of the district.[63] One hundred and twelve individuals were known to have been stricken with fever in Louisburgh and its environs, mostly with typhus, some with relapsing fever, and of these six had died. The investigators claimed that many cases had probably been concealed, a suggestion substantiated by the Louisburgh dispensary doctor.[64] Forty-four cases of fever were registered in Oranmore, County Galway, for the first six months of 1880, but, with the assistance of the local dispensary doctor and a clergyman, Sigerson and Kenny compiled a list of 132 cases and fourteen deaths for the same period. They attributed the recent fever outbreak in the district to 'privations', and, in an implicit criticism of government policy, observed that if the general distress had been foreseen and prevented, 'these destitution-diseases would not have affected the suffering poor, spread from them to their more comfortable neighbours, nor, extending still more widely, have made other distant localities pay tribute to disease and death'.[65]

Some places had distinctive features of their own. In Rosmuc in Connemara, for instance, the fear of losing employment on the recently inaugurated public relief works was an additional reason why families concealed the presence of fever, particularly among working males, disclosing it only when their lives were in danger.[66] In nearby Carraroe, which seemed to harbour an exceptional amount of illness, 'the half-fed, half-clad peasantry' appeared 'more forlorn' to the medical commissioners than any others they had yet encountered. Evictions were pending in the district and Sigerson and Kenny noted that there was no more effective way of spreading infectious disease than by compelling individuals who were sick with fever, or just convalescent, 'to quit their isolated dwellings and wander about, seeking shelter from others, probably at a distance and not yet smitten'. Distress was further evident in the dearth of clothing and footwear in the district: 'The men were almost all barefooted, even when using spades or "loys",' the doctors recorded, and the entire community, men, women and children, were clad in 'dilapidated pieces of flannel' which were too threadbare for patching. Sigerson and Kenny's observation as they embarked from Connemara's rocky shores captured the plight of the impoverished peasantry more graphically than a whole volume of official statistics. Their watching presence, according to the doctors, 'added not animation but desolation to a scene not to be paralleled in Christendom'.[67]

Typhus fever was the dominant disease in the various counties surveyed by the commissioners, with typhoid and relapsing fever detected in some localities. The primacy of typhus and the relatively low incidence of relapsing fever prompted some government apologists and minimisers, of whom T.W. Grimshaw, the registrar general, was the most prominent, to argue that the fever outbreaks could not be attributed to destitution resulting from crop failures and economic depression. These critics claimed that famine fever was in effect relapsing fever, and that typhus was a distinct disease and incidental to the prevailing distress. Sigerson rejected this proposition, contending that relapsing fever had 'no title to be termed famine-fever, *par excellence*'. His thesis throughout was the same as that propounded by Dr Dominic Corrigan at the time of the Great Famine, and subsequently by the eminent authority Dr William Stokes and others, that famine and fever were cause and effect. Sigerson argued that each of the three types of fever they encountered during their inquiry could occur in periods of distress and privation. The three conditions were, in the Mansion House committee's phrase, 'the direct offspring of frightful destitution', and the committee indicted local and central government for their failure to foresee and forestall these disease episodes.[68]

## Conclusion

The various relief committees that came into existence in the winter and spring of 1879–80 attempted to fill the void created by the inadequacy of the official response to widespread food, clothing and fuel shortages. Sigerson claimed that the intervention of these committees saved thousands of lives, though he believed that Indian meal was a poor substitute for the potato, the standard food of the general peasant population. Many of the individuals whom he and his colleague found stricken with fever and other diseases had subsisted for several months on the blighted potato's substitute, Indian meal, which was invariably insufficiently boiled because of a shortage of fuel, and consumed with water, which has no nutritional value, rather than milk, its traditional accompaniment. Inadequate or insufficient nourishment impaired individual and communal immunity to disease and exposed the general population to infection.[69]

This was particularly the case with children and young persons and, analogous to the experience of the Great Famine a generation earlier, this cohort was disproportionately struck down with fever in every district visited by the medical investigators. Again, as in the Great Famine, fever infected males to a greater extent than females. There was, however, a different dynamic at work during the 1879–80 famine, which resulted in more women becoming infected and dying. Many adult males had left the west to seek employment, in Britain and America mainly, and their womenfolk performed the hard physical labour that men had previously undertaken, increasing the possibility of infection at a time of reduced personal and communal resistance to malnutrition-related diseases. According to Sigerson, one of the more pronounced and painful features of the fever epidemic was excessive mortality among 'the mothers of the west'.[70]

The LGB, among other agencies, accused the peasantry of contributing to the generation and dissemination of disease by holding wakes, an allegation Sigerson rejected as baseless. He was equally dismissive of the purported drinking habits of the poor, and the implied link between heavy alcohol consumption, physical and mental debility and susceptibility to disease. Sigerson claimed that Kenny and he had encountered nothing but 'perfect sobriety' during their inquiry.[71]

The association between wakes, alcohol consumption and disease had a long pedigree in Ireland. For instance, in April 1832, at the height of a fearsome cholera pandemic, the Central Board of Health for Ireland, a government advisory body, counselled the public not to hold or attend wakes and warned against intemperance as a predisposing cause of cholera. The government and the Catholic Church supported both injunctions. In a pastoral letter, Archbishop Daniel Murray of Dublin urged individuals to abstain from alcohol, 'lest the body should fall a victim to premature disease and the unhappy soul to that sentence which declares that drunkards shall not possess the kingdom of God', and, he pronounced, any Catholic who ignored the board's advice regarding wakes and subsequently contracted cholera fatally would be guilty of suicide, self-murder,[72] which in Catholic eschatology had implications for burial in hallowed ground and for the afterlife.

As the LGB's stance attests, such beliefs were still current half a century later,[73] though Sigerson dismissed the possibility that they had any practical application to the diseases encountered in the west of Ireland in 1879–80. He did acknowledge that the general standard of peasant housing needed improvement as a preventative measure, but he rejected the suggestion that sanitary defects in people's homes had contributed to the fever outbreaks, insisting that the prime predisposing cause was the inadequacy of the food supply, a conclusion that conflicted with Dr Nixon's findings and reflected a different political ideology.[74]

Finally, Sigerson proposed a series of medical and general remedial measures, including more suitable conveyances to replace the antiquated ambulances then in use to hospitalise the sick; an improved medical service; the admission of clergymen to boards of Poor Law guardians; and legislation to ameliorate the socio-economic conditions of the peasantry, thereby cutting off at source the origin of many of these so-called destitution diseases.[75]

There was more than a grain of truth in a leading medical journal's analysis that the controversy over the presence of famine fever in the west of Ireland was ideological and politically opportunistic: 'The existence of famine fever was as much a part of the parliamentary programme of one party as its denial was necessary to the policy of the other.' The journal belied its apparent neutrality, however, by reproducing a substantial portion of Dr Nixon's report, which, its editorial writer claimed, reflected 'the real facts as to the sanitary state of a great part of Ireland', and he queried the reasons for allowing the residents of these districts 'to live like unclean beasts, and to spread to their neighbours the diseases propagated by their noisome mode of life'. The journal indicted the LGB for its failure to enforce the provisions of the mandatory Public Health (Ireland) Act, 1878, which gave extensive powers to rural and urban sanitary authorities, and it dismissed the board's public health remit as a 'disgraceful sham', claiming that the board had done 'everything in its power to obstruct the progress of sanitary reform in Ireland'.[76]

A good harvest in autumn 1880, the first in several years, gradually brought the famine and its attendant disease epidemic to an end. Nature's bounty afforded relief to the hungry and distressed peasantry, the beleaguered LGB, the defensive chief secretary for Ireland, and Gladstone's Liberal government, although it did not diminish in the least the evolving agrarian and political agitation or alleviate the chief secretary and the government's responsibilities towards Ireland. At the final ordinary meeting of the Mansion House relief committee on 15 August 1880, the chairman, Dublin's lord mayor, Edmund Dwyer Gray, MP, who was far from being a disinterested observer, claimed that large numbers of Irish people would have died from fever had they been dependent on government assistance, adding that it was their committee and the other charitable organisations that had saved the country from 'a terrible calamity'. He stated that the government had been warned twelve months earlier of the impending food crisis and its potential consequences, but their response was 'not sufficiently prompt to avert or assist in averting the famine'. Gray concluded that it was the government's duty to prevent the recurrence of these periodic famines in Ireland, a theme to which he returned at the committee's final general meeting on 7 December 1880, in the course of which he expressed the hope that the crisis they had just endured might be the last occasion on which the country and its people would have to appear 'as a beggar to the nations', a reference to the substantial sums of money and material aid donated by Irish expatriates and other charitable individuals in the United States and in various parts of the British empire and beyond in response to appeals for help from Ireland.[77]

Doctor Sigerson endorsed Gray's sentiments, observing that the country should never again have to resort to international humanitarianism to feed its people:

It would be a grave misfortune that the people of this island should be taught to rely on the charity of the world, where it was alike the duty of all classes in the country and of the government that had charge of its destiny, to take care that the possibilities of work as a resource for the people should be developed, and that the people should be enabled to look to labour, which ennobles men, instead of to pauperism, which degrades humanity.[78]

Such a concept – the promotion of personal responsibility, respectability and moral rectitude among the working population – which was widely shared among churchmen, politicians and others, carried a profound political charge. Gray, like his political leader Charles Stewart Parnell, attributed the country's socio-economic crisis and the potential debasement and demoralisation of its people to 'the condition of the land laws', and he demanded a resolution of the Irish land question. The Mansion House relief committee, despite the presence of many landowners and political conservatives in its ranks, gave its general imprimatur to the lord mayor's analysis, proclaiming that the country and its people should not be dependent on private charity, and that it was the government's duty and responsibility to redress Ireland's recurring subsistence crises and attendant disease epidemics, to unlock, in the committee's phrase, the socio-economic potential of a country closely bound to 'the richest nation in the world'.[79]

The 1879–80 famine was relatively short-lived and minor in scale compared to the Great Famine of the previous generation, even if, as Sigerson and Kenny's medical inquiry indicates, the number of deaths from starvation and hunger-related diseases was underestimated in the official returns. Several factors combined to mitigate the impact of the crisis; the most important was the voluntary relief effort initiated in autumn and winter 1879–80, which evoked an extraordinary international response – urgent, non-judgmental and exceptionally generous – and shed a favourable light on the expatriate Irish and humanitarianism generally. That private charitable endeavour served as a stark contrast to the tardy and grudging official response, to the government's singular lack of enthusiasm to take responsibility for the alleviation of famine and its consequences in Ireland. The extent, complexity and implications of the collective voluntary relief effort in Ireland and internationally, from autumn 1879 to the successful harvest of the following year, constitute the subject of this volume's next section.

# PART 2
# PHILANTHROPY

*It is agreed that the condition of things, under which
a fertile and in many places thinly populated island
is reduced twice in each generation to crave alms at
the doors of the nations, that a large section of its
people may not starve to death, is a shameful and
intolerable scandal.*

The Irish Crisis of 1879–80. Proceedings of the Dublin Mansion
House Relief Committee, 1880 (Dublin: Browne & Nolan,
1881), p. 75

*If you pour yourself out for the hungry and satisfy the
desire of the afflicted, then shall your light rise in the
darkness and your gloom be as the noonday.*

Isaiah, 58:10

CHAPTER 2

# The Australasian Response to the 1879–80 Famine in Ireland

Nothing is so efficacious in appeasing God's anger as almsgiving, and I have no doubt our people will discharge this duty towards their distressed brethren in Ireland, and thus secure for themselves the blessings of heaven.

> James Murray, bishop of Maitland, New South Wales, pastoral letter, 2 February 1880, *Freeman's Journal* (Sydney), 21 February 1880, p. 18

They *shall* not perish ... while we whose bread is sure
Have hearts to pity, hands to help, the poor,
And eyes in Ireland's hour of need to see
Queensland's, Australia's, opportunity!

> J. Brunton Stephens, 'The Famine in Ireland', *Brisbane Courier*, 28 January 1880, p. 3

They shall not perish, while we, whose bread is sure,
Have hearts to pity, hands to help the poor;
Our eyes in Ireland's hour of need shall see
Tasmania's golden opportunity.

> *Mercury* (Hobart), 12 February 1880, p. 2

## Introduction

On 6 May 1880, in an editorial reflecting on the Great Famine of the 1840s and previewing Ireland's prospects for the traditional hungry months of summer, the Dublin *Freeman's Journal* described the Irish

people as 'mendicants on the highway of the world'.[1] The country's beg-
gared status and the necessity to appeal to international humanitarianism, now and in the past, were recurring themes in press and political
commentary on the Irish famine of 1879–80 and were couched in variations of the *Freeman's* phrasing. References to starvation, beggary and
the country's political subjection and helplessness captured Ireland's
dependency on external forces, both metaphorically and in real terms,
following a succession of failed harvests in the later 1870s that precipitated the socio-economic crisis explored in the previous chapter. One
of these international agencies, the Sydney *Freeman's Journal*, portrayed
the reality of the Irish situation to its mainly Irish and Catholic readers
at the beginning of 1880: 'It is a matter of the deepest concern to us to
learn that Ireland is in dire distress, to end we fear in widespread famine
if the generosity of our common humanity will not step in and avert
such a calamity.' The writer dreaded the possibility of a famine on the
scale of the cataclysm that had desolated the country and swept away
2 million of its people a generation earlier.[2]

The prospect of famine in Ireland, the very word itself, appeared
to trigger personal or ancestral memories among the expatriate Irish
in Australasia, North America and elsewhere, many of them first- or
second-generation fugitives from the Great Famine of the 1840s. The
emigrants' response and that of the communities in which they resided,
their collective generosity and humanity, constitute the subject matter of
the following chapters, beginning with distant antipodean Australia and
New Zealand.

## Australia

News of the failed harvest in Ireland and the plight of the peasantry
began to reach the Australian colonies from early December 1879, arriv-
ing on 'every ship, almost on every breeze', as one Irish-born resident of
South Australia phrased it.[3] These tidings were often accompanied by
entreaties for help, particularly from the Irish Catholic clergy and religious sisters. One such appeal, from Sister Mary Francis Clare, a member
of the Poor Clare community at Kenmare, County Kerry, was published

on 9 December in the Adelaide *Express and Telegraph*. Clare, anticipating increased sickness following 'the winter's starvation', sought urgent assistance for the distressed poor of Ireland's south-west. She claimed that the provision of employment represented the best form of charity and, building on that premise, her community proposed to establish a training institution at their convent to prepare their female pupils for employment by teaching them 'plain washing, sewing, lace-work', and to provide suitable girls with the education necessary to apply for situations as governesses. According to Clare, the erection of the education and training facility at Kenmare would provide immediate local employment and would benefit hundreds of girls for years to come. Clare claimed that the Kenmare convent, due to its remoteness, the people's poverty, and the absence of resident gentry, was the poorest in Ireland, a situation that left the sisters wholly dependent on external assistance. She added that the current winter filled her with apprehension and dread, 'for the turf is rotten from the wet, and the misery of cold will be added to the misery of starvation'.[4] Clare, whose family name was Margaret Anna Cusack, was the renowned Nun of Kenmare, acknowledged at home and among the Irish diaspora for her many publications on history, literature, biography and religion.[5]

The Adelaide newspaper that published Clare's appeal signalled editorial support for her 'noble-hearted charity' and stressed the need for an urgent response. The writer referred to South Australia's 'handsome contributions' to earlier humanitarian appeals from India, China and Cornwall as evidence that they would not turn 'a deaf ear to the prayer of the suffering' in Ireland.[6] One respondent, Cork-born M.T. Montgomery, urged Adelaide's Catholic vicar-general to participate in forming a relief committee in the city, 'so that a generous response may be given to the touching appeal of a nation prostrated with affliction and distressed with sorrow'. He called on the Irish in South Australia to rally to the cause of their country:

> Sunk in grief, a prey to famine, victims to the inclemency of the weather, deprived of the means necessary for a mere existence, they feelingly implore you to help them in their hour of need. Do not

delay, for prompt exertion now might save many a poor fellow from absolute starvation.[7]

Numbers of concerned Adelaide residents requested their mayor, E.T. Smith, MP, to convene a public meeting to consider the deteriorating situation in Ireland. Smith despatched a telegram to the lord mayor of Dublin, inquiring if conditions in the country warranted assistance from the antipodes. A reply had not been received by the time 250 people assembled in Adelaide on 19 December 1879, to express their sympathy with the sufferings of the Irish people. The attendance resolved to raise a fund by subscription and to remit the proceeds to the lord mayor of Dublin for equitable distribution among the poor. They appointed a central committee, with Mayor Smith as chairman, and urged all colonists, irrespective of class, creed or nationality, to contribute to the appeal.[8]

On the following morning, 20 December, the Australian press reported on the duchess of Marlborough's initiative to raise funds among the English public to help alleviate famine and distress in Ireland. Her intervention prompted Kevin Izod O'Doherty, the former Young Irelander who had been transported to Australia for his involvement in the abortive 1848 rebellion, to call for a concerted philanthropic response from the Irish in Queensland, 'without distinction of creed or party'. Three government ministers, the speaker of Queensland's Legislative Assembly, and several members of both houses of parliament attended a preliminary meeting in Brisbane on New Year's Eve. Letters of support were received from James Quinn, the County Kildare-born Catholic bishop, and from Sir Arthur Kennedy, the Cultra, County Down-born governor of Queensland, who had witnessed the horrors of the Great Famine while serving as a Poor Law inspector in County Clare in the late 1840s.[9] Sir John O'Shanassy, who was born near Thurles, County Tipperary, and who had served as premier of Victoria on three occasions, presided over a similar meeting in Melbourne, and Patrick Alfred Jennings, born in Newry, County Down, and destined to be the first practising Catholic premier of New South Wales, discharged a similar function in Sydney. The moderators of the meetings in the three colonial capitals emphasised their humanitarian purpose and were at pains to distance themselves from charges of political manoeuvring or motivation. 'This was a question of practical charity,' Jennings stated. 'Let them sink politics, give help to the distressed first, and then teach them politics afterwards.'[10]

The mayor of Adelaide received an unambiguous message from his Dublin counterpart on the penultimate day of 1879, its cryptic wording emphasising its immediacy: 'Distress severe; assistance urgent'. The tenor of the message was immediately relayed to the mayors of the various colonial capitals and of other significant cities and towns. One South Australian newspaper warned that unless an immediate and magnanimous response was forthcoming, the homes of the Irish peasantry would be turned into 'pestilential dens of famine and disease'.[11]

Within days the Australian press had engaged with the famine appeal, deploying editorials, pictorial imagery and cartoons, and a great deal of indifferent verse to depict the extent of the food crisis and attendant diseases in Ireland, a country variously described, with considerable poetic licence, as 'The Emerald Isle', 'The Green Isle of the Sea', 'An Isle of Sad Destiny', 'The Cinderella of Nations'.[12] The illustrated *Melbourne Punch* depicted the sombre but bounteous figure of Victoria appealing for assistance on behalf of distraught Erin, who is portrayed crouching barefooted in front of a shaded Celtic cross. The *Advocate*, Melbourne's Catholic weekly journal, applauded its contemporary for its 'well-conceived and generous' full-page illustration, observing that the pictorial appeal on behalf of 'unfortunate Ireland' was creditable to 'Mr Punch's heart', and would have a more powerful impact than the most eloquent address, whether written or spoken. The *Advocate* parsed the design and imagery for its readers:

It represents Victoria appealing for help for Ireland, the personification of the former being a well-conditioned, fashionably dressed woman, who, whilst mutely but eloquently asking for help, holds up her pinafore to receive it. Hapless Erin is seated at the foot of a Celtic cross, thoughtless of her harp and shield on the ground at her side; her head resting in sorrow on her attenuated hands; her long, dishevelled

## HELP FOR IRELAND.

*"BIS DAT, QUI CITO DAT."*

Fig. 2.1: 'Help for Ireland', *Melbourne Punch*, 15 January 1880, p. 5.

hair hanging over her face on her lap, and the snow falling piteously on her lightly clad, shrunken shoulders. The sharp outlines of a fine but wasted figure are seen through the drapery; there are no sandals on the feet, which rest on a cold, marshy soil that evidently had but lately been flooded, and the pose of the figure, with all surroundings, indicates deep suffering and dejection.[13]

There was less urgency in those Australian publications that took their tone and frequently their news content from the British Tory press, especially *The Times*. The *Sydney Morning Herald* was thought to manifest a strong and stubborn anti-Irish bias. Its persistent denial of the existence of any untoward distress in Ireland during the winter of 1879–80 provoked a bitter response from the Irish community in New South Wales,[14] one correspondent claiming that the newspaper's jaundiced views were inspired by 'pure malignity'.[15] A similar animus prompted the suggestion in some Tory-leaning journals that funds subscribed for the relief of distress in Ireland would be diverted to political causes and purposes, which was a recurring theme, and not just in Australia, as we shall see.[16] In general, however, journalists displayed maturity and objectivity in distinguishing between humanitarianism and politics, promoting the former generously and vigorously while condemning unreservedly Irish agrarian and political agitation and its supporters.[17]

Against this generally sympathetic background, public meetings took place in Brisbane, Melbourne and Sydney between 7 and 12 January 1880. Government ministers, parliamentary representatives, leading churchmen, and other civic dignitaries were present at each venue. Sir Arthur Kennedy presided over the Brisbane meeting, the mayors of Melbourne and Sydney chaired their respective events. The governor of New South Wales made a personal donation of £25, acknowledging that aid from Sydney would be an act of 'fraternal friendship' and a memorial to their patriotism. The colonial secretary, Henry Parkes, who had little affection for Ireland or its people, offered his sympathy in lieu of a subscription, and apologised for his inability to attend the Sydney gathering.[18]

The meetings in the various colonial capitals shared similar features: exhortatory speeches, the passage of resolutions of support, and the election of relief committees, whose members were recruited from the pillars of the political, ecclesiastical and business establishments, individuals who served as lodestones, lent gravitas, and portrayed the relief appeal as genuinely humanitarian, non-sectarian and apolitical. When first appointed, the Melbourne central committee, which was representative of those in the other colonial capitals, consisted of thirty-seven members. Of the twenty-three whose biographical details were located, eleven were born in Ireland, seven in Scotland and five in England; six of the Irish committee members were practising Roman Catholics, three, possibly four, were Anglicans; one of the Scots was an Anglican, another a Methodist and the remainder were Presbyterians – one described as an Orangeman, another as a prominent Freemason; the religious affiliations of two of the English-born committee members could not be ascertained; of the remainder, one was a member of the Church of England, another a Methodist, and the Liverpool-born Jew Ephraim Lamen Zox was an Oddfellow and Freemason.[19]

The central relief committees were largely ornamental. The real work was done by smaller tightly organised executive committees, led energetically by Jennings in Sydney, O'Doherty in Brisbane, and O'Shanassy in Melbourne, despite the latter's close and crucial involvement in Victoria's acrimonious politics in the early months of 1880. In mid-January *Melbourne Punch* observed that the impending general election in the colony would benefit the Irish relief fund, and proffered the sardonic comment that a singular feature of any such election was the creation of 'a healthful desire in legislative breasts to assist in any laudable object which may be prominently before the public'.[20] The mayor of Adelaide, E.T. Smith, MP, English-born brewer, Freemason and devout Congregationalist, was described as the heart and soul of the movement in South Australia, 'the most genuine and ardent friend the suffering poor of Ireland have had in the Australian colonies'. Such an encomium, though sincere, was somewhat disingenuous. The author of the panegyric, M.T. Montgomery, the trenchant and waspish honorary secretary of the South Australian relief fund, was the real inspiration behind the colony's appeal, and thus the instigator of the entire Australian colonial response to the evolving crisis in Ireland.[21]

The executive committees in the various colonial capitals circularised influential people, including mayors of municipalities, shire presidents, magistrates and newspaper editors, encouraging them to promote the appeal in their respective localities.[22] Dilatory civic leaders were given short shrift in the local press. One Tasmanian publication directed a deprecatory editorial at the mayor of Launceston because of his reluctance to become involved, informing him that it was his 'plain duty' to support and advance the relief effort by every means in his power.[23] Scores of public meetings were held throughout Australia in the opening months of 1880, at which hundreds of platform speakers, possessors of varying oratorical gifts and powers of persuasion, appealed to their listeners' Christian duty, their common humanity, a feature which, according to one Ballarat advocate, distinguished civilised man from the savage.[24]

Several proponents contrasted current antipodean prosperity with Ireland's poverty and wretchedness and urged Australian colonists to share some of their bounty with their less fortunate fellow subjects in another part of the British empire. The lieutenant-governor of New South Wales described the colony as 'great, wealthy and happy'.[25] John O'Shanassy depicted Victoria as a land of 'plenty and comfort',[26] a colony that had just enjoyed its finest harvest ever, according to one provincial newspaper.[27] Similarly, Tasmania had experienced a harvest of 'exceptional bountifulness'.[28] In a prologue written for a theatrical performance in Adelaide in aid of the relief fund, South Australia was presented as a land teeming with golden grain, while Ireland starved.[29]

There were many references to the generosity with which Australian colonists had responded to recent humanitarian appeals from Lancashire, Cornwall, India and China.[30] A resident of Maitland, New South Wales, was reluctant to draw parallels between the current Irish crisis and the recent Indian famine, claiming egregiously that many Indians were 'blood-thirsty people', while the Irish were 'much nearer and dearer to them',[31] which suggests that under a common crown, some British imperial subjects were more equal than others. Adelaide's Catholic vicar-general expressed a similar sentiment, albeit more adroitly, observing that if the colonists could display generosity to those who were 'total strangers to them in nationality, colour, politics and everything else', their duty to 'their own flesh and blood, their own nationality and kindred' was infinitely greater.[32]

Inevitably, there were references to the Great Famine of the 1840s, several of those involved in the relief appeal having experienced that dread visitation.[33] 'There are many amongst us who well remember the terrible sufferings of the people in those days,' an emotional and emotive editorial in the Sydney *Freeman's Journal* of 3 January 1880 recalled, 'when the roads and the hill sides presented the ghastly spectacle of the skeleton dead and the fever-stricken dying, when to live was a misery and to be dead a comfort.' Sir Arthur Kennedy, governor of Queensland, who had lived and worked among famine victims in County Clare, admitted that he could never forget that great calamity: 'To see the frightful ravages which it committed amongst us, both young and old, was something to try the strongest and it tried me severely.'[34]

In general, those who recounted their earlier famine experiences were neither accusatory nor recriminatory nor demonstrably Anglophobic. There was little support among the Irish in Australia for John Mitchel's genocidal thesis of the Almighty sending the potato blight but the English creating the Famine.[35] On the contrary, many empathised with the strongly integrationist argument of the Richmond-based Jesuit Thomas Cahill that the Great Famine was providential, an act of God, and that England's response had been noble and generous. Such kindness, he stated, did much to extinguish anti-English prejudice among Irish people and would never be forgotten by them.[36]

Roger Vaughan, Sydney's English-born Catholic archbishop, made a passionate appeal to Australian generosity at the city's Masonic Hall on 12 January 1880, harping on many of the tropes that were addressed on other platforms and in the Catholic and pro-Irish press. He did so with greater intellectual rigour, learning and articulacy than most, while sharing the cloying sentimentality of many. Famine in Ireland was central to his address: Elizabethan famine; the famine of 1740–1, which accounted for up to 400,000 lives; the apocalyptic Famine of the 1840s, when 'it seemed as if the peasant world of Ireland, that noble race, was absolutely coming to an end'. Vaughan contrasted the two countries' respective situations: Ireland threatened and suppliant, Australia – 'in whose bosom the gold dwells' – a land of flocks and herds, cornfields and vineyards. The archbishop eulogised Daniel O'Connell as 'that king of men and tribune of the people', and attributed his death in 1847, mistakenly, to his exertions on behalf of the poor during the Great Famine. He cited Job, and concluded his exhortation with an extract from Oliver Goldsmith's 'The Deserted Village' (lines 51–6):

> Ill fares the land, to hastening ills a prey,
> Where wealth accumulates and men decay:
> Princes and lords may flourish or may fade;
> A breath can make them, as a breath has made;
> But a bold peasantry, their country's pride,
> When once destroyed, can never be supplied.[37]

Archbishop Vaughan did not deliver overt political opinions or statements, nor did he apportion blame, attributing earthly misfortunes to providence. Yet, sections of the Sydney press admonished him for his naivety in portraying O'Connell both as famine victim and model Irish patriot and reprimanded the archbishop further for his irresponsibility in 'renewing the memory of the bitterest animosities that ever cursed Great Britain and Ireland'.[38]

It was inevitable – given the nature and cause of the humanitarian appeal, the number and range of public meetings and the multiplicity of speakers and their opinions – that the political dynamic between Ireland and Britain would feature in the public discourse, and that the more politically attuned would attribute current Irish distress to the inequitable land system, to tenant insecurity, and to the lack of Irish self-government. One commentator, straddling both cultures comfortably, observed that spendthrift Irish landowners and their grasping agents stripped their unfortunate tenants as bare as if they had been rifled by bushrangers.[39] Some called for the abolition of landlordism and the introduction of peasant proprietorship in Ireland.[40] Others insisted, as had proponents of similar international appeals in the 1840s, that land reform would not of itself resolve the country's problems, which had, they contended, an inescapable political dimension. Ireland's impoverished condition would persist while it remained under what one pungent observer termed 'the jealous, palsying influence of English misrule'.[41] The solution was the establishment of a home rule parliament in Dublin's College Green. Those who advocated such a course were confident that once self-government was achieved – and here the Australian colonies served as a model – native entrepreneurs would revitalise the economy and lay the foundations for a better future for themselves and their country[42] – the classic, if naïve, analysis of Ireland's colonial situation, and its resolution.

Such sentiments were hardly grist to the charitable mill, and in general the platform speakers confined themselves to addressing the immediate famine crisis in Ireland and its resolution. While those of a clerical persuasion liked to remind their listeners that they were all God's children, the politicians bade them remember they were Queen Victoria's also, and as such deserving of sibling comfort and support. All Australian colonists, irrespective of their place of origin, were members of the British empire, and the Irish contribution to imperial consolidation, administration and protection was positively noted.[43] One Melbourne publication versified at some length on Ireland's defence of the imperial ideal, its fourteen extravagant quatrains encapsulated in the couplet:

And from the shamrock's tears of grief
The English rose caught new relief.[44]

Commentators agreed that Ireland's inestimable support for the empire entitled her to reciprocity in her current distressed circumstances. 'Australis' instructed the readers of one Queensland newspaper that British and Irish had fought side by side 'on the heights of Torres Vedras and on the battlefields of India'.[45] 'Cerberus' informed the inhabitants of the shire of Metcalfe in Victoria that soldiers from 'martial spirited old Ireland' were at that very moment formed in a phalanx around their queen, country and commerce, protecting them in the peace and safety of their homes from the world's warlike powers.[46] An Anglican clergyman in Victoria claimed that in addition to fighting England's wars, Irishmen had written some of her best ballads and poetry, adorned her bar and thrilled the House of Commons with their eloquence – a singularly inappropriate and ironic observation given the obstructionist tactics Parnell and the home rule party were then pursuing at Westminster – and concluded magnanimously that 'the sons of Ireland deserved well at the hands of all British subjects'.[47]

The Irish famine relief appeal was portrayed as a genuinely humanitarian endeavour, one in which all colonists should be involved. The widow's mite and the working man's shilling were as eagerly sought as the rich man's pound. The suggestion of inter-denominationalism noted in the composition of the appeal's initiatory committees was substantiated by the frequency with which clergymen of various Christian denominations shared public platforms.[48] The plight of the famine-stricken Irish also evoked the sympathy of the Jewish community in Victoria. A recently launched Judaic journal appealed to every 'Israelite' in the colony to help 'his suffering fellow creatures' in Ireland, positing a close resemblance between the Jewish experience and that of the Irish, and contending, fancifully, that of all countries with an ancient history, Ireland alone had not persecuted the Jews.[49]

The relief appeal was not aimed exclusively at Irish expatriates, or at individuals of any particular religious persuasion, but, as the Melbourne *Advocate* reminded its readers, Irish and Catholic colonists should not forget that the plea for assistance had 'a special claim on them'.[50] Similarly, Dr James Murray, bishop of Maitland, in an inclusive appeal pitched at 'all classes without distinction of race or creed', reminded his own flock that as Catholics they were especially beholden to Ireland, the source of those 'zealous priests and nuns' who conferred on them the blessings of their holy religion, adding, with a nod to St Paul, that Catholic Ireland had an inherent entitlement to their material gifts in return for tending to their spiritual needs and welfare.[51]

His hierarchical colleagues, those in Melbourne, Sydney, Brisbane and Goulburn particularly, threw their considerable episcopal and archiepiscopal weight behind the humanitarian appeal, while the parochial clergy were active promoters of public meetings and organisers of subscriptions. On 30 December 1879 James Alipius Goold, Cork-born archbishop of Melbourne, issued a pastoral invitation to the clergy and laity of the archdiocese to contribute to the relief of the distressed poor in Ireland: 'A cry for help comes to us from our suffering brethren in Ireland. Hunger and the discomfort of a winter, unusually cold and wet, weigh heavily upon them.'[52] The *Advocate* commented editorially on the archbishop's pastoral and on the distress in Ireland: 'The amount so subscribed will flow through the best-informed channels into the hands of the unfortunate people whose distress is most urgent, and who have the strongest claims on our sympathy.' The writer advised that the archbishop's appeal should take precedence over a similar plea for help from 'the patriotic Nun of Kenmare', which also appeared in its columns: 'Our own venerable prelate's appeal is entitled to the first consideration.'[53] A general collection was subsequently taken up in all Melbourne archdiocesan churches, yielding £1,500, and Melbourne's example was followed in Catholic churches throughout Australia. The hierarchy resisted pressure from some sections of the Catholic press to send the proceeds directly to their counterparts in Ireland for distribution among the Catholic poor.[54] The monies realised were remitted to the Dublin Mansion House relief committee in the normal way, through the central relief committees in the various colonial capitals, for equitable distribution among the Irish poor, regardless of their religious beliefs.

Domiciliary canvassing for funds complemented church collections and was extensively engaged in, although the process, which involved an element of pressure or compulsion, did not meet with universal approval.[55] Supplicatory letters and subscription lists were widely circulated. In South Australia, for example, 2,427 were distributed: 618 to hotels or public houses, 512 to unspecified establishments, institutions and committees, 437 to post offices, 319 to schools, 190 to stations or landed properties, 102 to district councils, 101 to banks, 89 to police stations, 25 to newspapers, 18 to municipalities and 16, inexplicably, to lighthouse keepers.[56]

Auctions, raffles, lectures, and the proceeds of river and ocean cruises swelled the relief coffers.[57] At Port Augustus and Stirling in South Australia a sack of flour was sold and resold until £50 was realised, an action described as 'a Yankee notion for raising funds'.[58] A clergyman in Hobart delivered a public discourse on 'A Friend in Need' which netted more than £10, after which the attendance joined in singing the doxology 'Praise God from Whom All Blessings Flow'.[59] Concerts and melodramas were staged, including one promoted by the Independent Order of Rechabites at the Oddfellows Hall, Balmain, where the order's secretary, by way of prologue, promoted the propriety and virtue of teetotalism.[60] Public concerts at Sydney and Adelaide, despite the well-publicised presence of the governors of New South Wales and South Australia, and their wives, were sparsely attended, due to incessant rain in the former and excessive heat in the latter. Those who braved the elements were exposed to a musical medley – in Sydney, Barker's 'Patrick Ma Cushla' juxtaposed with a Gluck aria, and Benedict's 'Erin' played in counterpoint to a Chopin polonaise.[61] The Adelaide programme was a more popular one, a melange of Irish and Australian balladry and sentimentality.[62] In Hobart, the performer's interpretation of the comic song 'Tim Flaherty' was well received by the 'lenient and hearty' audience, according to the local newspaper's patronising notice of the city's fund-raising concert.[63] *Pike O'Callaghan*, which was one of several stock Victorian melodramas staged, was described by a smug Brisbane reviewer as having 'just enough plot to sustain the interest of the audience, without making excessive demands on their imagination'. The performer who played the role of the eponymous O'Callaghan appealed to the attendance, in a specially modified version of the familiar air 'Ireland where the Grass Grows Green', to donate to the famine relief fund.[64] Dion Boucicault's *The Colleen Bawn* was staged at Ballarat,[65] and at Bendigo, where the performance was interspersed with warmly appreciated renditions of 'The Cruiskeen Lán', 'The Wearing of the Green' and 'The Powers of Whiskey', though the evening ended on a rather flat note, the size of the hall defying the lady ventriloquist's powers of delivery.[66]

The various fund-raising activities in the Australian colonies – which had an estimated population of some 2.2 million at the close of the 1870s – generated more than £84,000.

According to the final report of the Dublin Mansion House relief committee, Australasia contributed almost £95,000 for Irish famine relief, divided as follows:

- Victoria, £31,315
- New South Wales, £28,000
- Queensland, £12,069
- South Australia, £7,837
- Tasmania, £3,619
- Western Australia, £1,215
- individual subscriptions, £120
- New Zealand, £10,427
- Fiji, £315.[67]

## New Zealand

New Zealand's reaction to the Irish famine relief appeal resembled Australia's in its motivation and generosity. In 1880 Irish-born residents constituted almost 20 per cent of New Zealand's population,[68] and many of those who responded to the calls for assistance were personally invested in the plight of their homeland, their empathy reflected in the action of five gold-diggers who walked about forty miles from their claim to hand over £5, 'their mite', to the officers of the Nelson famine relief fund.[69] Other New Zealanders were prompted by a more expansive inheritance, the fellowship of a shared empire – 'the sympathy and benevolence of the colonists of this portion of the British empire', as the Greymouth Irish Distress Relief Fund Committee phrased it. A.R. Guinness, the Greymouth county chairman and a member of the relief committee, acknowledged that 'belonging to the British nation' afforded the privilege of assisting any portion of the empire that required help, mutuality that transcended any existing differences of opinion and demonstrated that 'they were a united nation'.[70] The 'various classes, creeds and countries' that constituted the Greymouth community subscribed £600, 'ungrudgingly and cheerfully', and the committee expected that the money would be 'distributed with the same broad and philanthropic spirit' that had motivated the donors.[71]

A similar inclusiveness characterised relief committees throughout colonial New Zealand. At the inaugural meeting in Dunedin on 16 January 1880, with only the scantiest information on the situation in Ireland available to the convenors and those in attendance, Rev. Dr Stuart stated that 'it was quite enough to awaken their sympathies and elicit their benevolence to be told that there was deep distress in Ireland, an interesting portion of the British empire, and that fellow subjects and fellow Christians were suffering from lack of bread'. W.D. Stewart, a member of the New Zealand House of Representatives, suggested that 'it was not necessary to inquire into the cause of the distress. It was quite sufficient to know that distress existed.'[72] The mayor of Dunedin, where £1,893 was eventually subscribed, may have captured the spirit and feelings of all who contributed to the Irish charitable appeal when he stated that their efforts were amply repaid by the knowledge that they were helping to alleviate, in however small a degree, 'the great misery' arising from famine in Ireland.[73]

Some advocates, among them Rev. Dr Stuart and Mr Justice Williams at the Dunedin meeting, referred to New Zealand's absence of poverty and its comparative prosperity, but others, contrarily, alluded to the commercial distress the colony was then experiencing, which had the effect of curtailing their response to the crisis in Ireland. The Christchurch and Wellington appeals, for example, were negatively affected by their concurrence with what the spokesman for the Christchurch appeal described as 'a period of great commercial depression' in New Zealand.[74]

As in Australia, some among the expatriate Irish in New Zealand were critical of the British government's response to the situation in Ireland. The originator of the Nelson relief committee, Irish-born Arthur McMurrough Kavanagh – a name with strong historical resonances in Ireland – expostulated: 'Poor Ireland! What must proud England's feeling be? Standing listlessly by at the door of our famine-stricken country, while all Christendom cries *shame*!' He claimed that England's treatment of Ireland had prompted numbers of colonists, formerly staunch supporters of the British government, to revise their opinion of the executive.[75]

One relief committee, representing Kennard goldfield and the town of Westland on the west coast of New Zealand's South Island, whose executive was almost entirely constituted of men with Irish surnames – O'Hagan, Dungan, Moran, Duggan – was more direct in its analysis, attributing the crisis in Ireland, like others of their countrymen at home and abroad, to the 'abominable' land system, and to the recurrence of bad seasons and harvests. The members hoped that the constitutional agitation then underway in Ireland would result in 'improved land laws', which, they claimed, would secure the country from 'these periodical scourges and enable the tiller of the soil to live in prosperity and contentment',[76] a sentiment they shared with their exiled brethren in Australia and elsewhere.

## Ireland acknowledges Australasian philanthropy

The generosity of the Australian and New Zealand response, the colonists' electric and eclectic sympathy with those suffering from famine and its consequences in Ireland, was avouched in a telegram from the lord mayor of Dublin, Edmund Dwyer Gray, Irish Parliamentary Party MP for County Tipperary and owner of the *Freeman's Journal*, and his wife Caroline, elder daughter of English-born Caroline Chisholm, who was feted in Australia for her community activism and her efforts on behalf of immigrants.[77] Gray subsequently addressed a public letter of gratitude to Sir John O'Shanassy in Melbourne which was intended for circulation throughout the colonies. Dublin's first citizen stated that the memory of Australian generosity 'will never be effaced from the mind of the Irish nation', and that Irish hearts were filled with admiration for such a people.[78] Antipodean bounty was fulsomely acknowledged in the Irish press, particularly in the news and editorial columns of the *Freeman's Journal*. At the end of January 1880, the newspaper commented:

> Those who give to the poor lend to the Lord, and no man who believes in the moral government of the world doubts that manifold blessings

will descend on those free communities beneath the Southern Cross for the promptitude and the munificence of their gifts ... The signal generosity of Australia has evoked throughout Ireland the strongest sentiments of gratitude and regard.

The writer concluded his encomium with the wish that the Australian colonies would enjoy all the positive attributes of the Old World but 'none of its manifold miseries – neither war nor famine, neither faction nor despotism, neither evil laws nor evil rulers',[79] an implicit attribution of current Irish distress to the country's circumscribed political and socio-economic situation, and a marked contrast to Australia's more favourable and privileged political status within the British empire.

The Mansion House relief committee, with Gray as spokesperson, was equally enthusiastic in its response to Australian generosity. In May 1880 the committee resolved to explore the best means of conveying Irish gratitude to the Australian colonists for 'the unprecedented munificence of their contributions'. At the meeting the lord mayor referred to 'the splendour of their subscriptions', and P.J. Smyth, who had succeeded Gray as Irish Parliamentary Party MP for Tipperary at the 1880 general election, and who was married to Jane Anne Regan, a Tasmanian with family links to Cork, stated that Australia had earned Edmund Burke's eulogium to America: 'With a filial piety and a Roman charity she holds the full breast of her youthful exuberance to the mouth of her exhausted parent.[80] The Mansion House relief committee claimed that the aid which saved 'the famishing Irish peasants at the most critical moment of the year' was that which the colonies literally showered upon them, and, the committee concluded fulsomely and genuinely, 'the effect of those huge anonymous remittances descending week after week struck the popular imagination with something of the wonder of a magic shower of gold'.[81]

The generosity of the Australian response, its warmth and spontaneity, its transcendence of religious, political, national and class boundaries, owed something to philanthropy, to stark memories of the Great Famine, to bonds of kinship among the Irish and to imperial ties among all colonists – a shared identity which implied reciprocal rights as well as obligations of loyalty and duty to queen and constitution. The response may have been partially triggered by a sentiment that the colonies were a racial melting pot, a distant peripheral location where immigrants could prosper, a land whose bounty could succour the suffering poor in the old country. This burgeoning sense of Australian identity manifested itself in the exhortation of one New South Wales resident to his fellow colonists to subscribe generously to the Mansion House appeal to disprove the novelist and traveller Anthony Trollope's view that the Australian colonies were inhabited only by 'blackfellows and kangaroos'.[82]

CHAPTER 3

# North America

Ireland is deeply indebted to her sons in Canada and the United States for their most generous aid in the period of her distress. There is no doubt that, were it not for the prompt, munificent offerings forwarded to our suffering people during the past months, we would have had to witness once more the heart-rending scenes of 1847.

Patrick F. Moran, bishop of Ossory, to Fr Jeremiah Ryan, Oakville, Ontario, 11 March 1880, *Irish Canadian*, 7 April 1880, p. 5

The generosity of America towards Ireland is unbounded, and already larger sums have been collected for the relief of that dear and suffering country than could have been expected.

Lady Georgiana Fullerton, Ayrfield, Bournemouth, England, to Rev. Daniel E. Hudson, 14 March 1880, *Ave Maria*, vol. 16, 10 April 1880, p. 295

## Introduction

The Mansion House relief committee's exuberant but genuine appreciation and acknowledgement of Australasian generosity was coloured and shaped by context, by the politics of time and place. As noted previously, the committee was one of several voluntary relief agencies established to combat Irish famine and distress, some of which were more ideologically and politically freighted than others. There was considerable public resistance in Australasia to the duchess of Marlborough's famine relief appeal because of a widespread perception that her committee was biased in favour of Irish landlords and the British government.[1] The Mansion House committee, on the other hand, was regarded as a genuinely humanitarian, non-sectarian and apolitical organisation, and did not attract any such animus.[2] In Australia and New Zealand – distant outposts of the British empire – where the Catholic Irish were in a minority and faced hostility, prejudice and sectarianism, the Mansion House committee's projection of itself as a philanthropic body stripped of religion and politics and established solely for the relief of an ever-deepening famine crisis in Ireland accorded with colonial sensibilities. The residents of the different colonies responded with compassion and generosity, as they had done to recent humanitarian appeals from Lancashire, Cornwall, India and China, and in Ireland's case did so with admirable leadership and cross-community purpose.

The reaction in the United States, an independent republic, was profoundly different: the Irish famine crisis was just as pressing, the sentiment equally humane, and the financial contributions comparably generous, but the political environment was dissimilar to that in Australasia. The difference in the American response was partly attributable to the decision by the recently inaugurated Irish National Land League to despatch a fund-raising deputation across the Atlantic, and the League's failure to specify from the outset the nature and purpose of the exercise, to differentiate between humanitarianism and politics. The presence and activities of Land League emissaries Charles Stewart Parnell, the League's president, and John Dillon in the United States and the nature and methodology of the political movement they represented divided American and Irish-American opinion and fragmented the response to Ireland's humanitarian crisis. Unlike Australasia, where the proceeds of colonial relief efforts were invariably remitted to the Mansion House relief committee, American funds were channelled in a variety of ways – by individuals directly to family and friends in Ireland, and through several agencies, most significantly the Land League, the Catholic Church, and James Gordon Bennett's *New York Herald* newspaper.[3]

The historiographical portrayal of the controversial mission's binary nature and purpose has been uneven. Most commentators have focused on the political rather than the humanitarian aspects, essentially because of Parnell's involvement and the venture's momentous impact on his political career. Parnell's part-American heritage, his personality and presence, and the compelling compound of politics and philanthropy expounded at various centres in the United States and Canada in the opening months of 1880 propelled the enigmatic member of parliament for Meath to the forefront of Irish nationalist politics and to international prominence.

Some scholars, such as R.F. Foster in his mid-1970s study of Parnell and his family, and the American historians N.D. Palmer, Merle Curti, and more recently Ely M. Janis, have attempted a more comprehensive parsing of the mission's humanitarian dimension.[4] Janis trawled American and Irish-American newspapers for the key themes of Parnell's public addresses and concluded that the most effective one was the famine crisis in Ireland. He contends that Parnell's decision to give priority to famine relief rather than the Land League's political agitation secured greater publicity and acceptance for the humanitarian message in America, both within and outside the Irish-American community. Janis, however, chose to concentrate on Parnell's politicisation of the 1879–80 Irish famine rather than pursue the American philanthropic response to the famine. For instance, his work mentions but does not detail Parnell's repeated denunciations of the famine relief funds that coexisted with the Land League's, nor does it examine these funds' modus operandi, not even that of the publicity-conscious *New York Herald*, though it does note Parnell's fractious relationship with the owner of that newspaper.[5]

The following survey of Parnell's North American mission and the wider humanitarian context within which it occurred acknowledges and is informed by Janis' work and that of the other scholars referred to above. It addresses the political aspects and significance of Parnell's undertaking, but aspires to a broader canvas, a more holistic assessment of transatlantic beneficence, a historiographical rebalancing of the political and humanitarian elements of the American and Canadian response to the 1879–80 famine in Ireland.

## The Parnell mission to the United States and Canada

On 21 December 1879 the rising nationalist politicians Charles Stewart Parnell and John Dillon embarked on a promotional tour of North America, their mission to raise funds for the fledgling Land League's political programme and, subordinately, for the relief of the hungry and distressed poor in Ireland. Parnell informed an enthusiastic and cheering crowd assembled at Queenstown to bid them farewell that their transatlantic venture would demonstrate that American hearts still 'beat warmly towards Ireland', that America would extend sympathy and practical assistance to the country's famine-stricken people, as it had done in 1847.[6]

The voyagers arrived in New York Harbour late on New Year's Day 1880, where they were met, according to Parnell's record of the event, by a 300-strong motley reception committee of distinguished judges, senators, merchants, Presbyterian ministers, Germans and miscellaneous others.[7] Such a gathering suggests homogeneity, uniformity of purpose and action, but it belies the reality of factional and fractious Irish-American politicking; the suspicions or outright hostility of some churchmen, newspaper interests and political conservatives; and the reluctance of many Americans and Irish Americans to contribute money to political causes in Ireland. These forces were particularly opposed to promoting the aims and agitation of the recently inaugurated Land League, which many regarded as meddling in European politics, in this case Britain's domestic affairs, a country generally perceived as well disposed to America. Despite their political reservations and differences, the various constituencies were anxious to display their sympathy for Ireland's starving poor and to contribute financially towards their relief. Cardinal McCloskey of New York and Bennett's New York Herald were perhaps the most prominent and influential exponents of the primacy of philanthropy over politics.[8]

The New York Herald drew a sharp distinction between the two impulses, encouraging the provision of food aid to Ireland but rejecting unequivocally any support for political or agrarian agitation. In a series of increasingly strident editorials throughout December 1879 in anticipation of Parnell's arrival in the United States, Bennett's paper questioned the Irish politician's motives for crossing the Atlantic – fleeing possible prosecution in Ireland and promoting 'a sedition fund' were among the suggestions – and all but demonised the movement he represented, depicting the Land League as a communist agitation

# HARPER'S WEEKLY.

## JOURNAL OF CIVILIZATION

VOL. XXIV.—No. 1204.] NEW YORK, SATURDAY, JANUARY 24, 1880. [SINGLE COPIES TEN CENTS.
$4.00 PER YEAR IN ADVANCE.

Entered according to Act of Congress, in the Year 1880, by Harper & Brothers, in the Office of the Librarian of Congress, at Washington.

BEWARE OF FOREIGN TRAMPS.

PAT RIOT. "Ah! you innercent Bridget, darlint, sure it's not a starvation of food that throubles us, *but it's money we're afther.*"

Facing page: Fig. 3.1: 'Beware of Foreign Tramps', *Harper's Weekly*, vol. 24, 24 January 1880, p. 49.

Pat Riot: 'Ah! You innercent Bridget, darlint, sure it's not a starvation of food that throubles us, *but it's money we're afther.'*

*Harper's Weekly*, which was founded in 1857 and based in New York City, was an influential American political magazine whose content and tone were consistently anti-Irish, reflected here in the use of negative Irish stereotypes. The cartoonist, German-born Thomas Nast, portrays the tension between famine relief and political opportunism, a continuing debate in the United States throughout Charles Stewart Parnell's fund-raising mission. Pat Riot (patriot!) bears a passing resemblance to Parnell. Bridget – predictably, an Irish domestic servant – offers him a miniature of a relief vessel, flying an Irish harp fore and the Stars and Stripes aft, and bearing the legend 'Full of Food for Ireland'.[9]

---

that threatened property rights everywhere. In a blistering leading article on 17 December the *Herald* denounced the agrarian agitation led by Parnell as 'a fierce and murderous crusade against common honesty – a war upon that first principle of sound morals recognised in all ages and countries, that it is the duty of men to fulfil their contracts'.[10]

The tension generated by these conflicting forces and the reaction they provoked forced Parnell to recalibrate, and within a few days of his arrival in New York, at a meeting at Madison Square Garden presided over by Judge Henry A. Gildersleeve, Parnell proposed to open two funds, one to promote the stated objectives of the Land League, the other for famine relief, and to keep the two separate so that donors could specify which of the funds they wished to support.[11] Parnell contended, however, and continued to do so at different times and locations in the United States and Canada, that the current distress in Ireland was a consequence of the prevailing system of land tenure, and that the organisation he represented aimed to sweep away landlordism and to convert the occupiers of land into owners, a process that was perceived as the essential first step on the road to political independence for Ireland.[12] The Great Famine of the 1840s, with its powerful resonances for the transatlantic Irish, was central to Parnell's argument and he returned to the Famine and its impact time and again in his North American platform speeches, in order to link the past with the political present, to awaken both consciousness and memory among the diasporic Irish, and to place the responsibility for Ireland's prostration and helplessness firmly on the country's iniquitous land system and mode of government.[13]

Parnell and Dillon launched an Irish relief fund on 9 January 1880, and appealed to the American people for subscriptions to alleviate distress in Ireland, especially in the Atlantic counties, Donegal, Sligo, Mayo, Galway, Clare, Kerry and Cork, where, they claimed, 250,000 people required three months' assistance to save them from starvation and pauperism.[15] They established an Irish relief office in New York, which Parnell's sisters, Anna, Fanny and Theodosia, attended regularly to receive donations.[15] In mid-February Parnell summoned twenty-three-year-old Tim Healy, the Dublin *Nation*'s London-based parliamentary correspondent, to New York to relieve the unsystematic John Dillon of the mission's secretarial duties.[16] Healy's impression on arrival was that the Parnell sisters worked diligently and took a great interest in 'the Movement'.[17]

Some weeks previously, in early December 1879, Anna Parnell had offered a spirited public defence of the Land League and her brother as president of that organisation, following an attack on both by the *New York Herald*, which predicted that the Land League would misappropriate for its own political ends any funds raised in America, an accusation that mirrored those in the opinion columns of the reactionary press in Australia. The *Herald* described the Land League as 'a lawless, violent and revolutionary movement for the subversion of the rights of property', and its leaders, Parnell and Davitt among them, as 'unscrupulous demagogues' who were 'exciting Ireland to violence, rapine, murder and revolution'. The writer encouraged the Irish in America to reject the politicians' overtures and to promote mass emigration from Ireland as the most effective means of addressing the country's current difficulties. 'Emigration, and not revolution, is the cure for the ills of Ireland and for the grievances of the Irish people,' he proclaimed, and he trumpeted the newspaper's message to that constituency and to its American readers generally: 'Not one cent for Parnell and his crowd, but millions to help emigration to this country', before exhorting: 'Let us hear no more Fenian nonsense, no proposition to "free Ireland" by processions three thousand miles off. That does no good; it only fills the pockets of adventurers and demagogues', by inference Parnell, Davitt, and the Land League leadership generally.[18]

Anna Parnell retorted by criticising the British government's support for Irish landlords and the provision of state assistance in the eviction process when tenants defaulted on their rents. She castigated the government's 'murderous programme', comparing it to official policy in the famine year of 1847, and accused the *New York Herald* of complicity and partisanship, of deliberately inciting 'the British government to destroy, by cold and hunger, hundreds of thousands of unoffending men, women and children'. Anna dismissed the newspaper's championing of emigration as 'an absurdity' and implored the wage-earners of America to support the Land League and its policies, thereby saving themselves from misery and Ireland from ruin.[19] Her sister Fanny was equally trenchant in her rejection of the *New York Herald*'s editorial stance on emigration, asserting that the Irish people had a right 'to happiness and prosperity in their own country'.[20]

Fanny Parnell was an early advocate of Irish-American intervention on behalf of the poverty-stricken and famishing peasantry in the west of Ireland. In late August 1879 she appealed to the readers of the Boston *Pilot* to help their countrymen 'in their terrible need', espousing the maxim: 'We should sacrifice our luxuries to other people's conveniences, our conveniences to other people's necessities.' She suggested that landlord negligence and unresponsiveness to the crisis in Ireland necessitated external humanitarian mediation, observing, with bitter irony, that threats of coercive legislation and wholesale evictions were 'the only answer which the Christian charity of the landlords has as yet seen fit to make to the cry of the starving'. Fanny proposed a public subscription and opened the fund with a personal donation of $75. The editor of the *Pilot*, John Boyle O'Reilly, endorsed her appeal, commenting that as sister to Charles Stewart Parnell, 'the unflinching Member of Parliament for Meath, and the originator and leader of "Obstruction"' – a reference to the policy of impeding parliamentary procedures and delaying legislation by radical elements of the home rule party – her name would be received with affection. The editor promised to acknowledge all subscriptions to the relief fund, and to remit the proceeds to Archbishop

John MacHale of Tuam, Charles Stewart Parnell, and the editor of the *Nation* newspaper for distribution among those in need.[21]

Anna, Fanny and Theodosia Parnell, members of an elite Anglo-Irish Protestant landowning family, were ecumenical in their approach to fund-raising, prompted by genuine concern for the hungry and distressed mainly Catholic Irish peasantry. According to one newspaper account, 'the three Misses Parnell' placed collection boxes in the New York Post Office and in many other business premises and divided the contributions equally among Archbishop MacHale and Sister Mary Francis Clare, the Nun of Kenmare.[22] Separately, Fanny promoted the latter's charitable appeals in the American press and personally contributed to her relief fund.[23]

On 4 January 1880, days after Charles Stewart Parnell's arrival in New York, an importunate and rather naïve Sister Clare appealed to the Parnell family to assist her charitable endeavours on behalf of Ireland's starving poor. She requested Fanny Parnell to organise a fund-raising fair or concert, informing her peevishly that all the current aid was being directed to Galway and Mayo at the expense of Kerry and other affected parts of the country, and she implored Fanny to intercede with her brother Charles on her behalf, to encourage him to transfer to her a portion of the 'immense sums of money' he would shortly receive. Clare claimed that as her name was so well known, vulnerable people throughout Ireland applied to her for assistance and she would require 'a large share' of whatever funds were available to meet their needs. She proposed that Fanny should obtain the money from her brother whenever he had 'any large sum' and remit it to the convent at Kenmare, 'as otherwise he may easily forget, with all he has to do'. Fanny forwarded 'the nun's petition' to the *New York Herald* for publication, with the comment that she would encourage Clare to apply directly to the Land League for some of the proceeds of that organisation's fund-raising endeavours. She observed in a postscript that Clare erred in believing that Parnell was able to supply her with money from the Land League fund; he did not have the authority to do so, she wrote, and none of the money passed through his hands.[24]

Tim Healy described Fanny Parnell as 'really clever'. He was particularly impressed by her article on the Irish land question in a recent edition of the *North American Review* – though her brother Charles' name was appended as author – and by a pamphlet, *The Hovels of Ireland*, which she had written for an American readership in order to raise money for the Land League's relief programme, and which, according to Healy, went through several editions within a few months.[25] The pamphlet, a sustained critique of the Irish land system, was informed by her own lively intelligence and her political and social radicalism, moulded by extensive reading on political economy and on Irish, European and American history. The preface, which was attributed to Charles Stewart Parnell – though, again, he is unlikely to have been the author – focused on the rights and duties of land ownership. It opened with the contention that property was made for the benefit and use of humankind and claimed as its central tenet that there was no such thing as absolute property in land. Fanny Parnell argued that the system of land ownership and land-holding in Ireland was responsible for the country's chronic misery, for the 'hopeless, voiceless poverty' that had enshrouded the great mass of the Irish people for generations. She herself had been imbued with all the prejudices of her Anglo-Irish Protestant and Tory family background until Ireland's social and political realities – 'the constant spectacle of tyranny and cold-blooded heartlessness on one side, and of suffering and degradation on the other' – had shattered her complacency. This defining dichotomy had provoked her anger and indignation and convinced her that peasant proprietorship was the only way to rectify the iniquities of the current system. 'The landlord belonged to the conquering race,' she claimed, 'and the laws of the country to which the conquering race belonged gave the landlord, and still give him, every power over his tenant short of direct murder.' Despite their current entrenched and seemingly impregnable position, Fanny Parnell pronounced that the Irish landlords' parasitic days were numbered, and with them England's sovereignty over Ireland. She appealed for American sympathy for her 'prostrate country' and support for Ireland's political struggle. 'Words are but little to ask,' she concluded, 'but words from a power like America resound all over the world, and can plead, trumpet-tongued, for a downtrodden cause.'[26]

Charles Stewart Parnell, on whom his sisters' and a large segment of his country's aspirations rested, regarded the other relief agencies as competitors. In particular, he provoked the ire of James Gordon Bennett, owner of the *New York Herald*, and Bennett became a trenchant critic of Parnell and his American mission.[27] There were several reasons for their mutual antipathy – Bennett's innate conservatism; his opposition to the Land League's political programme and its implications for property rights and ownership; and Parnell's refusal to link the Land League's fund-raising with Bennett's own humanitarian efforts in the *Herald*, because of his belief that Bennett and his newspaper were biased in favour of Irish landlords and the British government.[28] Parnell was equally critical of the Marlborough and Mansion House relief committees and launched attack after blistering attack on both, claiming that they were antagonistic to the Irish people and their aspirations, more concerned with relieving landlords and the British government of their responsibilities than aiding the starving Irish peasantry.[29]

Parnell's salvoes culminated in an open letter to the newspaper editors of the United States on 9 February 1880, with John Dillon as co-signatory. The pair referred to 'the terrible emergency of famine' which was pressing upon the Irish people, and they promoted the Land League's relief efforts at the expense of the other agencies. They claimed that the controlling force of the Marlborough fund was not the duchess but her husband, who, as lord lieutenant of Ireland, was responsible for the government's actions in the country. Thus, they contended, the actual as opposed to the titular head of the Marlborough famine relief fund was simultaneously engaged in promoting the appeal and in sending soldiers 'to bayonet the women and children' whose distress he was supposedly alleviating, driving them from their homes into the snow to perish of cold and hunger, and seizing their remaining provisions in partial satisfaction of their landlords' exorbitant rent demands.[30]

Parnell and Dillon directed similar invective at the Mansion House committee, stating that it was controlled by individuals whose primary concern was the preservation of the landlord interest in Ireland. They accused several members of the committee of 'eviction atrocities' and claimed that the hands of others reeked of 'the blood of the Connemara women butchered within the last few weeks', a reference to a recent eviction campaign in Carraroe, County Galway, which had been widely reported in the press. Parnell and Dillon observed that Irish people could not have confidence in such a committee, that it was cruel to compel the starving peasantry to apply for their food and survival to the very men against whom they were engaged in 'an unequal contest' for the possession and ownership of the land of Ireland. They accused both committees of conspiracy to divert American charity indirectly into landlord hands, of abusing American goodwill and humanitarianism for their own selfish ends.[31]

Parnell and Dillon's explosive and unashamedly partisan exposition of Irish landlordism and its trappings and of the shortcomings of the private relief committees in their open letter to the newspaper editors of the United States drew a near hysterical response from the *Freeman's Journal* in Dublin, whose owner, an apoplectic Edmund Dwyer Gray, was also chairman of the Mansion House relief committee, and a fellow elected member of the Irish Parliamentary Party at Westminster. The relationship between Parnell and Gray was already fractious. The two had previously clashed over the government's Irish university education legislation. Subsequently, the *Freeman's Journal* accused Parnell of rudeness towards several of his party colleagues, culminating in the charge that he had denounced those who opposed his line on the university question as 'a cowardly set of papist rats'.[32] An overly excited editorial in the *Freeman* criticised Parnell and Dillon's denigration of the Mansion House relief committee as 'an outrage to all decency', 'a gross and shameless libel ... reckless and nonsensical rant ... malign and almost maniac misstatement'. The writer claimed that their 'extraordinary emanation', which denounced everybody and everything except themselves, their followers and their agenda, was inspired by a 'spirit of jealousy' and was indefensible. The *Freeman's* editorial response coupled Parnell and Dillon in its strictures, but the former was the writer's critical target.[33]

Conservative newspapers and journals in the United States were equally outraged. The *New York Tribune* claimed editorially that Parnell's demonisation of the Marlborough and Mansion House relief committees, the violence of his language, and his subordination of philanthropy to political agitation were counterproductive, that his personality and his politics discouraged Americans from responding liberally to Ireland's famine crisis: 'Wherever Mr Parnell speaks,' the writer stated, 'suspicion is aroused, and benevolence is chilled.'[34] Similar sentiments and censure featured in the conservative and religious press in Ireland and Britain. The *Irish Ecclesiastical Gazette*, for example, which was politically hostile to Parnell, rejected his 'slanderous and untruthful' denunciations of the Dublin relief committees, and observed that 'if Mr Parnell had his way, the starving Irish might die unpitied like dogs in their kennels'.[35]

The polarised nature of the debate was reflected in the *Nation*'s robust defence of Parnell, and its repudiation of the views of its more conservative Dublin rivals, particularly the *Freeman's Journal*. In a swingeing editorial, the *Nation* rebutted the latter's misrepresentation of Parnell, its 'savage and shameful' innuendo, which, it claimed, was motivated by 'personal rage and bitterness'. The irony, according to the writer, was that Parnell derived his information on the savagery that attended the Carraroe evictions in early January from the *Freeman's* published accounts of these events, and the *Nation* reproduced lengthy extracts from its contemporary to substantiate its claim. The broadside maintained its caustic stridency to the last:

> We are sorry for the spectacle presented to the country by the *Freeman* in its vicious and spiteful attack on Mr Parnell. In that matter, as well as on other occasions before and since, it has shown a pettiness of spirit almost childish, and certainly unbecoming a journal claiming to be a great public organ. Such conduct is discreditable not merely to the newspaper, but to the whole country; it is harmful to the national cause, and, even with regard to the *Freeman* itself, it cannot be persevered in with either honour or advantage.[36]

Anna Parnell shared her brother's trenchant views on the composition and motivation of the Dublin relief committees and denounced both committees in the *New York Herald* a few days before Parnell addressed his open letter to the newspaper editors of the United States. The tone, language and content of the siblings' letters displayed strong similarities, which suggests a close communion between Parnell family members during Charles' fund-raising tour of the United States, or at the very least a harmony of ideas concerning Ireland's political and socio-economic status. Anna referred to the Carraroe evictions, as did her brother subsequently, during which 'famine-stricken women were bayoneted, knocked down and then clubbed with the butt end of the soldiers' rifles'. Anna attributed responsibility to the duke of Marlborough, who, as viceroy, was accountable for the actions of the Irish executive and its agencies. Thus, she claimed, the head of one of the relief committees – 'for in this matter it is impossible to separate the duke from the duchess' – was simultaneously engaged 'in driving the people he pretends to relieve from their cabins out into the snow to die of cold and hunger, in taking what little provisions they may have from them, and in clubbing, stabbing and shooting them'. Anna Parnell claimed that the duchess of Marlborough was complicit in her husband's actions: she did not repudiate them publicly and had associated herself and 'her benevolent enterprise' with a relief committee whose members were 'in full sympathy with all the atrocities already committed against the destitute Irish, and also with all that are intended'. Anna was equally critical of the Mansion House committee, claiming that nearly all the members were 'avowed supporters of the policy of extermination', though she exempted the Catholic clergy who served on the committee from her charge. Anna attributed responsibility for the current famine, which she described intemperately as 'one of the most fearful crimes of this century', to English misgovernance and Irish landlordism, and she called on the people of New York to respond humanely and generously to the crisis, and to have the courage to call those responsible, the British government and the Irish landlords, by their rightful name – 'murderers'.[37]

The influential English-born American journalist James Redpath, who had visited Ireland in February 1880 to report on the famine for the *New York Tribune*, shared and reinforced the Parnells' sentiments regarding the relief committees. When Edmund Dwyer Gray, Dublin's lord mayor and chairman of the Mansion House relief committee, cabled an additional appeal for assistance to the American and Canadian public in June 1880, highlighting the helplessness of the Irish peasantry until the crops were harvested in the weeks and months ahead, Redpath's public response was immediate and insistent: 'Not a single dollar should be sent from America to the Lord Mayor of Dublin in response to this appeal.' Redpath acknowledged the reality of the Irish situation and the suffering of the poor but advised that aid should not be forwarded to the lord mayor or the Mansion House committee, opining that both deserved American condemnation rather than American subscriptions and support. He distinguished between the committee's active and ornamental members, describing the former as representatives of a class of Irishmen, landlords, who were prepared to disgrace their country before the world rather than use their own financial resources to assist their suffering tenantry. He continued ever more scathingly:

> Instead of appealing to these rich landed proprietors to have pity on the victims of their avarice and holding them up to the scorn of Christendom if they refuse assistance, the lord mayor of Dublin uses the Atlantic cable as a beggarman's dog to catch a few more pennies for the paupers whom these merciless and mercenary miscreants have created.

Redpath linked the Irish landowners indiscriminately with the wealthy classes in Ireland and Britain, and more specifically with the lord mayor of Dublin, whom he castigated as 'a persistent beggar from America'. He linked them also with the duchess of Marlborough and her wealthy husband, the possessor of the sinecure of Ireland's lord lieutenancy, and with the British parliament and royal family. Redpath condemned this collective for its 'shameless and heartless indifference' to Irish suffering and for its refusal to take any responsibility for Irish distress. According to Redpath, the United Kingdom's wealthier classes' lack of engagement with Ireland's famine ought to provoke American indignation and disapproval rather than subsidies. In contrast to the prevailing sentiment of American non-interference in European affairs, Redpath claimed that America had earned the right to criticise England's dealings with Ireland, and he advised Gray to 'pass the hat again to your penurious queen ... your merciless landlords, and your close-fitted gentry, before *you* shout across the Atlantic to us'.[38]

Parnell's repeated denunciations in the press and on American public platforms of the various famine relief committees in Ireland prompted Gray to seek the support of the Irish Catholic hierarchy for the Mansion House committee's work. Gray informed Archbishop McCabe of Dublin at the end of January 1880 that if Parnell's statements continued and were believed, the committee would be discredited and American subscriptions to the fund would cease, and he appealed for the archbishop's public expression of confidence and support.[39] McCabe and the episcopacy generally responded promptly and positively to the lord mayor's appeal, attesting to the Mansion House committee's integrity and impartiality. Daniel McGettigan, archbishop of Armagh and primate of all Ireland, captured the mood among the hierarchy when he stated that the committee was 'engaged in the noblest work under the sun'. Some of the bishops referred to the Great Famine and compared the Mansion House committee favourably with similar committees in the 1840s. Archbishop T.W. Croke of Cashel, the most nationalistically minded and outspoken member of the Irish Catholic hierarchy, was more lukewarm in his support, querying the political sympathies of several unnamed committee members, but his was a singular perspective.[40] The *Freeman's Journal*, and presumably its owner, basked in the glow of the hierarchical response, editorialising that the bishops' collective expression of approval, confidence and trust constituted 'the most remarkable and valuable body of testimony to the usefulness, the fairness and the wise management of a public charity that has ever been made public in Ireland'. The writer, plunging to ever lower depths of deference and debasement, claimed that the committee had received 'the solemn approval, the warm praise, the thorough confidence, the hearty Godspeed of the episcopacy', whose collective sanctity, patriotism, pious devotion and noble charity were unequalled anywhere in Christendom.[41]

Against this clerical and political backdrop, Parnell and Dillon traversed the United States for the first ten weeks of 1880 and crossed into Canada to canvass support in Toronto and Montreal. They promoted their twin projects – the Land League's political and social programme and Irish famine relief – in sixty-two cities, adapting the tone and content of their message to suit their audience and location. One sympathetic American journalist, in his efforts to convey Parnell's platform presence and style, portrayed him as a striking figure, tall and graceful, with a clear and manly mode of expression. The directness of Parnell's sentences rendered them more like missiles than propositions, the reporter opined, and the speaker impressed his audience with the strength of his case and the intensity of his convictions.[42] W.G. Matthews, special correspondent of The Irish Times, who accompanied Parnell on his North American tour and who may not have been overly sympathetic to his political philosophy and programme, provided a rather similar analysis of Parnell's oratorical style and skills. He attributed Parnell's success to the simplicity and force of his language, every sentence containing a new fact or conclusion. 'This concentration of language and intense earnestness of manner are the two secrets of Mr Parnell's strength as a speaker,' Matthews stated. 'He makes no appeal to any passion or faculty but reason, and his triumph in gaining conviction and sympathy is unqualified.'[43]

## The modus operandi and politics of fund-raising in the United States

We have noted the welcome extended to Parnell and Dillon on their arrival in New York on New Year's Day 1880. Occasions such as this were theatrical set-pieces which offered considerable licence to reception committees and stage-managers, and the cities and towns subsequently visited featured variations of the following: insignia, banners and bunting; parades and processions and marching bands; reception committees, frequently complemented by military guards of honour and groups of musicians; addresses of welcome; interaction with representatives of cultural, social and philanthropic organisations; and in the evening a public meeting, attended by influential citizens and local dignitaries, and an audience, invariably several thousand strong, who paid what was considered a substantial admission fee of half a dollar – more for the better seats – and donated to the general collection that terminated the proceedings.

On 24 January 1880 some 50,000 welcoming individuals of different nationalities and religions thronged the streets of Cleveland, Ohio, which were illuminated by almost a thousand torchlights and enlivened by a dozen bands, several hundred banners and the wildest acclamation. The Irish-American Legion with drawn swords led the procession, followed by the militia guard with fixed bayonets. The golden eagle surmounted the American banners, and the rest were ecumenically decorated with orange and green. The motto 'God save Ireland from landlordism' was prominent. The lecture theatre – the Tabernacle – was emblazoned with banners featuring an incongruous mixture of scriptural and political exhortations.[44]

Parnell was accorded a more sombre reception at other destinations. He was welcomed to Philadelphia on Sunday, 11 January by Miss Bailey, 'a rich Quaker lady', who delivered an ode beginning: 'Give liberty or death, Parnell! Thy cause is ours.'[45] The sentiments and the time devoted to their recitation were modest compared to the offering Parnell endured at Chicago on 23 February, a dramatic rendition of Mrs Alexander Sullivan's 'The Famine of 1880', a seemingly interminable effusion of bathetic and sentimental rhyming couplets. The final stanza encapsulates the effort's tortuous style and risible sentiments:

Philanthropist and missioner lives oe'r St George's Channel –
Sends Bibles to the Pope of Rome, and to the tropics – flannel!
Prays godly prayer for *foreign* sin before her holy altar,
The while her hands twist at her back for Ireland's neck a halter!
In *foreign* lands protects the weak, with treaties – or with cannon!
And turns the dagger in the heart of her sister on the Shannon!
So generous to her foreign foes they praise her to the sky –
And leaves her Irish subjects *one* privilege – to die!
Come, nations of both continents, behold a Land of Graves!
Come, Russia, with Siberia! France, bring your galley slaves!
Come, leering Turks, with dripping knife, refreshed in Christian gore!
Bashi-Bazouk, hold up your head! Be ye ashamed no more!
O Empires of a humane world! Behold the Christian nation!
That *makes* her people paupers and grants them then – starvation![46]

Davitt provides a colourful account of Parnell's reaction, for which Dillon, who was present on the occasion, is likely to have been the source. The Chicago meeting, which was the largest of the entire North American mission, was already an hour late in starting, delayed by the scale of the procession through the city streets to the auditorium, and further threatened by the preliminaries that preceded the introduction of the speakers, not least 'the recitation of a long poem of welcome by a gifted lady', Emilie Gavin, 'a dramatic artiste' who was more than 6 feet tall, and a young woman of exceptional talent, according to Davitt, possibly sardonically. Parnell and Dillon were compelled to stand at the front of the platform, facing an increasingly restive audience, several thousand strong, 'while the handsome young giantess poured into them and over them for nearly half an hour an elocutionary torrent of praise and worship which the talented authoress had expressed in resounding verse'. The experience was 'an agonising ordeal' for Parnell, who, on returning to the privacy of his hotel room and in Dillon's presence, abandoned his customary *sang-froid* and, in Davitt's words, loosed a volley of 'lava-like language which swept everything before it'.[47]

Parnell or Dillon or both addressed these public gatherings, and their message was generally the same – the iniquities of the Irish land system and the plight of the peasantry. A secondary but consistent theme was denigration of the various famine relief agencies other than those linked to the Land League and the Catholic Church. Some of Parnell's speeches were more inflammatory than others.[48] At Cleveland he stated that Ireland was currently 'engaged in the greatest struggle ever raised in any country – a struggle for a nation to live upon the soil of its birth'. His claim that 'the time was coming when landlords and government would get sharper and worse terms' provoked the mass response: 'Give us the chance', and he concluded by charging the British government with deliberately conspiring to murder the Irish people.[49] At Buffalo, New York, where several German and American support speakers condemned Irish landlordism in vehement terms, Parnell excoriated the Marlborough and the Mansion House relief committees. He claimed that Ireland had a right to a separate nationality, which, if realised, should be defended and supported by every Irishman, by force if necessary, and, he added ominously, the landlords would have to go if a peaceful settlement could not be negotiated[50] Parnell complained to the editor of the *New York Herald* that the newspaper had suppressed the most important part of his Buffalo address and he repeated his criticisms of the two Dublin relief committees, stating that the Mansion House committee was 'mainly composed of government office-holders, Whig and Tory landlords and Castle flunkies, destitute of all sympathy with our suffering people and hostile to their aspirations'.[51] Parnell pursued the same theme in a speech at Rochester, New York, on the following evening, 26 January, which left the audience 'uncontrollable', according to newspaper accounts.[52] On 20 February he delivered an address at Cincinnati, Ohio, which became known as 'the last-link speech', one which was queried and parsed by contemporaries, and analysed and contextualised subsequently by historians: 'And let us not forget that this is the ultimate goal at which all we Irishmen aim. None of us – whether we are in America or in Ireland, or wherever we may be – will be satisfied until we have destroyed the last link which binds Ireland to England.'[53]

Clerical and lay guest speakers reinforced Parnell and Dillon's message on the ownership and occupation of Irish land. Rev. Henry Ward Beecher, an American Congregationalist clergyman, abolitionist and social reformer, in a radical address at Brooklyn in New York City, stated that he was in favour of 'the most serious, prolonged and earnest agitation of public sentiment in America for the emancipation of the Irish peasantry from their present condition', and, some days later, on 12 January, Wendell Phillips, attorney, abolitionist and advocate for Native Americans, denounced the Irish land system as 'tyrannous' before a 5,000 gathering at Boston. Phillips asserted that resistance against despotism was 'the righteous province of honest men', and, in a rousing conclusion, observed: 'When Ireland lifts her flag, with justice and liberty written in every fold, America must remember that Ireland was her best friend when she raised hers.'[54] The Irish contribution to American independence was a theme addressed by many American platform speakers, newspaper columnists and letter writers in their advocacy of Ireland's humanitarian needs.

Throughout his promotional tour Parnell was publicly acknowledged in various ways: several states suspended their legislative sessions temporarily in his honour and invited him to address the elected representatives, among them the New York State Assembly at Albany, Virginia (Richmond), Kentucky (Frankfort), Wisconsin (Madison) and Iowa (Des Moines); he was awarded the freedom of Buffalo and Rochester in New York State, Chicago and Springfield in Illinois, and Louisville, Kentucky.[55] The pinnacle of Parnell's mission was undoubtedly his address to the United States House of Representatives on 2 February 1880, which he delivered in the presence of his American-born mother and his sisters, and did so to considerable effect according to *The Irish Times*, which reported that Parnell's presentation was a model of clarity and composure, and the occasion itself a 'brilliant' success. Parnell's focus in his congressional address, as ever on his American tour, was on Ireland's feudal land tenure. He contended that the solution to the land question lay in the transfer of ownership to the occupying tenants, a social revolution that would bring an end to famine in Ireland and thus ensure that he and other Irish leaders would no longer have to appear as 'beggars and mendicants before the world',[56] a variation of a phrase hackneyed by usage during the famine crisis of 1879–80, but one which was emblematic of Ireland's colonial status.[57]

After two months in the United States Parnell offered an assessment of his and Dillon's reception and experiences in the various centres they had visited. On 1 March 1880 he reported from Des Moines to Patrick Egan, the Land League's treasurer, in Dublin:

> The greatest and most unusual interest is manifested in our movements, the citizens everywhere turning out to welcome us as the spokesmen of a suffering and struggling people ... The enthusiasm increases in volume as we proceed from place to place, military guards and salvoes of artillery salute our coming, and the meetings which we address, although high-admission charge is made, are packed from floor to roof. State governors, members of Congress, local representatives, judges and clergymen continually appear on our platforms, and the average contribution for the relief fund from each place we have visited up to this amounts to about £500.[58]

An incidental benefit of their campaigning, according to Parnell, was the substantial financial contributions that were channelled through the Irish Catholic hierarchy for the relief of distress in Ireland, which he attributed to his exposure of the composition of the Mansion House committee and the maladministration of the Marlborough fund, leaving the Catholic hierarchy and the Land League as the only proper and trustworthy mediators of Irish famine relief. He was surprised that 'the misrepresentations, calumnies, and falsehoods', as he described them, of a section of the New York and New England press had such little effect on public opinion away from the eastern seaboard. Parnell claimed that there was general support among Irish immigrants in America for the Land League's radical programme of land reform, and he believed that the funds they had generated would contribute to the inevitable transformation of the Irish land system. 'By this means,' he concluded, 'we shall have done something to prevent these recurring famines and thus save our countrymen from future misery, while we shall be spared the shame of seeing Ireland presented as a mendicant to the nations of the earth.'[59]

## Parnell in Canada

From Des Moines Parnell proceeded to Peoria and Springfield in Illinois and then on to St Louis, Missouri, before crossing into Canada. He and Dillon had previously appealed to the Canadian people to assist the famine-stricken peasantry in the west of Ireland, prompted by the urgency of the situation and the failure of the British government to perform its duty towards the country.[60] Patrick Boyle, owner and editor of the *Irish Canadian*, which he founded in 1863, called on Ontario's Irish Catholics to assemble in Toronto on Saturday, 6 March to welcome Parnell, 'that pure and earnest patriot', and Dillon, 'the son of one who knew how to suffer for his country'. County Mayo-born Boyle urged his fellow countrymen and co-religionists to provide the Land League deputation with material relief to meet the urgent food crisis in Ireland, and to demonstrate their moral support for the abolition of Irish landlordism, the agency of recurring famine in the country. Boyle's message was simply a reiteration of the one Parnell and Dillon had been promoting from the beginning of their North American tour.[61]

Parnell returned to these themes in his Toronto address, stating that famine in Ireland was an artificial rather than a natural occurrence, attributable to man and not to providence, specifically to landlords and the system of land tenure they espoused. He informed his audience that Ireland had been the beneficiary of the charity of every nation in the world, England alone excepted, and had it not been for the generosity of the people of Australia, Canada, India and the United States, the Irish poor would have succumbed to famine in their thousands. Parnell criticised the Mansion House relief committee as a pro-landlord body and urged his listeners to remit their subscriptions through the Catholic Church or the Land League, an exhortation that was reflected in and supported by one of the decidedly partisan resolutions adopted by the meeting: 'That the most proper mediums of relief are the friends of the people, the Irish clergy and the National Land League, who endeavour not merely to alleviate the distress but are working to remove its cause.'[62]

Parnell's North American venture came to an abrupt and premature conclusion at Montreal a few days later, when, on learning of the dissolution of the Westminster parliament, he decided to return immediately to Ireland to contest the general election. He left for home on the *Baltic* on 11 March 1880 and arrived at Queenstown ten days later to the strains of 'Hear, the Conquering Hero Comes', played by the Cove National Band. Michael Davitt, who was present for Parnell's homecoming, as he had been for his departure some three months earlier, introduced a Land League deputation whose welcoming address was excessive even by the inflated standards of such set-pieces:

Short as your stay has been in that mighty Western Republic, it has, nevertheless, been signalised by the most splendid and opportune service to the present wants of our starving people, while being at the same time, pregnant with encouraging hope for the future welfare of our Fatherland. While thousands of families, pauperised through the operation of an infamous land system, have been saved by your wondrous and indefatigable exertions from the fate which befell our famine-stricken kindred of '47 and '48, the heart of Ireland has followed in the wake of your triumphal progress among a generous and sympathetic people, and throbbed with expectant joy, as they pledged you the moral support of America to our struggle against felonious landlordism.

The address continued ever more fancifully, influenced no doubt by the coming general election and the headline opportunities afforded by the policies and actions of 'a truculent and unscrupulous government'.[63]

In an editorial marking Parnell's arrival at Queenstown on 21 March 1880 and his subsequent acclamation in Cork city, one of several constituencies he was to contest in the election, the *Cork Examiner* commended Parnell's American mission as 'an honest desire to serve Ireland', prompted by the twin aims of eliciting sympathy and practical support for 'his distressed fellow-countrymen' and of promoting his own political agenda. The writer's approval of Parnell's motives was tempered by criticism of his methods, particularly Parnell's characterisation of the Mansion House relief committee as a pro-landlord body, one disposed 'to use the money of charity to promote landlord purposes'.[64]

## Assessment of Parnell's mission to the United States and Canada

Parnell faced many challenges during the ten weeks of his American fund-raising venture, not least, as the *Cork Examiner* editorial demonstrates, in achieving a balance between humanitarianism and politics, and winning and maintaining the confidence and trust of different racial, socio-economic and political constituencies. He had to confront the sensitivities and aspirations of the Irish in America, the intricacies and competing interests of Irish-American politics, the suspicions of members of the Catholic hierarchy, the sensibilities and prejudices of those Americans who were offended by the presence of the Irish in their midst, and the hostility of sections of the American press. In general, he executed his mission adroitly, modulating or intensifying his rhetoric as occasion demanded, and in the process raised some £60,000 for relief purposes and another £12,000 for the Land League's political and social programme.[65]

Parnell's fulminatory outbursts against the Dublin famine relief organisations, augmented by those of James Redpath and others, had their intended effect, and contributions to the Mansion House fund from the United States in 1880 amounted to a relatively modest £11,245, a sum that contrasted tellingly with the £200,000 in American aid to Ireland channelled through the Catholic Church,[66] and the £84,000 the Mansion House relief committee attracted from Australia. Once again, context is key to explaining these differences. Parnell's flailing of the rival relief committees did not appear in the Australian press until the beginning of April 1880,[67] by which time the humanitarian response had climaxed and the various colonial relief efforts were being wound up. Furthermore, Irish expatriates in Australia viewed Parnell with a degree of ambiguity. In February 1880 his rumoured intention of returning home from America via Australia prompted an unenthusiastic response from the southern hemisphere. Irish Australians were prepared to welcome Parnell as a private visitor and to pay homage to his political leadership and achievements, but they were opposed to a political mission on the grounds that it might damage their relationship with their English and Scottish fellow colonists. Melbourne's leading Catholic publication, the *Advocate*, captured and reflected this view editorially:

> The community here, though in a measure heterogeneous, is chiefly English and the Irish people, who form a minority of it, are under an obligation to take no part in offending the prejudices of the majority. Good taste and good feeling impose that obligation on Irishmen here, and so much consideration is due to their English and Scotch fellow colonists, with whom, in the common interests of all, it is desirable they should live at peace.

The writer concluded that no constituent element of Australian colonial society – the Irish implicitly – had the right 'to introduce, or sanction the introduction of, an element of strife into its constitution'.[68] In the Australian colonies the fund-raising activities of both Parnell and the duchess of Marlborough were perceived as politically tainted, and the Mansion House fund benefited accordingly.[69]

The *Advocate*'s editorial stance was an example of what historian Malcolm Campbell, in his comparative analysis of the nineteenth-century Irish Catholic immigrant experience in the Australian colonies and in the United States, describes variously as 'the more inhibited colonial context', 'the more timid confines of empire'.[70] The leading article also captured the increasingly hostile, more pervasively sectarian environment that confronted Irish Catholics and Catholics generally in Australia in the final third of the century. Several factors contributed to their greater insecurity and polarisation in the 1870s and '80s, including the attempted assassination of Prince Alfred, the duke of Edinburgh, by a crazed Irishman in Sydney in March 1868, an incident that provoked a wave of anti-Irish and anti-Catholic hysteria and a Fenian witch hunt in New South Wales; the growth in membership and influence of the Loyal Orange Order; and a corresponding energising of the Australian Catholic Church under the influence of Cardinal Paul Cullen of Dublin and his nepotistic appointments to Australian bishoprics. As Campbell notes, republican America and colonial Australia constituted widely different political and ideological entities throughout the nineteenth century, differences that influenced the ways in which Irish immigrants engaged with their host societies. The United States, an independent polity, 'prescribed ideals of thought and behaviour and sanctioned actions by immigrants that were not regarded as appropriate in British colonies'. In both cases, according to Campbell, 'specific milieus proved tremendously influential in shaping the nature and tone of Irish immigrants' engagement with their New World neighbours'.[71]

Historians have tended to view Parnell's North American fund-raising mission through a political lens and to reduce to secondary importance its humanitarian dimension. In the main, they consider the venture a triumph, with consequences that impacted on Parnell's political career, Irish-America, and Anglo-Irish relations. According to Donal McCartney, the American tour propelled Parnell unquestionably to the leadership of nationalist Ireland and earned for him 'the title of the "leader of the Irish race at home and abroad"'. This, he concludes, was 'the ultimate significance of Parnell's American connection'.[72] Similarly, Ely M. Janis claims that the overwhelming response of Irish communities throughout the United States to Parnell's visit 'pushed the crisis in Ireland onto the front pages of the world's newspapers and gave succour to the movement at home while propelling Parnell into an altogether new level of prominence'.[73] Such evaluations fail to take into account the broader implications and repercussions, the negative aspects of Parnell's American project. The defensiveness which Parnell's rumoured visit to Australia engendered among Irish immigrants in the various colonies, and the bitter Orange backlash which his presence provoked in Canada – both British imperial dominions – suggest the need for a subtler, more nuanced interpretation.

## The *New York Herald* relief fund

But when thou doest alms, let not thy left hand know what thy right hand doeth

Matthew, 6:3

Merle Curti, the historian of American overseas philanthropy, places New York at the centre of the country's humanitarian intervention in the 1879–80 Irish famine, and he traces its origin to the revival of a committee inaugurated to address a similar crisis in the early 1860s. Parnell's impending visit to the United States, first mooted shortly after the establishment of the Land League in October 1879, may have provided the momentum for the committee's revival, and the emergence of others, although Curti does not refer to the latter possibility. The mechanics of American fund-raising, as surveyed by Curti, were broadly similar to those in Australasia. Ethnic and cultural ties, religious impulses and a common humanity were the essential motivating factors, and several agencies – particularly the press, the churches and Irish-American cultural, philanthropic and political societies – helped to vitalise, shape and direct these intangible forces. The staples of communal fund-raising endeavours were resurrected and deployed throughout

America: newspaper appeals; church collections; public meetings, lectures and sermons featuring admission charges and exit collections; auctions; sporting events; entertainments, concerts and theatrical performances, with Dion Boucicault featuring prominently as playwright and performer and responsible, as in Australia, for much of the repertoire.[74]

Boucicault, born in Dublin, a New York periodic resident from 1853 and an American citizen since 1873, also made a generous personal donation of $500 to the famine relief fund inaugurated by Sister Mary Francis Clare, the Nun of Kenmare, whose role will feature in the next chapter. The *New York Herald*, signalling its approval, linked the gesture to Boucicault's professional life as a playwright and particularly to his melodrama *The Colleen Bawn* (1860), a work based on Gerald Griffin's *The Collegians* (1829), which in turn was inspired by the true story of a young County Limerick girl who was murdered at her husband's instigation in 1819 and her body disposed of in the River Shannon. The *Herald* claimed, with some geographical licence, that Kenmare was 'the land of the Colleen Bawn' (Boucicault had transposed the tale to Killarney) and noted the dramatist's 'fine instinct' in remembering and assisting the land from which his characters and tale had sprung. 'It is the charity of the intellect finding the way to the heart,' the *Herald* commented grandly.[75]

The consciousness- and money-raising initiatives of a host of individuals like Boucicault forged and sustained an environment that encouraged benevolence, though none was vested with the drama and verve of the *New York Herald*'s own relief effort. On 4 February 1880, the *Herald* published an ominous and lengthy cabled report from its Dublin correspondent, whose essential message was that 300,000 people in Ireland were threatened with starvation and in need of immediate assistance. Dramatic sub-headings intensified the communication's urgency: 'Measures of relief instantly demanded. "Help Us Now or We Die!"' An abstract of the people's suffering and distress, which was compiled from applications by local committees to the Dublin relief agencies and labelled the *New York Herald*'s 'Famine table' by Anna Parnell, augmented the correspondent's report.[76]

Facing page: Fig. 3.2: 'The Herald of Relief from America', Harper's Weekly, vol. 24, 28 February 1880, pp. 129, 141–2.

Thomas Nast's sympathetic and supportive cartoon is an acknowledgement of the New York Herald's funding initiative for the relief of famine in Ireland. Harper's Weekly contended editorially that Ireland should be assisted through her current difficulties, despite its belief that the country's problems were self-inflicted – a 'want of thrift and prudence in the management of affairs'. The magazine's traditional anti-Irish prejudice was again evident in the writer's observation that 'there can be no worthier opportunity of benevolence than that of sending succour to this unhappy nation, which suffers as much from folly as guilt, whose faults are so hereditary as to be ingrained, and where the load of woe falls as heavily upon helpless women and innocent children as upon those who are in any way responsible for the terrible condition of things'. This censorious editorial attitude resurfaced in the following week's issue, the writer attributing the famine in Ireland less to a single year's crop failure than to 'improvidence during many years of plenty'. ('What May Be Done for Ireland', ibid., vol. 24, 6 March 1880, p. 155.)

---

An editorial announced that the Herald had opened an Irish relief subscription, headed by a munificent personal donation of $100,000 from the newspaper's owner and publisher James Gordon Bennett, Jr, and requested an equally generous response from its readers. The appeal was pitched at all creeds, classes and nationalities:

A crisis has come which appeals to the common heart of mankind. It would be a blot on the civilisation of the world, a disgrace to its Christianity, a stigma upon human nature, if those poor, wretched sufferers were permitted to starve when granaries are teeming with food, when ships are lying idle in many harbours, when untold sums of money are daily expended for luxuries and superfluities. Let the rich give out of their abundance, the comfortable out of their economy, the frugal poor from the promptings of willing hearts which have at some time felt want or the fear of it.

The newspaper proclaimed that the initiative was not politically motivated, nor was it intended as a reproach or an affront to the British government; its sole purpose was 'to save a wretched people from death by starvation'. The Herald announced that it would publish the names of all contributors of 25 cents or more and pledged that the proceeds

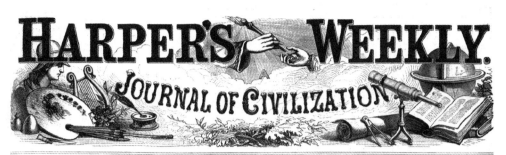

# HARPER'S WEEKLY.
## JOURNAL OF CIVILIZATION

VOL. XXIV.—No. 1209.]     NEW YORK, SATURDAY, FEBRUARY 28, 1880.     [ SINGLE COPIES TEN CENTS.<br>$4.00 PER YEAR IN ADVANCE.

Entered according to Act of Congress, in the Year 1880, by Harper & Brothers, in the Office of the Librarian of Congress, at Washington.

THE *HERALD* OF RELIEF FROM AMERICA.

would be equitably and efficiently administered in Ireland. The editorial concluded with the terse, dramatic exhortation: 'No true man or true woman should be deaf to the despairing cry. For God's sake, send us bread or money.'[77]

The *Herald*'s intervention prompted a mixed response from the American newspaper industry: some titles welcomed and promoted the initiative, others regarded it as vulgar, yet others, more cynical and worldly, queried Bennett's motivation: altruism or the marketplace?[78] *Puck*, a New York-based weekly comic and satirical magazine established in the 1870s by Joseph Ferdinand Keppler, an Austrian-born cartoonist, responded by launching its own fund – 'Puck's Parnell Fund' – to finance Parnell's repatriation to Ireland, 'in good order and as well conditioned as he ever was', rather than for the relief of Irish distress. The magazine, which took a jaundiced view of the *New York Herald*'s initiative, opened the subscription list with a $5 contribution, thereby ridiculing its contemporary's relief effort and disparaging Parnell and his politics. *Puck* announced that its fund would 'serve the cause of humanity and common sense by giving the public a chance to testify their disapprobation of a useless agitator who has used his own country's miseries as a stalking horse for the propagation of ideas which have always been his people's curse'.[79]

In Ireland, the *Nation* was firmly, if unsurprisingly, in the critical, sardonic camp, viewing Bennett's substantial financial contribution as a self-serving publicity-generating commercial exercise: 'The *Herald* has been distinguished for the bitter hostility which it has shown towards Mr Parnell's mission, but it has only excited intense odium for itself throughout the States, and now Mr James Gordon Bennett makes a bold stroke to win back his lost popularity.'[80] In the following week's more colourful commentary, under the rubric 'An English Plot', the *Nation* described the *Herald* as 'notoriously unscrupulous, mendacious and corrupt', the 'fawning slave and willing tool of the English government', and repeated its claim that Bennett's intervention was merely an attempt to salvage his tarnished reputation in America.[81]

Parnell had been invited to serve on the supervisory committee of the *Herald*'s famine relief fund, but refused, which was not surprising

THE AMERICAN MOSES.

JAMES GORDON MOSES to AARON PARNELL:—*This* is the way a professional prophet strikes the rocks!

Fig. 3.3: 'The American Moses', *Puck*, vol. 6, no. 153, 11 February 1880, p. 791.

given his fraught relationship with Bennett and his antipathy to the other private relief agencies. Days prior to the launch of the fund, the *Irish Times*' special correspondent reported that Parnell was 'at open war' with the *Herald* and its owner.[82] Parnell regarded Bennett's $100,000 donation as a 'patent advertising dodge', a financial speculation that defiled the name of charity, and he advised Irish Americans to ignore the newspaper's appeal: 'I hope no American Irishman will give the *New York Herald* one cent.'[83] Parnell was equally critical of the *Herald* and the Mansion House and Marlborough relief committees, objecting, often intemperately, to what he claimed was their pro-landlord and pro-government tendencies. Speaking at Peoria, Illinois, a month after the inauguration of the *Herald* fund, Parnell stated that the initiative's sole motivation was 'to support the landlords in attempting to put down the land movement'. He provoked laughter and applause among his listeners when he suggested that one way to resolve the Irish land question was to ship the landowners collectively, all 10,000 of them, to New York on vessels requisitioned from the federal government and to borrow and fit up the *Herald* office as a poorhouse for their reception. He concluded, with some panache and to renewed laughter and applause, that the transported landlords and Bennett would suit one another and would be very happy together.[84]

Despite Parnell's invective and the opposition of some newspapers and political figures, the *New York Herald* appeal proved effective, generating more than $320,000 among the American public in its first two months, with donations ranging from 25 cents to a single contribution of $25,000, plus an unquantifiable amount of provisions and clothing.[85] Some of the proceeds were directed towards provisioning a relief ship, USS *Constellation*, which left New York for Ireland at the end of March 1880, a relief mission that will be examined in a later chapter. The balance of the fund was administered by the *Herald*'s supervisory committee in Ireland, consisting of the lord mayor of Cork, William Shaw, MP, chairman; Colonel King-Harman, MP and landowner, Rockingham, Boyle, County Roscommon; Edward McCabe, Catholic archbishop of Dublin, who served as proxy for New York's Cardinal McCloskey; Professor Baldwin, possibly Thomas Baldwin, a public servant and author of *A Remedy for the Congested Districts of Ireland* (Dublin: W.H. Smith & Son, 1884); and George H. Hepworth, a New York Unitarian clergyman and evangelical preacher who was travelling with his family in Europe when Bennett appointed him to the committee.[86]

POOR MANS LINE
TO
EUROPE
STEERAGE TO
IRELAND CHEAP

HERALD

RELIEF
FUND

J.G. BENNETT

PARNELL
RELIEF
FUND

AGITATOR

TO OUR STARVING POOR—IF YOU WANT RELIEF, GO TO IRELAND.

Fig. 3.4: 'To Our Starving Poor – If You Want Relief, Go to Ireland', *Puck*, vol. 6, no. 155, 25 February 1880, p. 838. IMAGE COURTESY OF THE LIBRARY OF CONGRESS

Puck's cynical interpretation of the *New York Herald* funding initiative and of Irish famine relief generally is evident in the cartoon's introduction:

'Oh! Why weren't we born Irish? Is there all the Godlike justice and heaven-born equity about the Irish relief business that there ought to be? As matters stand now, the wisest thing for a distressed Irishman in America to do is to return to the ould country and scoop in his share of Mr James Gordon Bennett's fund. For, while poor Biddy Finnegan may be starving in Shantytown, her brother, Mr Tim Finnegan, in Clonmel, enriched with alien alms, is attending all the fashionable wakes in the neighbourhood.' (Ibid., p. 824.)

## The parliament of the dominion of Canada

In early 1880 the Canadian parliament voted $100,000, or £20,548 sterling, for Irish famine relief, the only stipulation being that beneficiaries should not be disenfranchised. The fund's disbursement was delegated to Sir Michael Hicks Beach, secretary of state for the colonies, on behalf of the British government, a decision that provoked some dissent in the Canadian parliament. Timothy Warren Anglin, the Clonakilty, County Cork-born member from St John, New Brunswick, contended that the money should be entrusted to the Mansion House relief committee, as the British government's response to the famine to date had been unenthusiastic and ineffectual.[87] Parliament disregarded Anglin's objections, and at the colonial secretary's suggestion the Canadian Committee for the Relief of Distress in Ireland, consisting of an equal representation from the Mansion House and Marlborough relief committees, was appointed to administer the fund. The committee agreed to expend the money on relieving the current food and clothing crisis and, with a view to creating sustainable employment, on developing piers and harbours in distressed districts and supplying boats and equipment to needy fishermen.[88]

The Canadian committee, which received the approval and £644 in additional funding from the *New York Herald* relief committee, contributed some £9,700 to the development of piers and harbours in 31 Irish centres, and expended more than £11,000 to acquire 192 new boats, repair 437 existing ones, and supply fishermen with 3,910 nets, 10,456 lines and 371,530 hooks. The vessels and equipment were distributed among sober, industrious, *bona fide* fishermen, defined as individuals who fished for sale for some portion of the year. The counties that benefited, in descending monetary order, were Donegal, Mayo, Clare, Cork, Galway, Sligo, Kerry and Leitrim. Although the fund was oversubscribed and only a minority of applicants accommodated, successful candidates profited almost immediately. Stocks of mackerel, herring, cod, ling and other species appear to have been plentiful in Irish Atlantic coastal waters and, according to the committee's report, the quantities that were caught and sold were soon valued in multiples of the outlay on boats and equipment. It was standard practice for the beneficiaries of philanthropy or their intermediaries to express gratitude to the donors, in this case the Canadian parliament and people. Though hackneyed, the exercise does not belie or detract from the significance of the assistance provided. A County Mayo correspondent, writing to the committee on 4 September 1880, captured the practical impact of the subvention on the subsistence economy of these fishermen-farmers. He had interviewed about thirty recipients of fishing nets and each man had earned between £7 and £8 in the interim. About twenty had each used some of the money to buy two young pigs which they fed on small or blighted potatoes that were unfit for human consumption and would otherwise have been discarded, and they hoped to realise £7 or £8 from the sale of these fattened pigs some months later. Others redeemed pawned articles and discharged debts to local shopkeepers for which they would have been processed, an action that would have forced them to dispose of their primary, perhaps only, asset, the cow that provided milk for their children. The approaching fishing season looked promising, the writer concluded, and the fishermen were anxious 'to earn the rent' and secure their domiciliary tenure.[89]

Curti claimed that the Canadian government's response to the 1879–80 famine in Ireland was more substantial than that of the United States, though he was impressed by the American voluntary relief effort, which he attributed to widespread and persistent publicity, the existence of surplus foods, the generosity of innumerable individuals, and sustained organisational endeavour.[90] As in Australasia, the Irish segment of the American population was motivated by kinship bonds and personal or inherited memories of the Great Famine of the 1840s. The broad American response was prompted by religious sentiment and a range of humanitarian impulses, with beneficial consequences for donors and recipients alike, subliminal, intangible, perhaps, but contributing to social cohesion and leavening. This was not an exclusively American phenomenon. As we saw in the previous chapter's conclusion, late nineteenth-century Australian society was similarly impelled and enriched.

Religion provided a strong bond for the Irish in North America, Australasia and elsewhere, Catholicism for the majority, the different Protestant denominations for the remainder, and the various churches, with their Christian ethos and allegiances, their associational cultures, structures, networks and supports in local communities, were uniquely positioned to respond to the clamour for assistance from Ireland. The next chapter examines the Catholic Church's role in the famine crisis.

CHAPTER 4

# THE CATHOLIC CHURCH

We, Irish priests and bishops, are custodians of morality and order. It is our duty to counsel peace and preach loyalty. But it is hard to instil loyalty or promote peace when there is a question of empty stomachs and an unsympathetic government.

Francis McCormack, bishop of Achonry, *The Irish Crisis of 1879–80. Proceedings of the Dublin Mansion House Relief Committee, 1880* (Dublin: Browne & Nolan, 1881), p. 13

## Introduction

In the historiography of the Irish Land War the Catholic Church's involvement with political and agrarian issues has largely occluded its wider social engagement, particularly its response to the threat and reality of famine and associated disease outbreaks that fused and fired political and agrarian agitation. Gerard Moran, in explicating the church's role in raising awareness of the 1879–80 famine and the clergy's contribution to relief operations, has been an exception. In his estimation, church leadership and commitment were vital to averting a calamity in Ireland's Atlantic coastal counties potentially as great as that of the Great Famine of the 1840s.[1]

This survey of the Catholic Church's role in the 1879–80 famine attempts to broaden perspective and analysis, assessing, for instance, whether proselytism, which was such a contentious issue during the Great Famine, featured. The chapter's primary focus, however, is on international appeals for assistance by members of the Catholic hierarchy and clergy, and particularly by religious sisters, who emerged from their convents and classrooms to reveal an astute grasp of secular affairs and opportunities, and who displayed a keen sensitivity to the social needs and realities of their communities. The singular contribution of Sister Mary Francis Clare, the Nun of Kenmare, whom some contemporaries regarded as the most renowned and significant Irish nun since Saint Brigid, is highlighted. At the time of the 1879–80 famine, her profile, at home and internationally, was remarkable, her fame attributable to the popularity of her literary and religious publications among the Irish worldwide. A combination of narcissistic-infused humanitarianism, energy and renown made Clare the most effective individual campaigner on behalf of the Irish poor during the famine crisis.

## The hierarchy

The Catholic Church, with a strong Irish diasporic constituency, both clerical and lay – an Irish spiritual empire, as some historians of Irish Catholicism have phrased it – offered a worldwide network for the relief of famine and destitution in Ireland, and dioceses in Australia, Britain, France and the United States in particular responded promptly and with generosity to the 1879–80 famine relief appeal, encouraged mainly by the Catholic hierarchy, clergy and religious sisters in Ireland.[2] Pastoral letters, drawing attention to the plight of the starving Irish poor and announcing church collections for their assistance, were issued in Ireland and internationally. One such, from Cardinal Manning of Westminster, was read in the archdiocese's churches at the end of November 1879. Manning referred particularly to conditions in the west of Ireland, where, he had been reliably informed, 'hunger, poverty and want' were more pronounced than at any time since 'the fatal famine of 1847', and he announced that there would be a church collection throughout the archdiocese on the following Sunday. Manning's intervention prompted an equally generous editorial response from the Nation: 'If all Englishmen were as well disposed towards Ireland as Henry Edward Manning, the Irish people would not, to say the least, have so much to complain of in the English system of government.'[3]

Similar appeals, featuring variations of Manning's distressing message, were made in virtually every diocese in the United States. The bishop of Detroit, for instance, addressed a circular to the clergy and laity of his diocese in late November 1879, in which he referred to 'the crisis in Ireland, the great want, and the danger of a universal famine among the brethren in the Isle of Saints'. The bishop observed that the Irish people's devotion to the Catholic Church was historic, their Christian heroism under the trials and sorrows of centuries admirable.[4] The American bishops' intercession prompted a later commentator, James J. Green, to suggest that the promotion of relief efforts to counter the 1879–80 famine in Ireland may have been the most significant al-truistic intervention by the Catholic Church in the United States in the later nineteenth century. Many of the American clergy were Irish and served congregations that consisted largely of Irish immigrants and their families, but, according to Green, the magnitude of the response and the scale of church collections suggest that the famine crisis in Ireland transcended mere Irishness and became in essence an American Cath-olic undertaking.[5] Such an assessment, which overlooks the response of Protestant churches and Jewish congregations and the individual con-tributions of followers of both religions and none, is too limited.[6] It is also likely that the bulk of the $330,000 and more generated by the *New York Herald* appeal in spring 1880 derived mainly from the non-Catholic sectors of American society.

The proceeds of church collections and other fund-raising activities were remitted to the Mansion House relief committee, or directly to the Irish Catholic hierarchy, particularly to the archbishops of Dublin, Armagh and Tuam, Edward McCabe, Daniel McGettigan and John MacHale respectively.[7] Most of the overseas dioceses left the disbursement of their contributions to the archbishops' discretion.[8] Some instructed McCabe, as a board member of the Mansion House relief committee, to forward their cheques and bank drafts to that organisation, others entrusted their remittances jointly to McCabe and Dublin's Church of Ireland archbishop Dr Richard Chenevix Trench, who also served on the committee.[9] Some American relief organisations adopted a similar approach. The Irish Relief Society of Richmond, Virginia, for instance, forwarded £733. 18s. jointly to Dublin's two archbishops. The secretary explained that the sum was contributed 'by all classes and by all denominations', and the society believed that the two prelates, who occupied 'a position far above any political party or denominational narrowness', would distribute the money non-discriminately.[10] Like the

Australasian hierarchy, most American bishops adopted a civic and inclusive rather than narrowly sectarian approach in allocating their funds. There were some, however, who eschewed such generosity of spirit and inter-denominationalism, M.A. Corrigan, bishop of Newark, New Jersey, for instance, who specified that all contributions from his diocese should be entrusted to 'the bishops or priests and not to a mixed committee',[11] meaning, presumably, a mixed religious body.

The Irish hierarchy's 1880 Lenten pastorals reveal episcopal awareness of the prevailing distress and its potential consequences, and the bishops' apportionment of blame and responsibility reflected their individual political and social beliefs and perspectives. McCabe, Dublin's ultra-conservative archbishop, noted the presence in the country of 'the dread spectre of famine' and the ineffectiveness of the government's response, but he urged forbearance and acceptance of God's will and advised the people of the Dublin archdiocese to place their trust and faith in the Lord rather than in politics and politicians to see them through their difficulties.[12] This was a stale reprise of the sentiments McCabe expressed in a pastoral letter in November 1879, in which he attributed failed harvests and food shortages to divine providence, condemned Land League agitation, and advocated the maintenance of the political and social contract.[13] McCabe's pronouncements incensed many nationalists, among them Michael Davitt, who, in a furious and scathing response, described the archbishop's opinions as insidious,

> the slavish doctrine of the great famine time once more; the mendicants' remedy again for the victims of the landlord system; alms from the public for starving tenants to pay rents with, seasoned with 'morality' – the morality that is religiously blind to the theft of rack-rents and the social sacrilege of eviction, but which is proclaimed from the house-tops in trumpet tones against the reformers who do not follow the footsteps of the modern Levites when they pass by the down-trodden or oppressed with averted eyes.[14]

Several members of the hierarchy preferred Davitt's more radical political and social vision to McCabe's. Patrick Dorrian, bishop of Down and

Connor, blamed the current Irish situation on a lack of employment and remuneration, contending that famine would not be an issue wherever wages could be earned. 'For industrious people to be left to starve is the greatest inhumanity and the weakening of all social strength,' he observed. 'It is the ruin of the commonwealth and therefore bad and indefensible government, for paternal duty is to supply food through employment.'[15] Francis McCormack, bishop of Achonry, was even blunter: 'We have unhappily to encounter the shameless abandonment of starving thousands by a heartless government.'[16] James Donnelly, bishop of Clogher, was in favour of legitimate agitation for political and social improvement, including land law reform, but he was strongly opposed to unconstitutional action, particularly any involvement with 'secret and illegal societies and combinations'.[17] This was a reference to the redresser activities of Ribbonmen and Whiteboys in many parts of rural Ireland, a theme that will be pursued in the concluding chapters of this volume. Laurence Gillooly, bishop of Elphin, believed that the existence of the various relief committees blunted the landlords' collective social conscience and provided them with the excuse not to engage actively with their tenants' difficulties. Gillooly insisted that landowners should be compelled to do their duty, observing caustically that a diet of Indian meal porridge for a month or two might provoke a more generous and humane response from them.[18]

Like Davitt, some of the bishops harked back to the cataclysmic famine of the 1840s, with which Indian meal was so closely and emblematically associated. Were it not for the generosity and speed of the international response to the food, clothing and fuel deficiencies in autumn 1879, Patrick Francis Moran, bishop of Ossory, observed, the press would have been compelled 'to repeat the harrowing recitals which ushered in the great famine of 1846'.[19] Daniel McCarthy, bishop of Kerry, expressed a similar sentiment in a letter to the American journalist James Redpath in mid-March 1880, predicting that without continuing external humanitarian intervention, the country would experience 'famine, dire and terrible', a repetition of 'the awful drama of '47'.[20]

Despite the peasantry's desperate plight, and the assumption of the moral high ground by the hierarchy in proclaiming it, Archbishop McCabe of Dublin saw fit to indulge in at least one episode of moral posturing, rejecting a donation for the relief of distress from the Ancient Order of Foresters, a friendly society with eighteenth-century Yorkshire roots, which was anathema to McCabe and to his archiepiscopal predecessor in Dublin, possibly because of its Masonic and anti-Catholic associations.[21] McCabe returned a cheque for £30 which the order's Dublin 'court' or branch had sent for the relief of 'the suffering poor', an archiepiscopal rebuff that provoked 'feelings of profound sorrow and regret' among the court's executive:

> That His Grace should consider, that his own spiritual children engaged in a work of benevolence and charity, unworthy to contribute through His Grace, to the relief of human suffering and still more, and above, and before all, that His Grace, should entertain even the shadow of a doubt, that the members of our society, nine-tenths of whom in Ireland are dutiful children of the Catholic Church, would belong to, or connect themselves with, any organisation whose working and principles would be out of harmony with the teachings of the church, pains and wounds us to the very heart.[22]

## Priests and parishioners

Members of the parochial clergy, and religious sisters to an unprecedented extent, acted as intermediaries on behalf of the underprivileged who lacked the skills and education, and in Irish-speaking areas the language, to publicise their plight and their need of assistance.[23] These interlocutors underpinned their appeals with empirical and often telling detail on the circumstances and living conditions of the poor in their parishes and school-catchment areas. At the end of January 1880 Fr Jerome Fahey, parish priest of Peterswell, Loughrea, County Galway, informed the bishop of Southwark of the increasing destitution among the district's 'sorely tried poor'. Most of his parishioners were disadvantaged, he wrote, even in the best of seasons. Many eked out a bleak mountain subsistence, inhabiting dwellings that were generally unfit for human occupation and often housed farm animals as well as themselves. Fahey compared their misery to that of the Galtee tenants, 'by which the better feelings of the British public were lately so painfully shocked', a reference to journalist William O'Brien's exposé in the *Freeman's Journal* of the wretched circumstances of Nathaniel Buckley's tenants on the slopes of Munster's Galtee Mountains.[24] Some of Fahey's parishioners discharged the annual rent on their holdings by working for their landlord on three days of each week – duty days – their labour valued at eight pence per day, without food. According to the clergyman, depressed agricultural prices coupled with the failure of potatoes and other crops had rendered the peasants' situation more desperate than usual, but, he added, they were peaceable and religious despite their travails and bore their sufferings with a patience that was 'worthy of a better cause'.[25] Fahey acknowledged the humiliation of begging but believed that he would have abnegated his duties and responsibilities as a clergyman had he allowed feelings of shame to deter him from attempting to assist his 'sorely afflicted parishioners'.[26]

Bishop Patrick Duggan of Clonfert, Fahey's episcopal superior, informed Dublin's archbishop in March 1880 that every parish in the diocese required outside help and that the clergy were 'harassed' by the urgency and scale of applications from their parishioners. He had provided the priests of his diocese with almost £2,000 from overseas donations which they distributed mainly among the 'respectable destitute', who, the bishop stated, would die rather than appear as mendicants before relief committees, and, by implication, would suffer a similar fate before seeking admission to a workhouse. Duggan was concerned that the country and its people were entering 'on a long period of distress' and he feared the collapse of the peasant economy. His assessment was as chilling as it was terse: 'Sheep rotting – credit gone – capital none – I fear a crash on every side', and, he added, it would take years to retrieve the situation.[27]

The acknowledgement by both Duggan and Fahey of the general perception of begging as shameful and degrading was a recurring theme throughout the crisis, as was the reluctance of those affected by food shortages to resort to the Poor Law for assistance. The Mansion House relief committee noted 'the invincible abhorrence of the workhouse entertained by the Irish peasantry', and from its privileged – and possibly rate-paying – perspective dismissed Irish workhouses, now forty years in existence, as 'half hospital, half prison' for 'the sick and worthless', 'expensive establishments for the accommodation of vagabonds and alms houses for the aged'.[28] These institutions – edifices of failure, loss of dignity and public shame – challenged the social ideals of personal independence, respectability and responsibility. The peasantry of Clonfert diocese, Fahey's sorely afflicted poor, and countless others throughout the affected western half of Ireland, were classic examples of the 'deserving' poor – humble folk, of necessity frugal and thrifty, and, as Dr George Sigerson attested in Chapter 1, essentially sober, their lot, in the words of the Mansion House relief committee, one of 'honest poverty'.[29] Such individuals treasured independence, personal dignity and self-sufficiency, however marginal and precarious. Their collective attributes and aspirations were genuine and deeply entrenched, part of the Irish peasant *mentalité*.[30]

Members of the Catholic clergy were critical of landlord inertia and lack of enterprise. Jerome Fahey claimed that labourers and small farmers were prepared to work in order to feed their families, but there was no work available, which he attributed to landowners' indifference and failure to act responsibly.[31] Similarly, Rev. Patrick Grealy, Carna, opined that the people of Connemara were 'energetic, hard-working, and economic', able and willing to labour, and anxious for the opportunity to demonstrate that they were not 'a race of sluggards and beggars'. Grealy deprecated the apathy displayed by the government and landowners during the opening months of the crisis. He believed that the landlords had the means to avert famine but, blind to their own and their tenants' interests, seemed disinclined to do anything.[32] Rev. Patrick Coyne, who presided over a mass meeting in mid-November 1879 at a bitterly cold Killanin, between Moycullen and Oughterard in County Galway, excoriated landowners and their 'heartless' agents for failing to discharge their proprietorial responsibilities and suggested that the appropriate penalty for such dereliction was the expropriation of their lands. In a fiery politically charged polemic before Michael Davitt, the principal speaker at the meeting, and the assembled thousands, Coyne blamed the 'vicious and iniquitous system of land tenure' for the 'ever recurring periods of destitution and famine' in Ireland, and claimed that the country would not experience prosperity or contentment until the system was remodelled, a sentiment shared by his curate, J.W. Mannin, who proposed a motion calling for peasant proprietorship as 'the only effectual remedy for the agricultural depression, and the only final and most satisfactory settlement of the land question'.[33]

In addition to informing members of the Catholic hierarchy in the United States, Britain and elsewhere of the deprivations, difficulties and suffering of the Irish poor, the clergy and religious sisters availed of the potential of the international press to appeal for assistance on behalf of the disadvantaged in their communities. They resorted to the letters pages of newspapers in countries where the diasporic Irish had settled, especially those publications favourably disposed to Ireland and to Catholicism, an exercise that revealed both the international dimensions of the Catholic Church in the later nineteenth century and an impressive awareness among the Irish, both lay and religious, of newspaper outlets, their potential and cross-fertilisation throughout the anglophone world. In his recent survey of Ireland's nineteenth- and early twentieth-century spiritual empire, Colin Barr's felicitous analogy captured the influence and impact of the religious and secular global Irish press: 'Like the orb lines of a spider's web, the newspapers of Greater Ireland reprinted one another's articles, reported one another's news, and inculcated a common identity that bound together the Catholic Irish from Boston to Ballarat.'[34]

In spring 1880 Canon James McDermott, parish priest of Buninadden, County Sligo, and chairman of the local relief committee, informed the readers of the *Advocate*, Melbourne's Catholic weekly journal, of 'the depressed state' of his parish and the need for external assistance. According to McDermott, about 400 local families lived on small farms measuring from a rood to 4 acres, and not one of them possessed as much as a single cow. Normally, these families lived off the produce of their land and their earnings from seasonal labouring in England, but in the previous year both means of support had failed them. 'Now,' McDermott concluded, 'those 400 families have no money, no food, except what the charitable have sent them, and no credit', a statement that could have emanated from almost any parish along Ireland's Atlantic seaboard. McDermott added that there was a stronger farming class in Buninadden parish who were normally more comfortable and secure, but their lands had flooded, with the loss of hundreds of acres of potatoes, oats and meadow, leaving them destitute. The clergyman offered a pithy summary of his parishioners' plight: 'manure and seeds, labour and hope, lost'.[35]

About the same time, John Molony, parish priest of Kinvara, County Galway, revealed the circumstances of his 'poor and sorely tried people' in the Sydney *Freeman's Journal*. He described Kinvara as a large, populous and extremely poor district, with inferior, occasionally unproductive, land, whose residents had been reduced to extreme poverty and suffering by crop failure. According to Molony, between 400 and 500 families required immediate assistance:

> Wherever we turn we meet persons whose pinched and shrivelled faces too plainly tell the sad story of their misery and woe. At all hours of the day, our houses are besieged by crowds of men, women and children, eagerly clamouring for food from those whose hands are empty and who have nothing to offer except perhaps words of comfort and hope.

This besieging of the senses, and the absence of employment for those who were able and willing to work – 'these saddening truths' – impelled Molony to turn for assistance to the charitable people of Sydney, many of whom, he wrote, were allied by blood and affection to those on whose behalf he appealed. In return, he pledged that his parishioners' prayers would be addressed 'to Him who regards whatever is given to His poor as lent to Himself'.[36] Molony's supplication was subsequently published in several New Zealand newspapers, modified for a local readership.[37]

The more radical members of the Irish Catholic clergy proclaimed their views on socio-economic issues and on the political situation in Ireland from the pulpit and on public platforms, and their opinions, which were relayed to the diaspora by a sympathetic press, reinforced the epistolary entreaties for assistance by members of religious communities. One such address, by a County Meath priest who was promoting a meeting at which Charles Stewart Parnell, as one of the county's parliamentary representatives, was to speak, was reprinted in December 1879 in the Sydney *Freeman's Journal* and the Adelaide *Express and Telegraph*, under the heading 'An Irish Priest's Vindication of Mr Parnell'. The clergyman captured the desperate situation confronting agricultural labourers and small and middling farmers throughout the country following the harvest failures of 1879:

> The weather has been wet beyond all precedent, so that the poor labouring man has only been able to get work for one or two days out of each week, and in consequence he has been starving for months. The potato crop is everywhere an utter failure, and all grass and corn has been so damaged as not to be worth gathering. There is no turf and there is no hope of fuel anywhere to anybody, so that starvation, cold and famine threaten with their grim visage the wretched and the ruined farmer ... What prospect for the winter has the farmer, where rain, rot and ravage have desolated his only hope of livelihood?[38]

## Ministering angels to the naked and hungry

Writing on New Year's Day 1880 – coincidentally, the day on which Parnell disembarked in New York to commence his North American fund-raising mission – the Irish correspondent of the *New Zealand Tablet* commented:

> Nuns from the cloisters have broken the long silence they held towards the world in an agonising cry for help. They tell us that the little ones in their infant schools, like the buds after a long frost, fall down unconscious from cold and hunger, and they appeal piteously for aid in their labour of self-sacrificing charity.[39]

The clergyman's dispiriting analysis that closed the previous section, and the circumstances that prompted Parnell's transatlantic venture help to contextualise and explain nuns' emergence from their conventual cocoons. The primary task of religious sisters was to educate children who attended the national schools under their aegis, but they owned to a wider social obligation, a commitment to the disadvantaged of the communities in which they resided.[40] During the 1879–80 famine religious sisters took on the additional responsibility of feeding and clothing their helpless and undernourished pupils, offspring of the agricultural labourers, farmers and others affected by food and clothing shortages.[41] Sister Mary Vincent Ryan of the Convent of Mercy, Clifden, County Galway, informed South Australian newspaper readers in mid-December 1879 that it was 'the sacred calling of a Sister of Mercy to advocate the cause of the poor', and she appealed for the means to open a soup kitchen and to purchase fuel and provisions, 'to save the poor of Christ in this hour of their need'.[42]

Religious sisters, like the clergy generally, were alive to the social sensitivities of the rural and urban poor. Sister M. Ignatius McCarthy, mother superior at the Convent of Mercy, Ballyshannon, County Donegal, informed the readers of the Melbourne *Advocate* that the poor of the town and district relied on the convent for assistance, and she drew attention to a cohort who might be classified as the hidden poor, 'decent tradespeople, and once well-to-do farmers, who would starve rather than beg public alms from the relief committee'. In many such cases, she wrote, the mothers of families confided 'the secret tale of woe' to the sisters, who in turn attempted to protect these families from 'exposure and starvation'. McCarthy observed that these individuals and others like them throughout the country would be better off in workhouses, but they had 'an invincible repugnance' to the very thought of these institutions, a statement that echoed those of bishops, priests and numerous other commentators. McCarthy added that the respectable poor would almost prefer to die of starvation than bear the shame and reproach that adhered permanently to a family compelled to seek refuge in the poorhouse. She explained that her community of religious sisters and others were advocates for the poor, because, next to the parish clergy, the sisters were most acquainted with their distress and needs. 'In our visits to the most destitute,' she explained, 'we see with our own eyes the sad havoc which the want of food, fuel, clothing and bedding has made on their desolate homes, their wan faces and their drooping spirits.'[43] Sister McCarthy's concerns reflected the yearning for dignity and respectability that existed in the ranks of the poor in late nineteenth-century Ireland, and an awareness among some in the higher ranks of society of the concept and reality of honest or virtuous poverty. McCarthy and others believed that the existing famine relief organisations, as public bodies, were not the appropriate agencies to serve the needs of the respectable poor and their families, and that a more discreet type of intervention was required.

In early March 1880 McCarthy informed Melbournians that Ballyshannon convent had provided 100 of the poorest and most ragged children of the town and neighbourhood who attended their national school with food and clothing throughout the current crisis. Their efforts had been funded by the Land League, the Marlborough relief committee, and Dr Michael Logue, recently appointed to the see of Raphoe, but they needed additional sources of income to support their endeavours until the new potato crop was ready for harvesting in September.[44]

Likewise, the Sisters of Mercy at Gort, County Galway, provided the distressed poor of the locality with a cooked meal each day and supplied a daily breakfast to almost 400 school children, some of whom walked up to four miles to attend. In May 1880 the sisters received a weekly grant of £6 from the *New York Herald* famine relief fund, but, according to the convent's mother superior, M. Aloysius Doyle, the sum was insufficient to provide for their needs, and she submitted several pleas to the *Tablet*, an English Catholic weekly, for supplementary aid.[45] The Presentation Sisters at Oranmore, County Galway, and the Sisters of Mercy at Skibbereen and Clonakilty, County Cork, turned to the United States, and petitioned Archbishop Blanchet of Portland, Oregon, to support their continuing efforts to provide cooked food to the poor, particularly to school children.[46]

On 1 March 1880 Sister Mary Vincent Ryan and her Convent of Mercy colleagues at Clifden, County Galway, acknowledged the receipt of £100 which Cardinal McCloskey of New York had sent to help feed and clothe nearly 500 children who attended their school, as well as the sick poor of the neighbourhood whom the sisters frequently found 'deprived of all the means of existence' when they visited them in their homes.[47] Ryan's parish priest, Patrick MacManus, lauded the Sisters of Mercy as 'ministering angels to the naked and hungry', and pledged that 'the prayers of the widow and the orphan, as well as those of the priest and the religious' would ascend before the throne of God for the intentions of the humane who supported their relief efforts. He added that 'those who give to the poor lend to God'. MacManus advocated 'mendicant importunity' in response to the government's dereliction in providing employment through relief works, claiming that thousands had died during the Great Famine because of a failure to engage in 'noisy mendicancy',[48] possibly because of the starvation-induced lethargy, passivity and fatalism that were such disabling features of the earlier famine.[49]

In spring 1880 the *New York Herald*, which was then promoting its own Irish famine relief programme, published a circular plea, 'A Wail from Skibbereen', from the Mercy convent located in the town. The editor noted that Skibbereen was the scene of such appalling horrors during the 1840s famine that the very mention of its name continued to evoke painful memories a generation later. The sisters detailed their work among the poor of the district to contextualise and support their appeal: they provided daily meals at the convent to hundreds of children and adults; enabled impoverished householders to remain in their homes by assisting with the payment of rent and the redemption of pawned goods; distributed food and clothing and ministered to the indigent sick in their homes. They concluded their plea with the terse cry: 'Save us or we perish',[50] which, as we saw in the previous chapter, was similar in sentiment and expression to one of the striking sub-headings employed by the *New York Herald* in launching its own famine relief appeal a month earlier.

The *Ave Maria*, a Catholic family magazine published weekly at Notre Dame, Indiana, was another American outlet for famine relief appeals from priests and religious sisters in Ireland. The editor, Rev. Daniel E. Hudson, was particularly concerned with the plight of Ireland's starving and deprived children, and he encouraged American Catholic school children to respond to their needs, however modest their contribution. Donations to the magazine ranged characteristically from 50c to $2, with the occasional contribution of $5 or more, and Hudson thanked his readers, 'in the name of the Blessed Virgin and the suffering poor of Ireland', for their generosity. He remitted the proceeds, relatively small amounts, to John MacHale, archbishop of Tuam, and to his successor John McEvilly, to Rev. Edward Murphy, a Galway-based Jesuit, to Presentation sisters at Mitchelstown, County Cork, and at Ballingarry, County Tipperary, and to Mary De Sales Lalor, at Abbeyleix Convent, Queen's County (Laois). Each recipient, according to the convention associated with such charitable interventions, acknowledged the donors' generosity, and offered their blessings in return. The elderly and venerable MacHale was rather patronising in his response, in contrast to Murphy, the recipient of several donations, who was effusive and sentimental. On 5 July 1880 Murphy acknowledged remittances of more than £125 to date for the children of Galway, which, he wrote, would help 'to feed and clothe hundreds of poor children, to send them to school and to Mass, to cheer their pure young hearts and wipe the tears of sorrow from their once bright, cheerful faces'. The mother superior of Mitchelstown's Presentation sisters was more reserved, though no less grateful, in acknowledging the modest £10 she received on behalf of the convent's 'poor, hungry children'.[51]

Rev. Edward Murphy, SJ was not the only individual concerned with Galway school children's fate and faith. Early in December 1879 the editor of the *New Zealand Tablet*, Bishop Patrick Moran of Dunedin, received an explanatory letter from an expatriate Irishman, E. O'Connor, who appended the Catholic School, Christchurch as his address, which suggests that he was a teacher at the school. In the previous October, the mother superior of Galway's Presentation convent had informed O'Connor of the deteriorating situation in Ireland and of her religious community's attempts to feed, clothe and educate some 500 children who attended their school, 'or else expose them to the claws of proselytists who are always about in this truly poor but Catholic city'. The editor did not publish the original letter from Galway, merely O'Connor's abstract, and it is unclear whether O'Connor was expressing his own or paraphrasing the mother superior's opinion on proselytism and its votaries.[52]

Bishop Moran, who was an articulate, polemical defender of faith and fatherland, used his editorial platform to denounce proselytists and their activities. He noted that the people of Galway were threatened by 'the extremity of physical want', and, he thundered, their spiritual interests were

> endangered by that army of harpies who are continually on the watch to rob the church of her children, and to transform the members of an open-minded honourable community into miserable time servers, professing, for the sake of temporal gain, adhesion to a creed in which they have no real belief.

The bishop located the origins of proselytism in Ireland in the Great Famine, claiming, erroneously, that 'it was in the evil days of the old famine that they began their miserable task'.[53] In December 1879, with famine in Ireland once again a reality, Moran observed that 'the tempter stands beside it, well content with the misery that seems to drive the victims towards his net'.[54]

Moran's reference to proselytism during the 1879–80 famine was one of only two encountered in the various sources consulted for this study, and his claim appears to have little or no foundation, though his allusion to netting, to the entrapment or ensnarement of vulnerable starving individuals would have been apposite had it applied to the Great Famine, which far exceeded the later famine in duration, intensity and impact. Proselytism, or 'souperism' as it was referred to in Ireland – religious conversion brokered by Protestant evangelicals in return for food and other forms of relief – was a feature, though its scale was frequently exaggerated, of some of the more afflicted parts of the country in the late 1840s and early 1850s, including west Cork, the Dingle peninsula, Connemara, and Achill Island, where the presiding spirit was the energetic and enterprising but misguided Church of Ireland clergyman and evangelical fisher of men Edward Nangle.[55]

The second reference to proselytism in 1879–80 occurred in a poem, 'Sister Clare', whose author, Lady Georgiana Fullerton, a high-born English convert to Catholicism, sent it to the editor of the *Ave Maria*, in acknowledgement of the fulsomeness of the American Catholic response to an appeal she had issued on behalf of 'those in Ireland ashamed to beg', individuals who personified the concept and reality of honest or virtuous poverty. Fullerton and others, including Bishop Duggan of Clonfert and Sister McCarthy of Ballyshannon, County Donegal, as noted above, believed that the respectable destitute were beyond the remit of the existing famine relief organisations, that public bodies were not the appropriate agencies to serve the needs of these individuals. 'There are wants and griefs,' Fullerton wrote, 'which can only be assisted by the secret and delicate ministrations of private charity.' In her subsequent acknowledgement of American Catholic generosity, Fullerton observed: 'Help coming from afar ... makes one value so well the Catholic union of heart and spirit which makes the children of the church one family, bound together by faith and love.'[56]

'Sister Clare', Fullerton's self-styled 'little poem' – a 148-line assessment of the Irish Catholic historical experience from the sentimental, though genuine and empathetic, perspective of this English aristocrat and Catholic convert – concerns the famine-afflicted Moran fisher-family, whose elder daughter Kathleen or Cathleen (both spellings appear in the text), a former pupil at Sister Clare's convent school, informed Clare of the deleterious impact of 'pinching want and hunger keen' on her parents and siblings, and of her father's painful, though faithful and honourable, rejection of offers of assistance because of their proselytist taint:

... But sooner will Pat Moran bear
To see his darlings dead,
Than send them to the souper's school
And sell their souls for bread.
We'll not deny the Faith at all,
We'll have no souper here;
Pat Moran's child shall never learn
To scorn Christ's Mother dear.

The remaining lines are a sustained criticism of 'the tempter's deeper art', and a paean to

> ... those of every creed,
> Of every race and land,
> Who to a suffering brother e'er
> Have lent a helping hand;
> Who never in his hour of need
> Have lured a man with gold
> To barter his soul's birthright, like
> The patriarch of old;
> Who never turned away with scorn
> From his impassioned prayer;
> Who never made a traffic of
> A starving man's despair.

The reference to the souper's school prompted a parenthetical interpolation by the *Ave Maria's* editor, Rev. Daniel E. Hudson, discounting the likelihood of proselytist activity during the current famine crisis in Ireland: 'It does not appear that during the present distress in Ireland the same open and shameless efforts have been made as in former times of famine to bribe with food the starving Catholic parents into sending their children to Protestant schools.' Hudson suggested that English and Irish public opinion would not countenance such meddling. His reservations were substantiated by Fullerton's explanation that she had written the poem 'after the famine of former years', which suggests that the sentiments expressed were a residue of the Great Famine of the 1840s and were resurrected and adapted to meet the current famine situation.[57]

Lady Georgiana Fullerton and the eponymous humanitarian enabler of her poem, Sister Clare, the Nun of Kenmare, together with the Catholic hierarchy, parochial clergy and religious sisters, were acutely aware of the power and reach of the press and the value of publicity, and, as the begetters and recipients of international famine relief aid, were equally conscious of the need to express their gratitude publicly through the same medium. The acknowledgements, while genuine and sincere, were usually as formulaic as the construction of the appeals themselves.

Michael Logue, bishop of Raphoe, for example, informed the arch-bishop of Boston that the donation of £500 which he had received from the archdiocese would relieve 'an immense number' of famine-stricken people in Donegal, and were it not for American generosity the peo-ple's advocates might long since have given up their supplicatory task in despair.[58] In April 1880 Laurence Gillooly, bishop of Elphin, thanked the editor of Portland's *Catholic Sentinel* for promoting the Irish famine relief appeal: 'May God bless you and the good friends who have joined you in sending in their sympathy and their help! We are in need of both and shall continue so until the harvest comes in to supply the poor with food.'[59]

## The Nun of Kenmare and her fund for the distress in Ireland

As noted in Chapter 2, Sister Mary Francis Clare's appeal to Australian generosity, which was first published in the colonial press in early December 1879, was instrumental in awakening the southern hemisphere to the famine crisis in Ireland. Clare, or the Nun of Kenmare as she was universally known, was among the earlier and was certainly the most enterprising of the religious interlocutors who engaged internationally on behalf of the disadvantaged in Ireland. She had an awareness of overseas newspaper titles that identified with or were sympathetic to Irish and Catholic issues, and she augmented this knowledge with a flair for publicity and organisation.

Clare's humanitarian appeal on behalf of the starving and suffering Irish poor provoked a mixed response in South Australia, where it was first published, almost a month before its appearance in the Sydney and Melbourne press. Adelaide's vicar-general, Rev. Frederick Byrne, refused to call a public meeting to organise subscriptions for the relief of distress in Ireland following the publication of her letter, despite calls from his parishioners to do so. He claimed that without the corroboration of a central relief committee in Dublin there was insufficient evidence to justify such an intervention. Byrne rejected Clare's appeal on the basis that money despatched to her would be limited to Kenmare and not extended to the Irish poor generally, and because of her stated intention to use the funds to enlarge and enhance the convent at Kenmare, which, he claimed, was already 'a magnificent pile'. Having thus rejected the Nun of Kenmare's supplication, the vicar-general proceeded to dismiss those who supported it as unthinking 'enthusiasts', individuals seduced by every passing fad.[60]

His clerical colleague in Adelaide, an equally blinkered and tactless Fr W. Prendergast, echoed Byrne's sentiments in a meandering semi-literate response to Clare's letter, which was prompted, he explained, by the necessity to deter swindlers and to prevent the perpetration of fraud on gullible citizens. Prendergast, who professed an acquaintanceship with the Nun of Kenmare and a personal knowledge of the town where she resided, advised strongly against sending money to her, claiming that it could be deployed more effectively in relieving Adelaide's poor, thereby missing entirely the point of Clare's solicitation – funds for the relief of distress in Ireland. He concluded, with a singular lack of grace: 'All praise to those who are ready to relieve the poor, especially the virtuous poor, and more especially the Irish poor, but let them first look for and see facts and not act in the dark as blind men or as fools.' Prendergast added the gratuitous comment that there were too many of the latter in Sydney and Melbourne, and South Australia should not follow their example.[61]

The editor of the *Express and Telegraph*, the Adelaide newspaper in which these unedifying clerical emanations appeared, displayed greater magnanimity and perspicacity than either of his correspondents. He reminded his readers of an account he had previously published, derived from the 31 October 1879 edition of *The Times* of London, which reported Cardinal Manning's authorisation of a general subscription among the 50,000-strong membership of Britain's Catholic temperance societies for the relief of the Irish poor, especially those in Kerry, for whom the Nun of Kenmare had made 'an urgent appeal'.[62]

M.T. Montgomery, who, within days, was to become the driving force behind the South Australian humanitarian response to the Irish food crisis, was scathing in his criticism of Prendergast's contribution to the public debate. 'There is not an Irishman throughout the colony,' he wrote, 'who will not blush with shame when he reads the letter written by the Rev. Prendergast on this subject.' Montgomery dismissed the cleric's epistle as 'mental ramblings', 'a composition of unpatriotic expressions, incoherent sentences, bad grammar and unintelligent [sic] English'. He was particularly critical of Prendergast's 'tone of studied insult to the talented and gifted lady known as the Nun of Kenmare', who had 'immortalised herself', he claimed, and whose name would be preserved in the collective Irish memory long after those of 'sham patriots and milk-and-water philanthropists' had faded to oblivion. Montgomery concluded stoutly by pledging to defend her 'noble character' against Prendergast's offensive charges.[63]

The *Express and Telegraph* devoted a lengthy editorial on 17 December to the Nun of Kenmare and her appeal, observing that her entreaty had been the subject of letters and articles in the British and Irish press, that committees had been formed in many cities in the United Kingdom for the relief of Irish distress – in some cases specifically for the poor in County Kerry – and that the movement had 'assumed national dimensions'. The writer stressed the 'collateral benefits' engendered by such charitable initiatives, claiming that they strengthened expatriate links to Ireland, increased sympathy and promoted kindly feeling between their compatriots and other colonists in Australia, and reminded both that they were 'subjects of one grand empire, having a common history and common interests, aims and sympathies',[64] a theme that was to feature throughout the entire Australian famine relief appeal.

The editorial writer's assessment of the Nun of Kenmare's humanitarian appeal, its popular reception and influence was more accurate and astute than Byrne's and Prendergast's negativity towards it. Sister Mary Francis Clare's intercession on behalf of the Irish poor in 1879–80 was herculean in its range and intensity. Her expositions of the situation of the Irish peasantry and her supplications on their behalf were not confined to Australian publications, but appeared in American, British, Canadian and New Zealand titles also – often repeatedly, and at tedious length – and generally with the editorial support of the journals concerned.

In an open letter to Catholics in the United States, undated, but probably written in the second half of October 1879, Clare stated that she was obliged to turn once gain 'to the well-off in America' on behalf of the poor in Ireland. 'Our harvests have failed,' she wrote, 'our potatoes are gone, the turf is rotten from the wet and famine and fever are staring us in the face in every direction.' This pithy and arresting summary of the situation in the western half of Ireland in autumn 1879 was followed by a serpentine and sentimental narrative that was characteristic of her writing style and general correspondence. She promised spiritual rewards in this world and the next to her benefactors; outlined the case and religious faith of a recently bereaved mother of seven young children; recounted the Kenmare religious sisters' desire to provide local employment during the coming winter, which she described as 'the best form of charity', in constructing a shelter for homeless girls – a variation on a theme in her Australian appeal; and in her four concluding paragraphs referred inconsequentially to unemployment among printers and bookbinders in Dublin, and to a pamphlet on the Blessed Virgin Mary – the latter a recurring topic in her literary works – which she had completed but had yet to publish as she required financial assistance to do so.[65]

The *New Zealand Tablet*, under the editorship of its founder, Bishop Patrick Moran of Dunedin, reproduced her American appeal at the beginning of January 1880, though he omitted the meandering concluding paragraphs. Moran referred to her plea as Clare's 'pathetic letter', and acknowledged the *Catholic Sentinel*, which was published in Portland, Oregon, as his source,[66] an illustration of the international reach and cross-fertilisation of late nineteenth-century Catholic newspapers and journals. Kevin Molloy, in his study of the *New Zealand Tablet*, observed that Moran derived copy from the *Nation* and *Freeman's Journal* in Dublin and from the Boston *Pilot*,[67] and, as noted here, from other Catholic sources also. Moran, a strong Irish nationalist, was a forceful and influential figure in early New Zealand Catholicism and, according to Molloy, in the later nineteenth century the *Tablet*, his creation, 'was, in effect, the national forum for those Irish in New Zealand of a nationalist and Catholic persuasion'.[68]

At the beginning of December 1879 Toronto's *Irish Canadian* published a similar entreaty from the Nun of Kenmare, supported by a letter from Dr Daniel McCarthy, bishop of Kerry, which Clare more than likely orchestrated, on the prevailing distress in Kenmare and its surrounds. McCarthy attempted to convey the circumstances of the inhabitants of 'this poor and mountainous district': the wet summer, which was the culmination of three years of unseasonable weather; the lack of employment; rising food prices, 'which to poor people means starvation'; the loss of the potato crop – 'the potatoes are nearly all black, and now the only resource is yellow meal', and that in insufficient quantities; the lack of fuel – 'the turf is rotten in the ground, hence the misery of cold is added to that of starvation'. Bishop McCarthy, anticipating 'a terrible want' of food and fuel, feared the coming winter and the possible recurrence of the fearful scenes of the Great Famine, and appealed for immediate help, not 'in the cause of abject charity', he stressed, but to meet an unforeseen emergency. McCarthy insisted that there was no desire to demoralise the Irish peasantry by creating a dependency on humanitarian assistance, an awareness and acknowledgement on his part of eighteenth- and nineteenth-century concerns and debates relating to poverty and its relief. He included an extract from the *Cork Examiner* on conditions in Kerry as evidence of the distress in the county:

> The farmers here simply exist; not with money in proverbial old stockings (landlords would have us believe to the contrary, but that article of faith is, like the stockings, worn out); not with wealth lying in sheep and dry stock; not with cash squandered in luxuries, but devoid of all, they live on the sufferance of the shopkeepers ... The farmers' lives are those of monotonous wretchedness, rising with the sun and going to rest with him; working in heat and cold; ill-fed, ill-housed and ill-clad; suffering all in order to fill the insatiable maws of landsharks and absentees, and scarcely lifted above the beasts they are housed with, save in the possession of the religion they have preserved so well.[69]

In McCarthy's version of events, Sister Mary Francis Clare, 'seeing the fearful distress around her', solicited assistance from the *Daily News*, which he described as 'the leading organ of English "Liberal" opinion', but the response was negligible, a miserly £9, which provoked the *Universe*, an English Catholic weekly, to exclaim:

> Here is proof irrefragable that the British public cannot yield credence to the existence of distress in Ireland. A couple of months ago a lady of the highest character, a lady incapable of exaggeration – the Nun of Kenmare – wrote a letter to the *Daily News* asking help for the destitute in her neighbourhood. What was the response? It is shameful, nay, almost incredible. The gifted, pious and tender-hearted woman received, as the result of the contributions of the wealthiest kingdom in the world, towards the relief of the suffering of its brethren in Kerry, the wretched sum of nine pounds sterling.

Bishop McCarthy's letter makes it clear that it was he who encouraged Clare to appeal to American humanitarianism, possibly in the wake of the rebuff administered by the British public. McCarthy and Clare arranged to send Peter O'Leary, an Irish-born London-domiciled journalist, as their representative in the quest for sympathy and more tangible support among 'the noble American people'.[70]

Clare introduced O'Leary to *Irish Canadian* readers – though the wording of her letter suggests that her communication was primarily intended for American publications – as 'the well-known press correspondent and ardent nationalist' who would shortly arrive in the United States to collect information for 'a very important literary work' she was preparing for publication, 'and to get some help for the great distress in the south-west of Ireland'. She claimed that O'Leary was too well known to require any commendation from her, his name a guarantee of his integrity and literary ability, and she encouraged her 'kind and generous American friends' to welcome him warmly. Clare believed that his presence among them would enable her 'to save numbers from starvation' and to assist Dublin tradesmen who had appealed to her for help. She claimed that they were as oppressed as the tenant farmers and attributed their plight and that of Irish trade generally to the expenditure of Irish money externally rather than on supporting home industries, adding that it was 'the work of a true patriot to raise the tone, social as well as political, of our native land, and to build up Irish trade', which is what she was attempting to achieve with her current enterprise. In a post-script, she announced portentously that she had appointed O'Leary as her special commissioner for the United States, Canada and Australia, 'to collect information for her new and magnificent work on "Distin-guished Irishmen at home and abroad"', which she was compiling to assist the 5,000 Dublin printers and bookbinders who, with their fami-lies, were suffering because there was insufficient work available to them. The *Irish Canadian* endorsed her petition, the editor commending her circular 'to every man in Ontario with an Irish heart'.[71] In this effusion at least, in which Clare's vanity and grandiosity are on more naked dis-play than in some of her other humanitarian appeals, the plight of the Kenmare and Kerry peasantry was linked with that of distressed Dublin tradesmen and both constituencies were very much secondary to her literary endeavours and ambitions.

Peter O'Leary visited Ireland between April and June 1879, returned in late October, and claimed that he witnessed in County Kerry privation and misery such as he had never previously encountered among a civilised people. He informed readers of the *Irish Canadian* that he had met the Nun of Kenmare, whom he called 'the greatest woman of our race', and he had agreed to promote her efforts on behalf of the distressed south-western peasantry and the Dublin printing and bookbinding trades. He observed that 'Sister Mary' was 'a most business-like woman' and any funds entrusted to her would be judiciously disbursed.[72]

O'Leary revisited and elaborated on these themes in the *Catholic Sentinel* and was even more effusive in his characterisation of the Nun of Kenmare, portraying her variously as 'the greatest woman of the Irish race', 'the famous authoress', 'this extraordinary woman, this literary star of the first magnitude, this meek and holy nun', who was attempting to rescue the defenceless Irish peasantry from starvation and hypothermia, and, he concluded, her charitable appeal deserved 'the greatest respect and consideration from Catholics and Irishmen'.[73]

O'Leary was an active and energetic advocate of her mission, on public platforms and in the American and Canadian press. He addressed a series of meetings in Canada in the winter of 1879–80. On 16 December 1879 he delivered a lecture in Toronto on the Irish land question and on the distress in Ireland, following which the Irish Relief Committee of Toronto was appointed.[74] In mid-January 1880 he reminded Canadians that the first necessity was the preservation of human life, not politics, for, he stated, 'talking political economy to a starving peasant, with a starving family around him, is sheer nonsense'. Food was the essential requirement, and the Nun of Kenmare was 'doing wonders' in her attempts to provide for the people. He promised that any aid sent to her would be distributed equitably and without delay.[75] Some three weeks later he disclosed that Clare, whom he described on this occasion as 'this truly great woman', 'one of the noblest women of our time', had pledged to 'forward boxes of the dear old shamrock, the emblem of our native land', to all who subscribed to her relief fund before 1 March. He mentioned also that Fanny Parnell in New York had subscribed £5 to Clare's fund, suggesting a link between her fund and the Land League's, and with Charles Stewart Parnell, who was then fund-raising in the United States.[76]

The *Catholic Sentinel* appears to have been Clare's preferred and most supportive American media outlet; others included the *New York Herald*, whose reach extended beyond an essentially Irish or Catholic base, the *Pilot*, and the *Irish American*.[77] On 11 December 1879, a month after publishing her initial entreaty, the *Catholic Sentinel* cast the Nun of Kenmare as a 'modern St Bridget', the religious world's most 'devoted heroine of charity'.[78] The following week's issue provided readers with an adulatory sketch of her life and religious beliefs, one which flattered by stripping a year from her age, and which Clare herself may have written or engineered. The editor's introduction, a servile conflation of piety and sentimentality, concluded by designating her 'this glorious bride of Christ'. The feature writer maintained the editor's unctuous tone. Clare, he wrote, 'was always of a deeply religious turn of mind', from childhood possessing 'an innate desire to do works of charity and help the needy'. This biographical confection was complemented by an encomium on Kenmare and the Poor Clare community by the Irish-born journalist S.C. Hall.[79]

Other journalists portrayed Clare in equally cloying and extravagant terms, fusing late-Victorian sentimentality with their own subliminal advocacy of the Irish famine relief appeal. According to the special correspondent of the London *Daily Telegraph*, whose account dated from February 1880, Clare was compelled to discharge her charitable work from 'her invalid's couch'. 'She cannot go about doing good, like her Master,' the writer proclaimed extravagantly, 'but her name is as music in the ears of those who need help on their way through what John Bunyan called "the wilderness of this world".'[80] James Redpath of the *New York Tribune*, who interviewed Clare on several occasions on the details of her own life and on the daily routine at the Kenmare convent, which he claimed was the most famous in Ireland, also referred to her 'delicate' health. Redpath described her as a brown-eyed little woman, 'with delicate and refined features, a pale and sweet face – with signs of the weariness that physical suffering leaves behind it'. He claimed that she was the most renowned Irish nun since Saint Brigid and that no Irish woman was ever so widely known during her own lifetime or exerted such a beneficent and widespread influence.[81] Redpath and his *Daily Telegraph* colleague each attributed Clare's authority and impact to her literary output, to the popularity and renown of her many published works among the Irish worldwide.[82]

Two Irish-born residents of Portland, Oregon, women who styled themselves 'Friends of the Nun of Kenmare' to preserve their anonymity, responded to Clare's entreaty in the *Catholic Sentinel* of 13 November 1879 by organising a collection among family, friends and neighbours which realised $165.[83] The Bank of British North America waived currency exchange charges, and the *Catholic Sentinel* agreed to bear the registration and postal costs to Ireland, announcing at the same time that its columns would remain open for a period to receive subscriptions and that it would continue to bear the transmission costs. Thereafter, the paper printed regular subscription lists, further charitable appeals and letters of acknowledgement and gratitude from Sister Clare and other beneficiaries, among them various members of the Catholic hierarchy in Ireland.[84] This was the broad pattern – the mechanics of famine-inspired humanitarianism – that featured throughout the anglophone world:

newspaper entreaties and publicity; fund-raising activities of multifarious kinds; the waiving of transmission costs and charges to Ireland by banks, postal authorities, rail and shipping companies.

The *Tablet* was the primary facilitator of Clare's charitable appeals to English Catholics, though the editor insisted that it was the government's responsibility to address Ireland's famine crisis, maintaining that private charity, whether domestic or foreign, was incapable of doing so.[85] In spring 1880 Clare submitted an overwrought plea to the journal, propelled, she wrote, 'by obedience and charity to make every exertion to obtain assistance for the distressed' in Ireland. Clare refuted claims that had begun to emerge in sections of the British Tory press, specifically that Irish adversity had been exaggerated, or that its severity had decreased, and she dismissed any similar statements that might serve as 'a balm to conscience' or excuse the common duty to provide alms. She claimed that the scale of Irish suffering had not been acknowledged until recently, which she attributed to the reticence of the Irish poor who knew that they would be accused 'of begging, and of laziness and of being demoralised' if they revealed the full extent of their wretchedness. Clare stated that a great deal of nonsense had been circulated about the demoralisation of the Irish people arising from the provision of gratuitous relief. 'One might suppose that Ireland was being strewn with gold dust and diamonds,' she observed sardonically, such had been the outcry, whereas the aid received amounted to no more than about a penny's worth of coarse food per head of population per day, which, she concluded, was scarcely enough to keep people alive, and if prolonged would render disease outbreaks inevitable.[86]

In a postscript Clare drew attention to an advertisement she had placed elsewhere in the journal publicising a bazaar and lottery to raise relief funds. She claimed that her initiative had received papal blessing and the support of the English nobility and others, suggesting that it was both legitimate and respectable: 'Bazaar in Aid of the Distress in Ireland', under the patronage of the countess of Denbigh, the countess of Gainsborough, Viscountess Maidstone, Lady Constance Bellingham, Lady Catherine Berkeley, Lady Frances Warburton, Viscount Camden, Viscount Bury, Viscountess Bury, Hon. Mrs Ross of Bladenburg, Henry

Bellingham, Daniel O'Connell, Derrynane Abbey, D. Shine Lawler, Killarney. The first prize, which she stated was donated by Pope Leo XIII, was 'a cameo of our Blessed Lady, of exquisite Roman workmanship, and his holiness' apostolic benediction on her work'. Other prizes included a crystal and gold locket, a gold cross and 'two beautiful Roman mosaic crosses', gifts of the Bellingham family.[87]

Two months later, in a lengthy, sinuous and overly emotional communication, Clare claimed that English Catholics had little knowledge of the current state of Ireland, that the country's adherence to Catholicism had resulted in misrepresentation in the English Protestant press, and that the Irish poor had incurred 'the everlasting hatred of Protestant England by their fidelity to their God'. She contended that if the north of England or Scotland were afflicted by famine, the British government would respond more promptly and effectively than it had done in Ireland. 'One thing is certain,' she wrote, 'there is widespread and most awful misery and desolation in almost every part of Ireland.' She appended extracts from two Irish newspapers (*Freeman's Journal*; *Cork Examiner*, both dated 26 April 1880) and communications from Catholic and Anglican clergymen in different parts of the country to support her claim, including one from Rev. W. Murray in west Cork, advocating legal amendments intended to protect Ireland from being cast as 'a periodical beggar before the nations of the earth'. Clare cited a sentimental letter from Bishop McCarthy of Kerry to an expatriate Irish priest in Liverpool: 'Were it not for the liberal donations of our American brethren, the famine of '47 would have again revisited many lonely and beautiful glens in your native Kerry.'[88]

The Nun of Kenmare invested an enormous amount of time and energy in fund-raising for the starving Irish poor from autumn 1879 through to the successful harvest of the following year, and, as her bazaar and lottery demonstrated, she was capable of considerable ingenuity and inventiveness in targeting potential subscribers in Ireland and overseas. She displayed her opportunism further in linking her humanitarian endeavours to the reputed appearance of the Virgin Mary at Knock, County Mayo, on 21 August 1879, and to related events in the village in the following January. Clare produced a pamphlet on the Knock apparition, dated Easter 1880, and addressed the vainglorious preface: 'To those generous friends who have contributed to my Fund for the Distress in Ireland, by which I have been enabled to give food and clothing to thousands of poor children in the convent schools in all parts of Ireland, and to assist several hundred priests.' She explained that the entirety of the fund generated by the sale of her Knock pamphlet would be distributed among the convents and Catholic clergy in the worst-affected parts of the country, and she promised to commission a priest to perform the Stations of the Cross at Knock, 'with lighted candles, both inside and outside the Church of the Apparition', to have a mass celebrated there in May 1880, and to make a financial contribution to Knock church for the special intentions of those who purchased her pamphlet. As further inducement, she informed potential subscribers that their donations would feed the hungry and clothe the naked and would support 'a *spiritual* work of mercy', her pamphlet in honour of the mother of God. Clare dedicated the said work to the highly respected and influential but aged and ailing archbishop of Tuam, Dr John MacHale, a dedication that implied hierarchical favour and support for her relief efforts.[89]

Clare outlined the objects of her Fund for the Distress in Ireland in an addendum to *The Apparition at Knock*:

- To supplement the often wholly inadequate relief provided by public funds;

- To enable priests exercise discretion in assisting 'their utterly destitute people', and to provide help 'in cases of severe sickness, or weakness', which, again, were beyond the remit of public funds;

- To provide convents with the means to assist the poor and needy in their communities.

She echoed the claims of other religious sisters that they had a greater knowledge and understanding of the poor and their needs and could expend money on food and clothing more expeditiously and efficaciously than others who had less time or experience. Clare repeated that food and clothing shortages prevented thousands of children from attending school and concluded: 'Never was there such an opportunity of helping a whole Christian people, and of obtaining so great a reward at so small a cost.'[90]

At the end of August 1880 Clare disclosed to the editor of Portland's *Catholic Sentinel* that she had fulfilled her promise to have a mass performed at Knock for the special intentions of those who had responded to her appeals for assistance during what she called 'this famine year'.[91] Three weeks later she reported in the same publication that she had begun to burn 'a lamp day and night' for the intentions of current and potential supporters of her efforts to assist Ireland's 'faithful poor'.[92]

Clare was careful to acknowledge the financial contributions, large and small, she received in response to her famine appeals, and to credit the essential role of newspapers and their editors in facilitating her entreaties on behalf of the famine-stricken Irish, a task that was eased by the clerical assistance provided by two lay secretaries and three of Clare's religious colleagues at the Kenmare convent.[93] At the end of April 1880 Sister Mary Raphael, on Clare's behalf, thanked the editor of the *Catholic Sentinel* and 'all those good, kind, generous people' who had contributed to the relief of Irish distress. 'Were it not for all the help we have got from America,' Clare's proxy observed, 'our poor people would be today in the workhouse or in their silent grave.' Sister Raphael's letter featured alongside acknowledgements from Bishop Laurence Gillooly, Archbishop John MacHale and Bishop John MacEvilly.[94] A few days later Clare expressed her gratitude for £7. 13s. 7d. received on behalf of 'the poor of this desolate locality', which, she stated, would assist 'some poor creatures who would otherwise be obliged to seek a home in the workhouse'.[95] On a larger scale, she acknowledged the receipt of $1,000 from the Irish Relief Committee of Philadelphia, which she assigned equally to the purchase of food and seed potatoes, adding that if the committee could provide her with an additional $2,000 she would be able to save her entire district from famine in the following year.[96] In May 1880 Clare informed the editor of the *Catholic Sentinel* that the distress was still deplorable and were it not for 'the generous assistance of munificent America', Ireland would probably be 'one vast graveyard' and 'the scenes of '46 and '47' would again feature.[97]

The many references to the Great Famine of the 1840s by those involved in the 1879–80 famine relief effort, including the Nun of Kenmare, is a reminder that famine was a recurring feature of Irish life, and that the trauma of the earlier catastrophe did not lead to the suppression of its memory, as some have claimed, at least not among the generation that experienced the event or the one that followed.

In mid-March 1880, in a prolix, labyrinthine communication to the editor of the *New Zealand Tablet*, Clare expressed her gratitude to Ireland's 'friends in Australia and New Zealand' for all they had done for the country, adding that she had been informed that her appeals had been responsible for acquainting overseas residents with the evolving famine crisis in Ireland. She criticised the various Irish private relief funds for their time-consuming bureaucracy, the rigidity of their approach to relief work, and their complete dependence on Indian meal as a substitute food for the lost potato crop, implying that she was more liberal and flexible in interpreting the needs of the poor and the sick.[98] Clare was also critical of the conservative approach adopted by the private funds administrators to the money they received, their practice of keeping a reserve rather than spending the entirety immediately, and the inadequacy of the sums they distributed to local relief committees, which, she claimed, reflected a failure of trust in 'God Almighty's great bank'. Her own inclination was to respond instantly to any genuine appeal from any part of Ireland, irrespective of the state of the funds under her control, buoyed by the firm conviction that the next morning's post would bring from America more than enough to cover 'the venture on providence'.[99]

Clare continued with this theme in a letter to the *Catholic Sentinel* on 19 March 1880. She reverted to her criticism of the administration of the Mansion House and Marlborough relief funds and hoped for a prompter and more generous response from those in charge of the *New York Herald* fund, but feared further delays, arising from the general practice of investigating and substantiating the extent of localised distress and of validating requests for assistance. This cautious, questioning approach was not caused by dilatoriness or any deficiency in compassion or sympathy, rather by fears of misappropriation, a justifiable concern given the experiences of similar relief efforts during the Great Famine.

Clare stated that she was 'heart-worn' with the entire famine relief process. She had persevered with her work on behalf of the Irish poor despite serious illness, which her doctor attributed solely to 'grief at the distress'. He had urged her for the sake of her health not to take the current situation so much to heart. 'As if I could help taking it to heart, as if our Lord did not take human sorrow to heart,' she exclaimed in a questionable conflation, before appealing: 'You will do all you can for me – not for me, indeed, but for dear Ireland.'[100]

Later, most likely towards the end of May 1880, Clare addressed a circular letter to her 'dear and munificent American friends', the readers of the *Catholic Sentinel*, which was pointedly political in tone and content, referring approvingly to the Land League and its activities for the first time. Her outburst may have been prompted by her own malaise and frustration at the continuing crisis in Ireland and the government's failure to intervene in any meaningful way. Clare appealed to her American readers to save Ireland from starvation, and once this was achieved to assist in freeing the country from 'the cruel injustice which leaves our people beggars before the face of the whole world', thus echoing the message Charles Stewart Parnell had delivered throughout his American mission some months earlier. There was a general awareness, she wrote, that Ireland was starving, and that England had let her starve, a situation that compelled Ireland to turn for assistance to the nations of the earth, and one that left England in disgrace:

Yes; feed us, oh, noble people! and then, in the name of the good God, free us! Stand by the Land League, stand man to man and your cause and ours is one; and England shall be compelled to change the laws which make Ireland a perpetual beggar and which exile her best and noblest sons.

Clare went further than in previous statements, claiming, misleadingly, that it was thanks to the United States alone that Ireland currently was not one vast graveyard. She appealed once again to American munificence, burnishing her entreaty with all her reserves of cliché and Victorian sentimentality. She had intended to write more fully on political matters, she explained, but 'grief and anxiety', 'constant and severe bodily suffering', and 'the immense correspondence' in which she was engaged prevented her from doing so. She stressed the need to have a fund at her disposal to enable an immediate response to urgent cases, for, she wrote, returning to one of her recurring tropes, 'people may die while committees are considering or waiting to meet'.[101]

## Assessment of the Nun of Kenmare's role in the 1879–80 famine

In December 1880 Timothy M. Harrington, editor of the *Kerry Sentinel* and later a prominent Parnellite MP, claimed that Sister Mary Francis Clare had raised and spent £15,000 in assisting the poor and needy, an approximate match to her own estimate of $75,000, and one that has been generally accepted by her biographers and historians of the international relief effort.[102] One commentator, John White, believes that the figure should be revised upwards, that her various initiatives realised more than £20,000.[103] He claimed that much of this money was distributed through local branches of the Land League, an assertion that conflicts with Clare's that her fund would be administered through the Irish convent network and the Catholic clergy, and with the paucity of references to the Land League in her international appeals. The occasion of Harrington's statement was a 'great indignation meeting' at Kenmare on Sunday, 5 December 1880, called in response to a threatening letter which Clare had received from London. The hyperbole and praise which the platform speakers, clerical and lay, lavished on her that day might have brought a blush even to the well-rounded roseate cheeks of the fifty-one-year-old Nun of Kenmare![104]

Clare's unremitting efforts to awaken people's consciences and to raise funds on behalf of those affected by famine in 1879–80 relieved many hungry and vulnerable individuals in Kerry and elsewhere in Ireland, and possibly saved lives. She resorted to various stratagems to publicise her humanitarian endeavours, appealing to people's materialistic impulses by raffling trinkets and novelties, and to expatriate Irish sentimentality with her offer of shamrock. She complemented the material with less tangible, more spiritual rewards: her own prayers and those of her religious sisters at Kenmare, and the ceremonial performance of mass, the Stations of the Cross, and candle-burning at Knock, the site of the reputed apparition of the Virgin Mary. Given the context and nature of her intervention, such inducements were hardly necessary, and at this remove appear tawdry and ill-judged, resurrecting the discredited whiff of the sale of indulgences. More appropriately and conventionally, Clare appealed to people's humanity and their Christian obligation to assist the sick and the starving. Her own powerful personality towered over the whole enterprise: her literary fame and achievements; her physical and emotional malaise; her increasing political stridency as the crisis deepened, and her lack of restraint in drawing attention to these issues; her narcissism and braggadocio; her proclaimed links to the papacy and her imputation that she was one of Christ's chosen. She included in her publicity material encomiums and expressions of gratitude from individuals such as Daniel O'Connell of Derrynane, the Liberator's grandson, and from the bishop of Kerry, clergymen of different denominations, and relief committees throughout the country.[105] Clare basked in their acclaim, citing, for instance, a letter from a fellow Kenmare resident to a Dublin newspaper:

> If there was no 'Nun of Kenmare' many a cold grave would be filled through starvation ere this. Such a benefactress is worth a legion of speechmakers; for while they are talking, she is working ... carrying out her heaven-born ideas of saving a wretched, starving people from disease and death.[106]

Clare recorded in one of her two autobiographical offerings that she regarded her mission on behalf of the Irish poor as 'a most sacred trust', which accorded with the motivation and sentiments publicly expressed by other religious sisters, and that it was her bounden duty to discharge this trust or confidence with the utmost care and commitment, even to the detriment of her own physical and emotional health.[107] She put it more simply and affectingly in an interview with the American journalist James Redpath: 'In the rural districts the poor have no one to look up to but the priests and nuns.'[108] Clare's involvement in the 1879–80 famine embodied the dedication of Irish female religious to education and to charitable work in the nineteenth century, and reflected the social and moral authority with which they were vested and which they exercised.[109] There is a lingering suspicion, however, that Clare's interposition was not entirely disinterested or altruistic. Her own writings on the famine and on other topics reveal her as a shameless self-publicist, egotistical, vainglorious, emotional, and central to the drama.

The Nun of Kenmare's narcissism was an essential component of her personality, which in turn fuelled her famine relief work, and her commitment to the latter characterised the humanitarian effort of the Catholic Church and community in Ireland and internationally during the crisis. The Mansion House relief committee commended the 'energy, firmness and administrative capacity' of the clergy and 'their loyalty to the suffering people', referring primarily though not exclusively to the Catholic clergy.[110] The Catholic Church in Ireland provided direction and leadership: the prelacy lent spiritual and moral authority; the parochial clergy were frequently involved with local relief committees and in aid distribution networks; religious sisters in convents throughout the country educated, fed and clothed school children. Each of the three constituent elements used overseas news outlets and their own international contacts to appeal for assistance to the diasporic Irish and the humane worldwide. The Catholic Church's role in the 1879–80 Irish famine crisis, the assumption of moral leadership in the relief effort, which was generally acknowledged as a genuine ecumenical and inclusive humanitarian endeavour, epitomises – and substantiates – Gearóid Ó Tuathaigh's recent reflections on the church's authority and influence in late nineteenth-century Ireland, the cultural dominion the institution had attained over much of the country by the century's close.[111]

Expatriate Irish Catholic communities and the overseas Irish generally benefited morally and more tangibly from their involvement in relieving famine in Ireland, not least in renewing and strengthening their sense of Irishness, in cementing their bonds with the Irish nation. Their efforts, augmented by international beneficence, produced a substantial return in money, food and clothing, and the next chapter, the final one in this section on philanthropy, will explore the disbursement of the proceeds among the needy, a process that required a different form of organisation to that involved in consciousness- and finance-raising, necessitating centralised administration, committee structures at local level, and distribution mechanisms that ultimately involved the United States and British navies, the Irish rail network, and a flotilla of currachs and other small craft.

CHAPTER 5

# DISTRIBUTION OF INTERNATIONAL AID

So soon as her cargo is on board, you will proceed in command of the *Constellation* to Dublin ... You will make known to the [*New York Herald* relief] committee that this cargo of provisions is contributed by a few generous-hearted citizens of the United States to relieve the wants of the suffering people in Ireland, whose condition has caused extraordinary sympathy in the American mind.

R.W. Thompson, secretary of the navy, Washington, to Commander Edward E. Potter, 25 March 1880, *New York Times*, 26 March 1880, p. 2

Private charity, domestic or foreign, is wholly inadequate to the social crisis in Ireland, which can be met only by State interference, prompt and liberal ... It behoves the government to move, and promptly, in this matter. A month, a week, is an era in a question of such awful moment.

*Tablet*, 10 January 1880, editorial, pp. 37–8

## Introduction

The Dublin Mansion House relief committee estimated that £830,000 was subscribed worldwide for the relief of distress in Ireland in 1879–80. Fifty-eight per cent of the total, £480,000, was remitted to the various voluntary relief organisations and initiatives: £180,000 to the Mansion House fund, £112,000 to the duchess of Marlborough's, £60,000 to the Land League's appeal in North America, and the balance of £128,000 was accounted for by the Philadelphia fund, the *New York Herald* appeal, and the Canadian government and people. Private subscriptions despatched through the agency of the Catholic Church in North America to bishops and priests in Ireland were valued at £200,000, and individual remittances from North America and Australasia to friends and relatives in Ireland were conservatively estimated at £150,000.[1]

The published accounts of the Mansion House committee, though certified by a Dublin firm of chartered accountants, are open to question. Analysis of the Marlborough fund indicates that the Mansion House committee's calculated total of £830,000 was an underestimate. The Marlborough committee was dissolved on 15 April 1880, following the defeat of Disraeli's Conservative government in the general election and the automatic termination of the duke of Marlborough's appointment as viceroy in Ireland. At the time the Marlborough fund amounted to £112,484, with some £15,000 awaiting allocation. For some months afterwards the four trustees appointed to manage the fund continued to receive international donations, and the trustees issued a final report in October 1880 which showed that the Marlborough relief appeal had generated a total of £135,245, some 20 per cent more than the Mansion House committee's reckoning.[2] Furthermore, the Mansion House committee failed to acknowledge the Nun of Kenmare's Fund for the Distress in Ireland, which attracted and disbursed some £15,000, though this money may have been included in the total realised by the general Catholic appeal.

## Methodology and philosophy

According to the figures provided by the Mansion House committee, the United States was the largest source of aid, though only a relatively small portion, £11,245, was directed to its fund, which the committee attributed to the 'strong attacks' made in America upon its constitution and motives, an oblique reference to Parnell's repeated fulminations against the committee and its activities, which were noted in Chapter 3.[3] In contrast, the people of Australia and New Zealand did entrust their subscriptions to the Mansion House committee and left the fund's distribution entirely at the committee's discretion. Those in the southern hemisphere who responded to the appeal did so unconditionally, albeit with an expectation that their contributions would be disbursed on a non-discriminatory basis. The mayor of Geelong in Victoria, for instance, in forwarding £650 to Dublin, explained that the money had been contributed by 'various classes, creeds and countries' (nationalities), and their wish was that it would be allocated 'on the same broad and benevolent basis'.[4]

Some in Australia suggested that a portion of their donations might be used to encourage emigration from Ireland. One such, the Ballarat correspondent of the *Advocate*, Melbourne's Catholic weekly journal, stated that entire families rather than individuals should be so assisted, claiming that neither Victoria nor any other colony was 'a good place for an unprotected Irish girl'.[5] The chairman of the Perth relief fund in Western Australia informed the lord mayor of Dublin that there was a shortage of domestic servants and farm labourers in the colony and that Irish emigrants should be encouraged to travel to Australia rather than to the United States. 'There are few places where an honest, sober and able-bodied working man *can do better*,' he wrote.[6] The linkage of relief subscriptions to emigration was very much a minority advocacy, however, and the general expectation and desire among Australian colonists was that the relief funds be deployed expeditiously, at the Dublin Mansion House committee's discretion, for the alleviation of immediate distress. Similarly, as we have seen, the *New York Herald*'s editorial suggestion that some of its fund should be used to promote Irish emigration to the United States received short shrift from Anna and Fanny Parnell, among others.[7]

There was no shortage of demands on the funds that had been forwarded from Australia, New Zealand, the United States, Canada, Britain, France and elsewhere. Petitions for assistance rained down on the Mansion House and the other relief committees from the affected western half of Ireland, mostly through the agency of the different religious denominations, particularly the Catholic hierarchy and clergy. Several tropes can be identified in these anguished appeals: the reality and severity of the prevailing distress; the ensuing mortality from starvation and famine-related diseases; the scarcity of casual employment; the general withdrawal of credit and the necessity to pawn personal clothing and bedding, which resulted in cold and misery combining with hunger and disease to increase the suffering of the poor; landlords' dereliction of duty towards their tenants; boards of guardians' parsimony and their extreme reluctance to grant outdoor relief; and – repeatedly and consistently – the great antipathy with which the famishing, the distressed and the sick poor regarded workhouses and their auxiliary institutions.[8]

Individuals who interacted with the private relief organisations on behalf of the afflicted peasantry stated that these features were reminiscent of the Great Famine of the previous generation. At the end of January 1880 the parish priest of Addergoole, Ballina, County Mayo, observed: 'We have the bitter scenes of '47 re-enacted', the 'ghostly memories of the famine years' resurfacing like 'a spectre from the tomb'.[9] Reports of coastal dwellers resorting to shellfish and seaweed for their survival, and the spectacle at Drumsna, County Leitrim, of hitherto comfortable individuals 'tottering along at a funeral, more like skeletons than living men' added substance to the clergyman's claim.[10] A more general reminder of the Great Famine was the public works programmes to provide employment – the standard official response to famine and periods of distress in Ireland – and the proven inappropriateness and ineffectiveness of this type of intervention, typified by the exaction of enervating physical labour on hungry enfeebled individuals as a test of destitution. Even worse was the non-implementation of such programmes. In early July 1880 the parish priest of Belmullet, County Mayo, stated that the public works promised for the locality and elsewhere had not materialised, and it was solely due to the endeavours of the voluntary relief agencies that the scenes witnessed during the 'bad times' – the Great Famine – were not repeated.[11]

The Mansion House relief committee assisted more than 500,000 people through the agency of 840 parish-based distributive networks, which were staffed and managed by almost 10,000 individuals: 1,404 Catholic and 835 Protestant clergymen, 508 medical practitioners, 977 Poor Law guardians, and 6,171 lay volunteers. The committee explained that its strategy was 'to gather together the representative men of all religious and political hues in a neighbourhood', trusting that they shared the committee's 'sentiments of honourable responsibility and scrupulous economy'.[12] There were only three instances of the different religious denominations refusing to co-operate on the same committee, in Connemara parishes where the Protestant clergymen were members of the Irish Church Mission Society, an organisation dedicated to converting Roman Catholics in Ireland to Protestantism.[13] The difficulty was resolved by establishing distinct committees in each of the parishes concerned, and providing grants to both. The Mansion House central relief committee, conscious of its responsibility to account for the usage of public funds, adopted an overly bureaucratic approach to administering relief. The committee's scrupulosity, its desire to place its integrity above suspicion, imposed a considerable burden on local relief committees and generated a mountain of statistics and paperwork. The central committee demanded from each of its 840 subordinate committees estimates of the numbers of individuals entitled to relief; weekly returns; each applicant's circumstances; the number and age of family members; the extent of the family's landholding (if any); the amount and duration of relief afforded to each applicant; 'with such other particulars touching population, valuation, amount of poor rate paid and other available resources of any kind, as should afford the central committee some basis of comparison between the necessities of different districts'.[14] Such demands, which were reminiscent of the bureaucracy associated with relief distribution during the Great Famine, delayed the response unnecessarily, prolonged the suffering of the starving, and frustrated the Nun of Kenmare and others who were conscious that expeditious intervention would diminish suffering and save lives.[15]

The Mansion House committee's essential and uniform rule was to restrict the format of relief to food, fuel and clothing; money was never given to relief applicants, an embargo that featured during the Great Famine also. The vast bulk of the Mansion House fund was expended on food for the hungry, invariably Indian meal, which was regarded as 'the humblest and cheapest' substitute food available. The committee explained:

Ground Indian meal had come to be the ordinary sustenance of the Irish peasantry for several months of the year; its cheapness enabled a small sum to spread relief over an astonishingly large area; while the unpalatable nature of the diet was little likely to tempt those who were not reduced to a dire pitch of destitution.

The latter observation carried the stench of the old workhouse test, extending that concept from the public sphere and the public purse to voluntary and private relief interventions. The Mansion House committee, influenced by the experience and lessons of the Great Famine but alive to society's perennial fear of demoralising charity recipients by fostering dependency, felt compelled to explain that it did not require work in return for assistance, claiming that a labour test was impracticable in the current circumstances and would not be attempted.[16]

The Mansion House and the Marlborough relief committees adopted different distribution models, the former a parish-based system, the latter a Poor Law union-centred network. The chairmen of the various boards of Poor Law guardians became ex-officio the conduit for the material relief both committees despatched from Dublin, and for its distribution among various relief committees within their respective unions. James Hack Tuke, the English Quaker philanthropist who was esteemed for his relief efforts in the west of Ireland during the Great Famine, revisited Connacht and the country's north-west in the opening months of 1880 and concluded empirically that the Mansion House distribution system was quicker, more efficient and direct than the Marlborough committee's, but more open to abuse. According to Tuke, there was little supervision of the lists of names supplied to or compiled by local committees, and occasionally too much depended upon 'the opinion, or good nature, or easiness, of an individual'.[17]

## USS *Constellation*

On 25 February 1880, following legislation in Congress, the federal government of the United States authorised the secretary of the navy to designate a vessel to transport a relief cargo to Ireland, and appropriated

the funds necessary to cover the costs. The *New York Herald* famine relief
fund, which had been launched three weeks earlier and which prompted
an immediate and generous response, was responsible for 25 per cent
of the food and clothing on board, and a handful of private donors
contributed the remainder.[18] The *Constellation*, a sailing vessel built in
1798 and once commanded by Commodore Charles Stewart, Charles
Stewart Parnell's maternal grandfather, was assigned to the task, and was
freighted with barrels of seed potatoes, meal, flour, tinned meat, clothing
and footwear, some 500 tons in total according to the manifest, though
it transpired on arrival in Ireland that the consignment was considerably
less, closer to 325 tons.[19] The vessel, under the command of Edward
E. Potter, and with a crew of ninety-six, left New York on 27 March
and berthed in Cork Harbour three weeks later, on 20 April, after 'a
very anxious and boisterous passage', according to Potter.[20] The latter's
instructions were to deliver the *Constellation*'s cargo to the *New York
Herald* relief committee in Dublin for allocation at their discretion, but,
according to the *Cork Examiner*, 'dreadful weather' on the crossing forced
Potter to divert to Haulbowline in Cork Harbour to repair structural
damage to the ship.[21] The secretary of the navy informed Potter prior to
his departure that the *Constellation*'s visit would enable the Irish people
to realise that '"peace hath her victories no less renowned than war",
and that, in this age, these victories do more to create amicable relations
between the people of different nationalities and to draw them closer
together than the roar of battle'.[22]

The *Cork Examiner*'s editorial writer compared the *Constellation*'s
arrival to that of the *Jamestown* relief vessel, under the command of
Captain R.B. Forbes, in 1847, observing that 'the evil time' had not yet
passed and the need for external assistance was still 'sore and urgent'.
In an inside page, the *Cork Examiner* devoted a full column to the earlier
mission, under the heading 'Reminiscences of the Famine of '47–'48'.[23]
On the following Saturday, a supplement to the newspaper contained a
two-column feature, 'The Great Famine Year: The sufferings of the Irish
people in '47–'48', which focused on the *Jamestown* mission. The article
was compiled from Captain Forbes' published account of the voyage,
including correspondence addressed to him outlining the people's

distress in 1847 and the urgency of their need.[24] In one such letter, dated 29 March 1847, J. Kennedy of Ballydehob in west Cork detailed his efforts to feed some 280 starving individuals. Kennedy stated that the local people carried an odour of decomposition about them, 'the smell of the grave', as they phrased it, and he described the whole country as one vast tomb.[25] These references to the Great Famine and the *Jamestown* relief effort linked past and present and contained an implicit political message, Ireland's subject status, and such connections and inferences were a recurring theme in press reports and public addresses during the *Constellation*'s short presence in Ireland.

It was standard practice, a courtesy, for local representatives and dignitaries to present addresses of welcome and gratitude to the commander and officers of relief vessels on their arrival in Ireland and while in port. Rev. Stephen C. Ashlin, Roman Catholic administrator at Queenstown and spokesman for the welcoming committee, informed Commander Potter and his officers on the evening the *Constellation* docked that the residents of the town were 'deeply sensible of the large generosity of the great American people. They came to the rescue in the hour of need and their charity would never be forgotten.'[26] On the following day, the lord mayor of Dublin, Edmund Dwyer Gray, representing the Mansion House relief committee, arrived in Queenstown and expressed the country's 'deep debt of gratitude' to the United States for coming to her assistance. He referred to American generosity during the Great Famine and once again, he said, they turned to 'the same generous hands' for help. Gray observed that the ship's cargo would relieve distress and would serve as evidence of 'the kindly feelings of the people of the United States towards Ireland'.[27]

On 23 April 'the principal citizens' of Cork, led by the mayor, William Shaw, MP, who was also a member of the Mansion House and the *New York Herald* famine relief committees, arranged to hold a public banquet for the commander and officers of the relief vessel, 'in recognition of the splendid generosity of the great American nation in sending the *Constellation* to this country laden with stores for the relief of a suffering people'.[28] At a meeting of the Queenstown town commission on the same day a proposal was made to entertain Commander Potter and his officers at the town's expense, which provoked one of the members, Charles Guilfoyle Doran, a civil engineer and former president of the town commission, to exclaim: 'Entertain them in a famine-stricken country!' An angry discussion ensued, one which was 'not conducted in the best taste', according to the newspaper report. The motion to issue the invitation was eventually carried, despite Doran's continuing dissent. He queried the public entertainment of individuals 'coming with relief to a country which is a pauper in the highway of nations', an echo of similar objections during both the Great Famine and the current crisis, and, he insisted, it would be 'impolitic and imprudent to ask those gentlemen to dine on the gravestones' of people who had died from famine or its attendant diseases.[29]

Doran had been a key figure in the Irish Republican Brotherhood (IRB) throughout the 1870s, its leader in Munster, and secretary to the organisation's supreme council until he stepped aside in March 1878, two years before the *Constellation*'s arrival in Cork Harbour on its famine relief mission.[30] His was the voice of advanced Irish nationalism and his trenchantly expressed views captured the frustration and anger that Ireland's political subjection and dependency on external agencies engendered in many of his fellow citizens.

The *Cork Examiner*, reflecting a more acquiescent and conservative nationalist constituency, dismissed Doran's intervention as inappropriate, describing his objections as 'the emanations of a narrow spirit', which, if 'tinged with any trace of sectional feeling', would be even more offensive and reprehensible. The editorial writer reminded his readers that the arrival of the *Jamestown* in 1847 was celebrated 'with all sorts of festive rejoicing', overlooking the inconvenient fact that much of the rejoicing was singularly vulgar and unseemly.[31] He claimed that Doran was misusing language when he strove to invoke the name of the poor as a reason why those who represented their benefactors should not be acknowledged and entertained.[32]

Commander Potter rejected any address of welcome or appreciation containing political references or sentiment, which resulted inevitably in bland and formulaic presentations and in the redaction of some. The Cork Land League's address, for instance, referred to the *Constellation*'s 'mission of love and charity' – which was ironic, given Parnell's lack of love and charity for the partial begetter of that mission, the proprietor of the *New York Herald* – and to 'the noble generosity of the American nation'. The Land League did manage to include an implicit reference to Ireland's political situation by contrasting the country's colonial status with that of the United States: 'When we refer to the free land of America, we cannot but recall the noble institutions whose laws based upon justice accord to its subjects the largest measure of freedom and secures to the tiller of the soil the full fruits of his labour.'[33]

In their presentation, the people of Queenstown and the Great Island referred to the *Jamestown* voyage during what was described as 'one of the darkest periods of our strange history'. They acknowledged the assistance provided then and on the present occasion but expressed frustration and humiliation at their country's continuing need of such charitable relief. Potter demanded the deletion of the following passage before he would accept the address:

Why do periodical famines desolate our land? Why are the blessings of heaven blighted among us? Why, with strong hands and willing hearts, are we paraded before the nations of the earth? These are questions we do not put and could not rightly put to your government or to you. To the government of England we have often put them, and just as often have been answered by unreasoning majorities within the Senate House, and by a want of practical recognition outside. Hence have we tenfold greater reason to be grateful for the timely aid which your generous nation sends us. Time was when Irish hospitality was no empty word – when the stranger coming on an honourable mission to our shores was welcome to all the comforts of a happy home. But Ireland was then a nation; she is a prostrate country now. Worse still, the gaunt spectre of famine is stalking through the land, cries of famishing thousands are ringing bitterly through our ears and multitudes of our people are flying affrighted from our shores.[34]

Similar sentiments were frequently expressed during the *Jamestown* mission in 1847, as were references to the country's sense of shame and humiliation as recipients of universal charity, 'mendicants on the highway of the world' as one Dublin newspaper expressed it editorially.[35]

The *Cork Examiner* reminded its readers that it was not American policy to intervene in European politics or disputes, and the newspaper rebuked those who sought to make political capital out of the *Constellation*'s presence by including controversial statements and claims in addresses of welcome. The editorial writer advised people to confine themselves to expressions of collective gratitude to 'the American nation for the grand display of generosity' towards Ireland's starving poor.[36]

The newspaper's editorial admonishments, servility and sermonising infuriated Doran, who, in a scathing response, referred to 'the ridiculous inconsistency of banqueting the very benefactors whose charity we are receiving within earshot of the wailings of famishing thousands', and to the absurdity of 'a nation of paupers in the midst of their misery feasting their benefactors'. He continued, critically and with deadly cynicism:

Judging by the luncheons, balls and illustrious assemblies that have arisen out of this purely Irish misery, one would imagine that Irish famines were specially invented for the purpose of affording certain classes of society an opportunity of making merry and of interchanging fashionable greetings, and that affording relief was, after all, but of secondary importance.

Doran misquoted St Augustine: 'The superfluities of the rich are the patrimony [sic] of the poor', appending the arch observation that if the saint were alive and preached such a doctrine in Cork, a jury would be found to convict him of communism, and, in a sly reference to the *Cork Examiner*, suggested that 'a newspaper would not be wanting to justify the verdict'.[37]

Nonplussed, the said newspaper devoted five and a half columns two days later to reporting the banquet given by the mayor and citizens of Cork to Commander Potter and his officers in the Assembly Rooms on the South Mall, and to listing the names and credentials of many of those who attended. As on a similar occasion in 1847, the fare on offer was rich and abundant, and was itemised and described with great relish in the *Examiner*. Each of the banquet's ten toasts was followed by an appropriate musical item. In keeping with protocol, the mayor proposed the first of the acknowledgements, to the queen and the prince and princess of Wales, but he did so routinely, without preface, fanfare or sycophancy. There was considerably more enthusiasm in his tributes to the president of the United States and to Potter and his officers. The mayor referred to the former as 'the elected and chosen governor of a free people', 'the man who rules the destinies of the freest people upon earth'. In acknowledging Potter's 'mission of charity and benevolence' and the generosity of the American people, he reminded them of the *Jamestown* relief expedition in 1847. 'Since the foundation of the American republic,' the mayor stated, 'there always existed a strong bond of sympathy between the two countries', and he expressed his appreciation of 'the gallant nation which had done so much for them'.[38]

Rev. George H. Hepworth, the representative of the *New York Herald* relief fund in Ireland and the consignee of the *Constellation*'s cargo, responded to the toast acknowledging his country's beneficence.[39] He stated that America did not regard the donation as an act of charity, but as a 'fraternal kindness'. When Commander Potter 'dropped his anchor in Queenstown harbour', the clergyman continued, 'he stood upon the deck of a vessel that represented the profound commiseration, condolence and sympathy of a whole nation for a people who had nothing to eat nor wherewithal to be clothed'.[40] Hepworth's address, which was laced with biblical allusions, was fanciful, inflated, pompous and more than a little tedious, and his biographer's claim that her subject's after-dinner speeches, as reported in the Irish newspapers, were 'eloquent, tactful and diplomatic' was woefully wide of the mark.[41]

The remainder of the evening's toasts and responses were as politically innocuous as those that had gone before, and the occasion ended on the same note of goodwill and benevolence with which it began, aided no doubt by the champagne, hock and claret that accompanied the repast and toasts.[42]

Commander Potter's sensitivity regarding the internal affairs of the United Kingdom and his determination as the American government's representative to remain politically neutral throughout his time in

Fig. 5.1: 'The Eviction by Hubert O'Grady' (New York: A.S. Seer Eng. Print, 1881).
IMAGE COURTESY OF THE LIBRARY OF CONGRESS, www.loc.gov/item/2014637107/

Ireland may have been tested by Hubert O'Grady's charged melodrama *The Eviction* which Potter and some of his officers attended at the Theatre Royal, Cork on Friday, 23 April 1880. O'Grady's play, which the lord chamberlain's office had licensed for public performance in the previous November, was a product and a reflection of its time – the early months of the Land League and the Land War – and its title was a pointer to its content and its socially disruptive potential. Evictions – forcible dispossession from land and homes – with their attendant protests and publicity were one of the key agents of political mobilisation in Ireland in the late 1870s and early 1880s. According to the theatre historian Christopher Fitz-Simon, O'Grady was 'the author of the most original and also the most politically and socially provocative body of Irish plays that were first seen during the final quarter of the nineteenth century', and Fitz-Simon regards *The Eviction*, with its powerful visual effects and 'remarkable political commentary', as O'Grady's finest drama.[43] It was no less than 'a sermon preached from behind the footlights', in the estimation of one the playwright's contemporaries.[44]

*The Eviction*, which opened in Cork on Monday, 12 April before an enthusiastic audience, was billed as O'Grady's 'new and powerful Irish drama', though it did not find favour with the nationalist *Cork Examiner*'s pompous and pedantic theatre critic, whose commendation was limited to the performers and the production's 'artistic and novel' scenery. 'The new drama has such a strong "no-rent" flavour,' he wrote, 'and is so inflammatory in its style that it cannot fail to attract crowded houses at this particular period, when the *kettle* of popular excitement is *boiling over* in the county, and when *spouting* is so much the rage.' The reviewer noted the crowded state of parts of the theatre in contrast to the empty benches of the previous weeks when, he claimed, entertainment of a vastly superior kind was on offer, a dichotomy that prompted the supercilious reflection that 'the amount of good taste once boasted of in the community has lost some of its original quantity'.[45]

*The Eviction* was performed by O'Grady's Irish National Company and was scheduled to run from 12 to 17 April, but its popularity and commercial success resulted in the ensemble's re-engagement for another week, and the company marked its retention with an expanded and more varied programme: O'Grady's first play *The Gommoch* (simpleton or clown) in four acts; Dion Boucicault's *The Colleen Bawn* and *The Shaughraun* (wanderer), and other stock productions.[46] The company's final performance, scheduled for Friday, 23 April, was advertised as a 'grand monster programme for the benefit of Mr and Mrs O'Grady'. The entertainment consisted of a mélange of poetry recitations, including 'The Charge of the Light Brigade'; orchestral scores; a dance by O'Grady – his 'celebrated' Irish reel; *The Eviction*; and 'the celebrated comedy' *Perfection*.[47]

Commander Potter and some of his officers, the United States consul and the mayor of Cork attended at the special invitation of the playwright and the Theatre Royal's managing director, and the American guests were enthusiastically received by the audience. 'The performance was excellent in every respect', according to the *Cork Examiner*'s representative – presumably a different reviewer to the opening evening's –

and O'Grady thanked his 'distinguished visitors' and the rest of the audience for their attendance. There is no record of whether Potter and his fellow American naval officers were as engaged and moved and possibly enraged as the Irish members of the audience by the topicality, content and political propaganda of *The Eviction*. The event's 'great success and the great numbers' who were unable to gain admission prompted an additional, final performance on the following evening.[48]

On 4 May 1880, the day on which the queen conferred the Order of Victoria and Albert on the duchess of Marlborough in recognition of her endeavours to relieve distress in Ireland – to the chagrin of many Irish nationalists and their sympathisers – the lord mayor and the corporation of Dublin honoured Commander Potter's contribution by bestowing the freedom of the city on him, and in the evening more than 1,300 people attended a ball in his honour. The *Freeman's Journal* devoted more than two columns to listing those who were present, and the newspaper's leader writer availed of the occasion to reflect at length on the 1847 *Jamestown* relief mission.[49] Subsequently, Potter and some of his officers travelled to Galway, where they visited Queen's College, dined with the county clerk, and attended a ball. After returning to Queenstown, they gave 'a dancing party' on board ship for several hundred people as a gesture of appreciation for the civilities and kindness extended to the officers and crew while in port.[50]

It appears that members of the *Constellation*'s crew may have availed too liberally of Cork city's hospitality. The *Cork Examiner*, under the heading 'The American Tar and the British Red Coat', reported on a Saturday-night fracas between a *Constellation* crewman, who appears to have 'cultivated a taste for Cork whiskey', and a British soldier, which resulted in the former having to seek treatment at the city's North Infirmary. On the following evening there was an interracial quarrel on board the *Constellation*. According to one newspaper report, a good many of the crew were 'coloured men' whose religious beliefs did not permit any type of amusement or entertainment on the sabbath. Some of their white colleagues proposed a dance as a means of entertaining public visitors to the vessel on Sunday, 2 May, but the 'darkies' – the *Cork Examiner*'s crude expression – who were 'adept at the tambourine' refused to provide the music. In the ensuing altercation, a pistol was discharged, blows were exchanged between blacks and whites, and iron belaying pins were used as weapons. According to the newspaper's overblown account, several crewmen were 'severely cut', and 'the deck presented a bloody scene after the battle'.[51] A partial retraction and a more sober version of the affray appeared in the following day's edition, the newspaper claiming that the affair was merely a row between a few drunken sailors and that no dangerous wounds had been inflicted.[52] Unsurprisingly, Commander Potter did not refer to either of these drunken episodes in his report to his naval superiors in Washington.

The *Constellation* embarked from Queenstown without fanfare on the afternoon of 11 May and did so with the addition to its crew of about forty men who were working their passage across the Atlantic. Some, according to the *Cork Examiner*, were naturalised American citizens, and all were keen 'to try their fortunes' and avail of the opportunities open to them in the United States. The newspaper added: 'Having faithfully discharged the noble mission on which she was sent by the generous American government and its people, she will be allowed to depart as quietly as she unostentatiously and unexpectedly entered our harbour three weeks ago.'[53] After returning home, Commander Potter conveyed to the secretary of the navy the 'heartfelt gratitude of the Irish people to the United States government' for the assistance afforded. He reported that the attention and courtesies showered on them in Ireland as representatives of their government 'were bewildering in their multiplicity and almost overpowering in their demonstration'.[54]

These public displays of gratitude were, however, less perplexing and overwhelming than those extended to Captain Forbes and the officers of the *Jamestown* during the Great Famine a generation earlier. The reception accorded both vessels was broadly similar: the presence of politicians, clergy and other dignitaries on welcoming committees; addresses of salutation and gratitude; serenading by local bands and endless speechifying; balls and banquets, lunches and dinners, and other entertainments. Although the format was much the same in each case, the tasteless and inappropriate exuberance and excess that were characteristic of the 1847 reception did not feature to the same extent in 1880, which might be explained by the relative scale of the two crises and the changes that had taken place in the Irish political, social and demographic environment in the quarter century after the Great Famine.

## The mechanics of aid distribution

There was a substantial degree of co-operation between the Mansion House, the Marlborough and the New York Herald famine relief committees in distributing the proceeds of their fund-raising endeavours, underlining the urgency of getting food and clothing to the hungry and needy, and the challenges presented by the large numbers affected, the remote scattered locations of their homes, and infrastructural deficiencies throughout the west of Ireland. Sea transport was the obvious and most effective means of distribution. At the beginning of February 1880, the Admiralty assigned a squadron of Royal Navy vessels from its Haulbowline base to distribute food and clothing along the Atlantic coast and offshore islands. HMS Goshawk, the fastest and most powerful gunboat in the fleet, was the first vessel detailed for this work and was allocated to the Mansion House committee, together with the gunboats Orwell, Bruiser and Imogene, while Valorous and Hawk served the Marlborough committee, an arrangement that continued until Prince Alfred, the duke of Edinburgh, took command of the relief squadron. Thereafter, he allotted a ship or ships as requested by the committees.[55]

These naval vessels were also employed to ferry LGB inspectors on investigative missions to the west coast islands. In February 1880 the Goshawk was placed at the disposal of twenty-three-year-old Henry A. Robinson, recently appointed to the inspectorate, and for two weeks he visited successively the Galway and Mayo islands of Dinish, Furnace, Gorumna, Lettermullan, Lettermore, Crappagh, Inisbarra, Feenish, Miveenish, Mason, Iniskea, Blue, Turbot, Turk, Omey, Freagh, Roe, Inisboffin, Inishark, Inisturk, Clare and Achill, and in each he examined the condition of the inhabitants and the state of their homes. Some of these offshore outposts were better circumstanced than others. The residents of the thickly populated islands in Kilkieran Bay, County Galway, appeared 'remarkably healthy' to Robinson, though he found it difficult to equate their health with their primitive homes, which he characterised as nothing more than 'piles of mud and stones'. Robinson singled out Blue Island in Roundstone Bay for the filthy state of the people's cabins, describing their condition as 'quite beyond conception'. Further north, he examined about thirty of the fifty residences that were clustered together on the south-eastern side of Inishark, and what he saw convinced him that the island's poverty was 'absolute and unfeigned'. Robinson recorded:

> The houses were bare and empty, and the clothing was scant and ragged; many of the children, indeed, had nothing on whatever except an old red pocket handkerchief or a patch of flannel pulled over their shoulders, and no better criterion of the genuineness of their want could there be than the pale and emaciated appearance of some of the women.

He noted that some householders possessed pigs, which were almost as thin as their owners. The islanders were mainly dependent on fishing, but heavy gales had prevented them from putting to sea, and the Indian meal that one of the relief committees had distributed to every family on the island was the only addition to their diet of boiled seaweed. The people on Inisboffin were better off than those on Inishark, but poorer than on any other island Robinson had visited. Inisturk, Clare Island and Achill were comparatively prosperous. There was an abundance of stock on Clare Island, supplying eggs and milk to the inhabitants, but potatoes were unavailable. In contrast, Achill, which was densely populated, appeared to have a plentiful supply of potatoes, and its people were well fed and properly clad. They possessed pigs and fowl and many had cattle, but none could avail of credit, which, according to Robinson, was 'gone'.[56] Robinson's reports, and those of his fellow inspectors, while primarily intended for the LGB and for the application and administration of the Poor Law, are likely to have influenced decision-making among the various relief agencies, not least the most effective way of distributing the food and clothing which the *Constellation* brought from the United States.

Fig. 5.2: C.W. Cole, 'On US Frigate *Constellation*, Queenstown' [1880], C.W. Cole Sketchbook, National Library of Ireland, PD 2196 TX9. IMAGE COURTESY OF THE NLI

Cole's sketch shows the duke of Edinburgh, attended by Captain Potter, commander of the American naval vessel *Constellation*, being received on board by members of the *New York Herald* relief committee: Colonel King-Harman, Dr Hepworth, and others whose names are written at the foot of the drawing. The Stars and Stripes flies from the fore of the ship.

On 23 April 1880, three days after the *Constellation* berthed at Haulbowline, the duke of Edinburgh, on board the yacht *Lively*, arrived in Cork Harbour to take possession of its cargo.[57] He and the representatives of the *New York Herald* relief committee decided on the following distribution plan:

- *Amelia*: north-west Mayo
- *Bruiser*: west Galway
- *Goshawk*: Sligo

- *Hawk*: the islands off the Donegal coast
- *Imogene*: Donegal, having previously delivered fifty-five barrels of seed potatoes, fifty-five barrels of corn meal, thirty barrels of flour and ten of oatmeal to Baltimore for distribution in west Cork
- *Lively*, the squadron's flagship: Galway and the west coast of Ireland generally
- *Orwell*: islands off the Galway coast
- *Valorous*: Cork's southern and western coast.

Any remaining cargo was distributed by rail.[58]

On arrival at their coastal or island destinations the vessels discharged their relief cargoes onto currachs and other small craft for landing and distribution on shore. Henry A. Robinson, who supervised the first such operation off the west coast, captured both the excitement and the exigency of the occasion: 'Before the vessel was ten minutes anchored, the sea was black with boats running into one another, coming stern on alongside, getting their ropes entangled with the screw and with each other; every island sending its contingent to add to the excitement and confusion.'[59]

An officer on board *Lively* recorded his impressions of relief supplies being unloaded from *Valorous* in Kilkieran Bay:

> The effect of the crowded boats and canoes on the calm water, the heavily sparred trim man-of-war *Valorous*, and the rakish 'can't-we-go' looking yacht *Lively* bearing the flag of the Admiral the Duke of Edinburgh, with islands and mountains all round the horizon, combined with the very apparent good work done, with bags of meal being boated away in all directions, gave food for the eye and heart to all right-minded people.[60]

Once landed, the cargoes of food and clothing were assigned to the local relief committees for distribution among those in need. James Berry, assistant secretary to the Carna relief committee in County Galway, obtained 300 barrels of meal, 250 barrels of flour and 300 barrels of potatoes from the *Constellation*'s cargo, which he brought to his home place, Mynish, where, as he described it, he and 'the priest divided them on the people', an arbitrary process, but one presumably that was formulated on local knowledge of those most in need, though, given the experience of the Great Famine, the possibility of misappropriation, here and elsewhere, cannot be discounted. On 1 June 1880 Berry informed his sister Mary in the United States that 'Ireland was scarcely ever in a worse state of poverty' than in the spring of that year, and the summer to date had proved even worse. He reported that the potato crop looked promising, but the people's indebtedness was such that subsequent failure would strip the country of its population within twelve months.[61]

Berry's assessment of the Carna district was substantiated by the parish priest, Patrick Grealy, who informed a correspondent in mid-May 1880 that the locality was not fit for human habitation. He claimed that not more than one-third of the population could live in any sort of comfort on the land. Grealy stated that the poor of the district were, and always had been, half naked and half starved, their current food 'a mess of Indian meal, eatable seaweed, nettles and dockens boiled together', and even this unsavoury mess was not available in sufficient quantities. He described ten destitute but industrious and virtuous families in the parish, comprising eighty-seven individuals, as suitable for an emigration scheme currently being promoted in Connemara. These families, he wrote, had nothing, they were 'as poor as Job on the dunghill'.[62]

The duke of Edinburgh, whom Berry described as a 'humble wise fellow', of dark complexion and balding,[63] was obliged to surrender command of the relief squadron to a senior naval officer, Captain George Digby Morant, and return home following the death of his mother-in-law, the empress of Russia. The duke of Edinburgh, like the duchess of Marlborough before him, was subsequently honoured by Queen Victoria, his mother, for his role in the Irish famine relief effort. He was vested with the Order of St Patrick in recognition of his services in distributing food among the west of Ireland peasantry, an acknowledgement that provoked a scathing response from the infuriated American journalist James Redpath, among others.[64]

Morant informed the Admiralty that between 3 February and 1 August 1880, when their mission terminated, the relief squadron delivered 856.5 tons of Indian meal, 453 tons of seed potatoes, 30 tons of oats and barley, 110 bales of clothing and a considerable quantity of loose clothing to the western islands and parts of the Atlantic coast that were difficult to access, extending from Tory Island off County Donegal to Baltimore in west Cork, and he estimated that they had served a needy and vulnerable population numbering almost 37,000. The Mansion House and Marlborough committees were the main suppliers of relief cargoes, though the squadron also attended the *New York Herald* committee, and distributed seed potatoes and corn supplied by the boards of guardians of some western Poor Law unions. Morant witnessed 'extreme destitution' in the early months of the year in Connemara and on the islands along its coastline and was convinced that there would have been deaths from starvation in these areas without the intervention of the voluntary relief agencies. Morant offered a sympathetic, quasi-nationalist analysis of the situation in the west:

> Distress did not appear to have come suddenly from the failure of last year's harvest, but apparently had been getting worse and worse as the people each year had been getting poorer and poorer, until the crisis arrived last winter, when all credit having been stopped by the shopkeepers, and the potatoes that had been saved from last harvest having been eaten, the poorest were on the verge of starvation; it was then the relief committees came to these poor people's rescue in time to avert starvation.

Morant claimed that the food and money provided by the agencies had bridged the food gap, and by the beginning of August 1880, with the new potato crop ready for harvesting and consumption, the distress that had prevailed since the previous winter had begun to ease. He referred specifically to one relief work which the Marlborough committee had initiated in the Kilkieran district of Connemara, one that offered both immediate and longer-term benefits and was thus of lasting utility to the residents of the locality. Since the middle of June some 2,200 men and women had laboured on building roads and small piers for five days of the week, for which each worker received one stone of meal for each day's endeavour, food payments that enabled them to leave their potatoes in the ground until maturation. The relief works themselves were of a useful and permanent character, according to Morant, though some were left unfinished as the various public relief projects were scheduled to terminate on 1 August.[65]

There were discrepancies in the cargo manifests compiled separately by Morant and the relief squadron's paymaster, George S. Goddard. According to the latter's return, the fleet carried 547.5 tons of potatoes, 790.5 tons of meal, 53.5 tons of oatmeal, 99 tons of flour, 5 tons of rice and 30 tons of seed corn, plus 6 casks of pork, 1,008 jars of Liebig's meat extract and 110 cases of soup. Goddard itemised Morant's 110 bales of clothing and the considerable quantity of loose clothing, and in the process offered both colour and perspective on the extent of the clothing shortages and the implications for school-going children and workers particularly: 1,588 blankets, 3,683 petticoats, 613 frocks, 391 boys' suits, 34 boys' jackets, 28 boys' trousers, 30 women's jackets, 60 girls' boots, 453 flannel shirts, 751 'loose dresses and lengths of 10 yards material', 200 men's suits, 906 chemises, 188 packets of trimmings, 306 guernseys, 606 flannel jackets, 460 quilts, 16 'bags of old worn clothing', 20 assorted bundles and 204 hats. In a series of additional remarks, Goddard noted that 334.5 yards of material 'to make up' were carried on HMS *Lively*, 32 sets of implements for road and pier making on *Valorous*, 291 construction implements on *Hawk*, and clothing for 40 children and 20 women on *Imogene*.[66]

The duke of Edinburgh continued to add his royal weight to ongoing relief appeals in England following his departure from the relief squadron and from Ireland for his mother-in-law's obsequies. He informed members attending the Royal Geographical Society's annual dinner in London on 31 May 1880 that the distress in Ireland, while not on the scale of 'the historical Irish famine', was 'excessively severe' and that its dimensions and impact had not been exaggerated. He acknowledged and praised the duchess of Marlborough's relief efforts and the American humanitarian response, and he appealed publicly for continuing subscriptions to the various relief funds. The duke advocated more permanent works, together with support for existing fisheries and the creation of new ones along the west coast as a means of preventing the recurrence of famine and distress. He observed that the land in many places was incapable of sustaining the population and claimed that 'the same thing' would recur unless the commercial possibilities of fishing were recognised and promoted.[67] The duke's statement, with its suggestion of government neglect and lack of investment in Ireland's resources, economy and infrastructure, afforded opportunities for nationalist propaganda and political manipulation.

Nationalist analyses of the 1879–80 famine tended to focus, explicitly or implicitly, on the tardiness and inadequacy of the government's response, which enabled the claim that Ireland's colonial status, and its lack of political independence and executive power, had placed the country in a vulnerable and servile position, one that created a dependency on aid agencies and external philanthropy and denied Ireland the opportunity to redress its troubled society and economy. The Mansion House relief committee captured this sentiment in a bold, concluding reflection on the necessity for the committee's inception and humanitarian endeavours:

We deem it a duty to record it as our opinion that the tax upon the humanity of distant communities, the uncertainty of the results, the shame of craving alms throughout the world and the danger of demoralisation in distributing them, were all too great to have been left for so long a time to be the only resource of an immense area of a country, possessed of unappropriated national funds of its own, and bound closely to the richest nation in the world.[68]

The 1879–80 famine brought misery, distress and death from starvation and malnutrition-related diseases to Ireland. The scale of mortality is difficult to determine, but, for several reasons, was infinitesimal compared with that of the Great Famine: the later famine was less intense and of shorter duration; the population was considerably smaller and less vulnerable; the rural economy had evolved and modernised in the third quarter of the nineteenth century; diet had diversified, with less reliance on the potato and a greater acceptance and usage of Indian meal as an alternative food; the relief operation was more sophisticated and communication networks were better. The government expended more than £2 million in supporting the relief effort, much of it in grants and loans in relation to public works.[69] This was almost double the amount generated and disbursed by the voluntary relief agencies and organisations, but the government received little credit for its investment. Its maladroit and tardy response to the crisis cost it the propaganda war, gave impetus and substance to the newly established Land League, fuelled the subsequent Land War, fanned the home rule flames, and placed Parnell in the van of the quest for political independence.[70]

Philanthropy, the theme of this volume's second section, was and remains essentially, though not exclusively, the prerogative of the privileged classes, those with the resources and time to assist the distressed and disadvantaged. In the late 1870s it was the victims of famine and life-threatening diseases in Ireland who required such interventions. The volume's third and final section shifts the focus to a different kind of responsive social engagement, from the beneficence of the wealthier sectors of society to lower-class agrarian protest and mobilisation, specifically the activities of clandestine societies in late nineteenth-century rural Ireland.

# PART 3
# MOONLIGHTING

*Law, peace, and justice, at our feet shall fall,*
*And the white-shirted\* race be lords o'er all!*

[Thomas Moore], *Memoirs of Captain Rock, the Celebrated*
*Irish Chieftain, with Some Account of His Ancestors, Written*
*by Himself* (London: Longman, Hurst, Rees, Orme,
Browne & Green, 1824), p. 129

\* The costume adopted by the Whiteboys, Shanavests, and other Rock associations.

CHAPTER 6

# Secret Societies and the Land War in Late Nineteenth-century Ireland: The Royal Irish Republic as archetype?

Then hurrah for Captain Moonlight, he still maintains our right.
Success attend his rifle crack where'er he roams tonight.

'I Am a National Moonlight Boy', C.P. Crane, *Memories of a Resident Magistrate, 1880–1920* (Edinburgh: T&A Constable, 1938), p. 81

Before the Land League was established at Millstreet it was a quiet and peaceable neighbourhood. It was only an out-station of the Macroom police district and consisted of a sergeant and five constables. After the League began to boycott and moonlight, it had to be made the headquarters of a resident magistrate, a district inspector of the R(oyal) I(rish) Constabulary, with a force of about seventy police, who had to be strengthened at one period by a company of infantry.

National Archives of Ireland, INL Carton 10, Outrage Reports, Cork, 1880–1888

## Introduction

Rural social protest was the customary response historically in Ireland to failed harvests and food shortages, to inequities in the countryside, or the perceived iniquities of the empowered and entitled, particularly unscrupulous landlords and their retinues of lawyers, agents and bailiffs. Traditionally, protest from below was unsophisticated and violent, cloaked in oaths of secrecy and makeshift disguises and uniforms, and the young men involved were usually single, with little or no education and limited employment prospects, and disproportionally drawn from the ranks of small farmers and agricultural labourers.

Late nineteenth-century peasant protest drew its inspiration and direction from agrarian secret societies of earlier generations, notably the oath-bound distinctively clad Whiteboys of the 1760s and '70s, whose opposition to excessive rents and tithes, evictions and other grievances featured many of the enforcement tactics their lineal descendants were to embrace so enthusiastically more than a century later: nocturnal house searches for weapons and money; intimidation; punishment beatings; houghing or maiming cattle; and numerous other violations of public order.[1]

A succession of emblematically named secret societies followed the first Whiteboy outbreak: Hearts of Steel or Steelboys in the north of the country, Rightboys in the 1780s, Rockites in the early 1820s, Ribbonmen, and Terry Alts, among many other collectives – all drawing from the same deep well of agrarian grievances and discontent and reflecting the broader social and political concerns and sympathies of the communities that spawned them. According to historian James S. Donnelly, Jr, the initial Whiteboy movement of 1761–5 gave rise to a complex tradition of peasant protest throughout much of Munster and Leinster. 'Many of its features (uniforms, quasi-military organisation, oaths of secrecy and loyalty, codes of approved behaviour, rituals of intimidation and punishment) reappeared in a regular succession of major eruptions of rural unrest during the late eighteenth and early nineteenth centuries',[2] and, Donnelly might have added, much later into the nineteenth century.

The government responded to these expressions of rural social protest by enacting draconian legislation. The 1776 Whiteboy Act, 15 & 16 Geo. 3, c. 21, made certain offences against persons, property or the public peace capital crimes, and greatly increased the coercive power of magistrates in searching for weapons and in dealing with suspected Whiteboy activity.[3] The 1831 Whiteboy Amendment Act, 1 & 2 Will. 4, c. 44, mitigated the severity of the 1776 Act; offences such as breaking into houses, malicious injury to property, sending threatening letters, and procuring firearms by threats were punished by transportation, penal servitude or imprisonment rather than the death penalty.[4] (Penal servitude differed from imprisonment in requiring hard labour of those so sentenced; imprisonment literally meant confinement.)

By the 1880s Whiteboyism had become a term of convenience, one the police and prosecution services employed generically to describe serious agrarian crime, which they classified as follows:

- Offences against the person: homicide (murder, manslaughter); firing at the person; administering poison; aggravated assault; assault endangering life; assault on bailiffs and process servers; cutting or maiming the person;

- Offences against property: incendiary fire and arson; burglary and robbery; taking and holding forcible possession; killing, cutting or maiming cattle; demanding money; demanding or robbing firearms;

- Offences affecting the public peace: riots and affrays; administering unlawful oaths; intimidation (by threatening letters or notices; otherwise); rescuing prisoners; resistance to legal process; attacking houses; injury to property; discharging weapons into dwellings.

The Irish authorities categorised these types of public order offences as outrages, and perpetrators on conviction were given disproportionately harsh sentences compared to those handed down to persons convicted of non-agrarian or ordinary crime.[5]

In the later nineteenth century, the period of the Land War, the term Whiteboyism had general currency among the police, the judiciary and the Irish administration, but Moonlighting was the expression in common usage in the Munster countryside. Both appellations appear to have applied particularly to the nocturnal activities of armed and masked groups of men who broke into the homes of individuals who had, or who were suspected of having, transgressed the communal code of conduct – the unwritten, though universally understood law of the countryside, which derived its authority and compliance from the popular belief in the moral economy of the poor[6] – and in the process threatened, humiliated or assaulted the occupants, often with great brutality, and seized arms, ammunition, and money to purchase weapons. The evidence suggests that the authorities were particularly concerned about the discharge of firearms during these midnight incursions.

Whiteboy offences and agrarian unrest generally escalated as the Land War intensified between 1879 and 1882. One indication was the increase in the number of recorded agrarian outrages, from 2,590 in 1880 to 4,439 in the following year, and of outrages generally (including agrarian) from 5,609 to 7,788.[7] In an address to the grand jury at the opening of the Munster winter assizes at Cork on 6 December 1881, the presiding judge, John David Fitzgerald, excluded ordinary crime from his review and focused solely and at length on agrarian crime in the assizes' jurisdiction. The courts of assizes – or simply assizes – dealt with serious criminal offences, sat at intervals, and were presided over by one or two senior judges. Counties Clare, Kerry, Limerick and Cork, which was divided into East Riding and West Riding, and the cities of Cork and Limerick constituted the Munster circuit.[8] Justice Fitzgerald, drawing on statistics compiled by the constabulary, informed the grand jury that in the four months since the previous assizes in August, 240 indictable agrarian offences had occurred in Cork West Riding, 233 in Cork East Riding, 223 in Kerry, 191 in County Limerick and 174 in Clare, a total of 1,061, including 4 homicides (2 murders in Clare, 1 in Cork East Riding, and 1 case of manslaughter, also in the East Riding), which was a considerable increase on the total of 607 for the same four-month period in the previous year. Fitzgerald concluded from these statistics that life in Munster was insecure or had been rendered so miserable as to be worthless. He stated that 'a spirit of lawlessness and disorder' prevailed, 'an insolent defiance of law' which threatened to undermine the very fabric of society, and, he added, 'an overwhelming military force' was required to execute 'the process of the law'.[9] The agrarian crime figures cited by Fitzgerald and his comments on them substantiate historian Terence Dooley's claim that during the first phase of the Land War, 1879–82, rural Ireland was violent and dangerous, and, as William J. Smyth noted, at the peak of the agitation in 1881 Munster was the most violent of the country's four provinces.[10]

A particularly active secret society located at Millstreet and its hinterland in north-west Cork, an area with a long tradition of peasant protest, was responsible for many of the 240 indictable agrarian offences returned for Cork West Riding. This society – the incongruously named Royal Irish Republic, which combined redresser elements, agrarian violence in the traditional pattern, overlapping Land League membership, and Fenian allegiance and ideology – and its second-in-command turned approver, Daniel Connell, constitute this chapter's subject matter.

## Moonlighting: north-west Cork

On the night of 7 August 1881, a party of about twenty armed and disguised men broke into the home of thirty-five-year-old Thomas Cudmore, a comfortable farmer who resided near Millstreet. In response to the intruders' demand for weapons, Cudmore handed over a double-barrelled gun, a powder horn and an ammunition pouch, and one of the raiders stole his gold watch which was on the bedroom table. According to Sub-Inspector Thomas Fitzwilliam Starkie of the Royal Irish Constabulary (hereinafter RIC) at Millstreet, Cudmore's home was the eleventh in the district raided for firearms during the previous four days, and thirty similar house attacks were to occur over the next three weeks,[11] a level of activity indicative of a sophisticated local intelligence network, surveillance and organisation.

On 7 December 1881, four months after the violation of Cudmore's home, the same gang, similarly armed and disguised, invaded the dwelling house of the widowed Catherine Fitzgerald at Mushera, a mountainy district 5 miles south-east of Millstreet, and in the process assaulted and beat her severely, cut off the moustache of her servant, Andrew McCarthy, with a sheep-shears, and threatened to clip her three young daughters' hair. According to the police report on the incident, some of the intruders wore hats with plumes and feathers and 'sported foxes' tails for whiskers', while others attempted to conceal their identities beneath handkerchiefs and wideawake – wide-brimmed – hats.[12] Mrs Fitzgerald was ostracised for having paid her rent secretly to her landlord and for

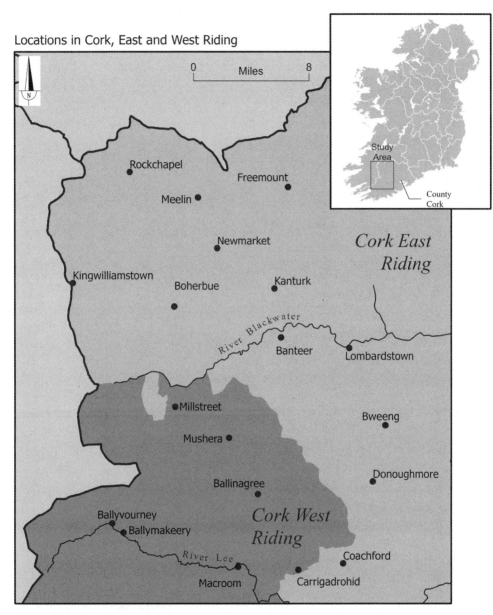

Locations in Cork, East and West Riding

Map 6.1: North-west Cork.
IMAGE COURTESY OF MIKE MURPHY, DEPARTMENT OF GEOGRAPHY, UCC

dealing with Jeremiah Hegarty, a boycotted shopkeeper and general merchant in Millstreet.

Hegarty was a divisive figure in the district. He was a magistrate and a member of the Millstreet board of Poor Law guardians, a landowner, extensive grazier, land agent, sub-agent, land grabber and money lender, whose speculations enabled him to prosper while his neighbours suffered from economic recession and depressed agricultural prices.[13] Hegarty's general opportunism rendered him obnoxious, and he became the target of sustained communal criticism and disaffection which lasted for much of the 1880s.

On 21 December 1880, almost a year before the assault on the Fitzgerald household, a resolution was passed at a meeting of the Millstreet Land League to boycott Hegarty and his family, and on the following day placards were posted throughout the town to that effect: 'Take notice, you are cautioned against having any dealing with J. Hegarty of Millstreet, or his family. Neither buy nor sell them anything. Shun them as you would lepers. If you disobey these orders, may the Lord have mercy on you.'[14] Another notice, which was far more inventive and incendiary and with unusual features, including a disparaging and offensive reference to a wicked black person and a more esoteric one to Ireland's patron saint, called on the people to banish 'the polluting tread of landlords' from 'the sacred soil of Erin' and to exterminate land grabbers, 'those barbarous hounds of discontent'.[15] Land grabbers took possession of farms from which less fortunate individuals had been evicted, usually for non-payment of rent, and Michael Davitt, the Land League's founder and leader, cast them as a key prop of landlordism, 'the buttress of the rack-renting evil and the worst foe of the struggling tenant'.[16] Hegarty was one such land grabber, mean, hateful and merciless, a 'nefarious Sambo', according to the boycott notice. 'Boycott him,' the writer instructed. 'Let no man dare from this day forth have any dealing with him; let no man work for him; let him be shunned as if accursed by the avenging spirit of St Patrick ... Mark this man with the indelible stigma of bigot.'[17]

Captain Moonlight, successor to Captain Rock and Rory of the Hill and eponymous commander, essence and representation of Moonlighting, or agrarian secret society illegal activity, appended his name to the following threatening notice, whose formality of language, structure and style parodied official pronouncements and exposed the government to ridicule by subverting its authority. The notice was not directed at Hegarty specifically, but at the perpetrators of a range of objectionable activities, such as occupying evicted holdings, non-compliance with the enforcement of boycotting, or fraternising with the constabulary. Transgressors who persisted with their defiance were threatened with death:

> A proclamation. Moonlight. Whereas it now becometh known to me that in the town of Millstreet, and in the parish of Drishane and Cullen, that there are ungrateful renegade Irishmen to be found capable of occupying the farms of the evicted. That in the town of Millstreet are to be found Irishmen base enough to converse with the bigoted and the boycotted. That also in that town are to be found ten Irish women mean and despicable enough to converse in public and in private with the blood-thirsty spirits of the Royal Irish Constabulary. Now we, Captain J.L. Moonlight, governor general and general governor of this district for the time being with the advice, consent, and approval of my privy council do hereby make, order, and sayeth that such disgraceful and abominable workings shall now cease. This is to be the first and last warning to be given to those concerned. I shall not hesitate now to use cold steel in the upholding of my government, so let all beware.[18]

Boycotting, a word recently coined from the ostracism of Captain Charles Cunningham Boycott, Lord Erne's English land agent in the Lough Mask area of County Mayo, was a technique of nonviolent intimidation that remained within the law if skilfully implemented. It depended for its effectiveness on the complete disruption of the business and social life of its victims and proved to be a powerful weapon. The process was employed against land grabbers, landowners, and agents, indeed anyone who supported the institution of landlordism in any way. Others, such as gombeen men – individuals who took usurious advantage of their neighbours' financial difficulties and vulnerabilities – were also targeted, and Hegarty was both land grabber and money lender. 'Grabbers' were castigated in vicious ballads and public notices, and shunned, in Charles Stewart Parnell's phrase, as if they were lepers of old.[19]

Two local Millstreet men were convicted at the Cork assizes in March 1881 of boycotting Hegarty, and each was sentenced to twelve months' imprisonment, the judge referring to 'the malignity' with which they had persecuted their victim. Hegarty testified in court against the defendants, and the verdict was marked by rioting in Millstreet. His house was besieged, its windows broken, and shots were discharged into the homes of some of his supporters. Hegarty's most significant ally was the parish priest, Canon Arthur Griffin, an outspoken critic of boycotting and of the Land League and agrarian activism generally.[20] The clergyman's cloth afforded him little protection; one of his cows was attacked and maimed, as punishment and as a public warning, following his defence of the boycotted shop owner. Police reinforcements were drafted into Millstreet in the wake of these public order offences, and eight armed constables were assigned to guard Hegarty's home.[21]

At mass on the last Sunday of August 1881, as the boycott continued, Canon Griffin condemned the prolonged assault on Hegarty's character and business interests, whereupon 'a perfect chorus of coughing' erupted in the church. Undaunted, the parish priest denounced boycotting and outrages in the district and the connivance of the local community in their perpetration and continuation. Griffin claimed that the people appeared 'to have banded themselves together in a sort of secret society', an illegal act that contravened the laws of God and man. At the conclusion of his harangue from the pulpit, and long before the termination of the service, most of the congregation left the church,[22] demonstrating that Moonlighting at the time exerted a more compelling authority than either the clergy or the constabulary, at least in unruly north-west Cork.

Griffin may have been prompted by a Moonlighting incident that had occurred on Sir George Colthurst's property at Rathcoole, some five miles from Millstreet, on the previous evening, 27 August. Colthurst's tenants were celebrating his marriage, drinking porter and making merry, when, approaching midnight, 'a party of black men' appeared and shot and wounded five of the revellers. The interlopers wore large loose-fitting overcoats and tall broad-brimmed slouch hats, and were variously armed with rifles, revolvers and bludgeons. They had blackened their faces, hence the reference to black men, shaded their foreheads and eyes with thick veils and had wrapped large mufflers around their necks and the lower part of their faces to conceal their identities.[23] Sometime later the police arrested the son of one of Colthurst's tenants for participating in the raid, and in a search of his home found documents denouncing landlords and rack-renters.[24]

The colourful, rather sensational newspaper account of the scale, intensity and consequences of the attack was subsequently modified,[25] but there was no doubting the gang's intent – the assertion of Captain Moonlight's presence and authority in the district. The bulk of Colthurst's Rathcoole tenants had paid their rents some days previously, with a 15 per cent reduction. The Moonlighters may have been expressing dissatisfaction at the scale of the rent abatement, or disapproval of the rent settlement, or of the marriage celebration itself, with its implicit and traditional display of deference, which marked the economic and social disparity between landlords and tenants, the owners and occupiers of land. The Moonlighters' intervention reflected a changing political and social landscape in the early 1880s, a new ordering of rural affairs and hierarchies. Even the Catholic Church was not immune, as a notice posted in Millstreet on Christmas Day 1881 indicates: 'Who is feasting the tyrants of the country? Father Griffin. Who is getting the best men in the parish into prison? Father Griffin. If you give him one penny at Christmas you will get buckshot.'[26]

## Daniel Connell: approver

On 27 December 1881, three weeks after Catherine Fitzgerald was assaulted in her home at Mushera, the constabulary at Macroom, acting on information received – apparently from one of the men involved in the raid on the Fitzgerald household – arrested Daniel Connell on charges of administering illegal oaths and possessing weapons in a proclaimed district. The police found incriminating documents, Thomas Cudmore's watch, and discharged revolver cartridges in Connell's possession, and they discovered four loaded revolvers in an outhouse on the farm where he was apprehended. Five others were also arrested – the farmer, his two sons, and James and Jeremiah Twohig, brothers who were 'strongly suspected' of being involved in the attack on the Fitzgerald household and in similar house-raiding incidents.[27]

The documents found on Connell were regimental orders issued and signed by Captain Moonlight, the nominal leader of all such nocturnal groupings, and the documents recorded the sentences passed and punishments prescribed for several individuals who had violated the Moonlighters' prescribed code of communal conduct, which was universally known and feared.[28] In a classic example of clandestine sanctions and the brutality of their enforcement, three named individuals were to be shot in the legs, two for paying rent, the other, James Sullivan, for purchasing goods at Jeremiah Hegarty's boycotted shop in Millstreet, and Sullivan's wife and daughter were to endure the public humiliation of having their hair shorn for the same offence; two males were to be similarly cropped, one for terminating a labourer's employment, the other for what was described as story-telling to the local priest, and a female was sentenced to the same hair-clipping punishment for talking to a policeman in Macroom and for cursing the Moonlighters.[29]

The townspeople jeered and taunted the constabulary as they escorted Connell to Macroom railway station for transfer to the county jail at Cork.[30] This public expression of feeling and support was an uneasy compound of endorsement and apprehension, a moral sanctioning of Moonlighting and its objectives, buttressed by a subliminal but well-grounded fear of midnight retribution. As Maura Cronin notes:

> Agrarian movements were held together as much by intimidation as by genuine communal solidarity or belief in a moral economy. Captain Right (or Fear Not, or Rock) [or Moonlight!] was obeyed not only because he stood for the interests of 'the people' but also because he could visit dire punishments on those same people if they offended against the code for which 'he' stood.[31]

Shortly after his imprisonment, Connell, who was described by one Cork newspaper as a man not 'of the very best antecedents',[32] betrayed both the community and his accomplices by becoming a police approver, unlocking the secrets of the Millstreet illegal combination and implicating a large number of his house-raiding associates.[33] An approver was an accomplice to a crime, who, on detection, turned 'queen's evidence', that is he or she agreed to testify against the other accused, usually – and in Connell's case specifically – to secure immunity from prosecution. Approvers differed from informers in that the latter were invariably motivated by the prospect of financial reward.[34] Connell's action adds substance to Cronin's contention that oath-bound agrarian secret societies were secret 'only insofar as the precise identity of their members was hidden from the authorities – and that only until the inevitable informer or approver spilt the beans'.[35]

On 9 January 1882 the RIC, acting on Connell's information, arrested fourteen men and lodged them in Millstreet jail: seven were from the town – two bakers, two grocers, two labourers and a weaver; the others included a farmer, two farmers' sons and an assistant national schoolmaster, and this was the socio-economic stratum – small farmers, farmers' sons and labourers – from which additional arrests were subsequently made.[36] A parliamentary return, listing the names and occupations, by province and county, of those arrested for involvement in nocturnal attacks in the two-year period June 1880 to June 1882, confirms this socio-economic profile, although, if the Millstreet evidence is indicative, the return is a gross underestimate of the numbers involved in such attacks. Not surprisingly, most of the arrests were linked to Munster and Connacht counties, including thirty in Cork East Riding, twenty-six in Cork West Riding, and twenty-four in Kerry. The West Riding cohort consisted of fifteen farmers' sons, four labourers, a farmer, a shopkeeper, a shopkeeper's son, a weaver, a shoemaker, a cooper and a schoolmaster. Ten labourers constituted the largest component of those arrested in the East Riding; the remainder consisted of eight farmers, four shoemakers, a dairyman, a schoolmaster, a blacksmith, a van driver, a clerk, a stone dresser, a publican and, uniquely in the return, a farmer's daughter. Thirteen farmers were arrested in Kerry, along with five labourers, four farmers' sons, a carman and a servant. The eighty arrests in counties Cork and Kerry resulted in twelve convictions, with two cases pending. The collapse of the remaining cases may have been due to insufficient evidence, or to juries' failure to convict, either through fear or empathy with the defendants' cause. In County Mayo, where thirty-two individuals were arrested, the occupational profile displayed less diversity: thirteen farmers' sons, ten labourers, eight farmers and a blacksmith. The conviction rate, 6 per cent, or two of the thirty-two arrested, was even less than that for Cork and Kerry.[37] These returns indicate the authorities' difficulties in securing convictions and suppressing agrarian crime and outrages during the convulsive Land War years.

The fourteen Millstreet prisoners were variously charged with raiding houses at night, terrorising the occupants, and stealing weapons, which appears to have been the primary purpose of these incursions.[38] In the following months some fifty additional individuals – mainly labourers, farmers' sons and tradesmen from the town and parish of Millstreet, some from the parish of Ballinagree and a few from Boherbue – were arrested and charged with Whiteboy offences on Connell's testimony and on the evidence of Hannah Reardon, a twenty-year-old poorly educated itinerant dressmaker who was dubbed 'the female informer'. Reardon, who was from Brosna in north-east Kerry, acknowledged that she had made 'caps and other articles of uniform' for the Moonlighters, the 'banded brothers' as she called them.[39] The prisoners were additionally indicted on the altogether more serious charge of treason-felony, in this case membership of a Fenian network, the Royal Irish Republic, which was designated 'an unlawful, treasonable and seditious conspiracy', designed to overthrow the government, depose the queen and establish an Irish republic.[40] Conviction on such a charge carried a maximum penalty of life imprisonment under the Treason-Felony Act, 1848.[41]

## The Protection of Person and Property (Ireland) Act, 1881 and its impact on Millstreet

Previously, ten individuals from the Millstreet district had been incarcerated in Limerick jail under the Protection of Person and Property (Ireland) Act, which became law on 2 March 1881, while another absconded before he was arrested.[42] The PPP Act, or the Coercion Act as it was more commonly known, which suspended habeas corpus, was the government's draconian and rather desperate response to agrarian crime, increased lawlessness, and contempt for the existing law and law enforcement in the Irish countryside. W.E. Forster, chief secretary for Ireland, argued in the House of Commons that the law of the land was largely ineffective, because individuals were afraid to prosecute those who planned and perpetrated outrages, or to give evidence in court, or to return honest verdicts in jury trials. Forster categorised those who were responsible for outrages variously as surviving members of 'the old Ribbon and other secret societies of former days'; Fenians, taking advantage of the current disturbed state of the country to pursue their own political and constitutional ambitions; and a large number of individuals whom he cast as 'the *mauvais sujets* of their neighbourhood' – village tyrants who through fear and intimidation exerted authority and control over the districts in which they resided.[43] The PPP Act, which was intended to counter the threat these forces and individuals posed to the country's security and integrity, empowered the lord lieutenant to issue a warrant for the arrest and detention without trial of anyone 'reasonably suspected' of treason, or of violence, intimidation, incitement or disrupting law and order in a proscribed district. Cork West Riding, which included Millstreet, was proclaimed immediately after the enactment, along with eight Munster and Connacht counties.[44]

Under the act's dispensation, local police named the suspects and the RIC sub-inspector or the resident magistrate of the district provided the information on which arrest warrants were prepared and issued.[45] John Creedon, a twenty-six-year-old bachelor farmer, a wealthy and substantial landholder, Land League member and Poor Law guardian, was arrested, in tandem with his brother Cornelius and another local man, John O'Sullivan, following an attack on the home of the boycotted Jeremiah Hegarty on 25 March 1881. The trio were suspected of armed assembly at night, attacking a dwelling house and assaulting one of the occupants. Hegarty and John Creedon were competitors for a vacant holding which the latter ultimately acquired, but Hegarty's involvement increased the purchase price and the two were on bad terms as a result. According to his arrest warrant, Creedon had been active for some time 'in fanning the excitement at Millstreet against Hegarty'. The Millstreet board of Poor Law guardians, of which Hegarty was a member – though not on the popular side – protested at Creedon's arrest. The board claimed that there was insufficient evidence for the prisoners' detention and demanded their immediate release.[46] The guardians' intervention in what was essentially a political and administrative matter underlined the gradual supersession of the traditional representation on boards of guardians during the 1870s and '80s, the transfer of power and influence from ex-officio guardians, drawn essentially from the landed gentry and their retinues, to tenant farmers and other popularly mandated local politicians.[47]

Andrew Connor, James Mahony and John Riordan were arrested under the PPP Act in June 1881 on suspicion of attacking the dwelling house of Patrick Geron some weeks previously, administering an illegal oath, and robbing firearms. They were part of an armed and disguised body of men, numbering between twenty and thirty, who broke into Geron's house and compelled him to swear that he would reinstate a farm labourer whom he had ejected from his cabin and employment. The raiders discharged several shots within the house and took a weapon belonging to Geron. The latter's spouse and their sons informed Sub-Inspector Starkie that Mahony, who was addressed as captain, was the group's leader, and they identified Connor as one of the raiders. Mahony, who had been imprisoned for nine months in 1867 for Fenianism, was described in his arrest warrant as a thirty-six-year-old shoemaker and militiaman, married with five children, and in 'poor circumstances'. He was committed to Limerick jail, but released on health grounds within two months, on 10 August 1881. His accomplice, Connor, who was a draper's apprentice, aged twenty, single, and in fair circumstances, remained in prison until 31 March 1882. Sub-Inspector Starkie described both as 'bad' characters.[48]

Riordan's arrest warrant has not survived, but it appears that the police were not privy to his role as captain of the Royal Irish Republic in Millstreet prior to Approver Connell's disclosures. Once the authorities became aware of the situation, they discharged Riordan from custody, along with Thomas McCarthy, a local schoolmaster, who was also one of the leaders of the Millstreet Moonlighters. The police rearrested the pair on their return to their hometown on 11 April 1882, charged them with treason-felony, and returned them for trial to the Cork summer assizes and the possibility of life imprisonment, an outcome that would have been altogether more satisfactory from the authorities' perspective than simply detaining them under the Coercion Act.[49]

The extra-judicial arrest and detention without trial of the ten individuals from Millstreet, who were variously suspected of attacking dwelling houses, boycotting, and intimidation against the payment of rent, removed the physical presence and influence of a troublesome cohort from this disturbed district. The PPP Act is likely to have had the same result in other parts of the country, as almost a thousand suspects were apprehended and imprisoned nationwide, while countless others fled, mostly to America, to avoid a similar fate. It is equally likely, as the anarchic state of the country in the winter and spring of 1881–2 tended to show, that the vacuum created by their removal was not long in responding to nature's law.

## Daniel Connell and the Royal Irish Republic

Following the imprisoned Connell's decision to become a police approver and inform on his erstwhile comrades, Sub-Inspector Starkie of Millstreet RIC was summoned to Cork on 8 January 1882 to interrogate him. Starkie provided the inspector general of the RIC with a series of briefings on Connell's personal details, the information he provided on the Millstreet Moonlighters, and the impact of these disclosures. In the sub-inspector's estimation, Connell, who was in his late teens, was an individual 'of considerable shrewdness and ability'. He had trained as a carpenter, though he seldom worked at his trade. In 1877 he enlisted in the army, but deserted fifteen months later, and subsequently joined the Queen's County militia and later the 109th Regiment, rising to the rank of lance-corporal. While serving in that regiment Connell was charged with drunkenness and during his hearing disclosed that he had deserted from the army, whereupon he was court-martialled, convicted of desertion and fraudulent enlistment, and sentenced to 112 days' imprisonment, on completion of which he was ignominiously discharged from the forces.[50]

Connell returned to Millstreet and in May 1881 was recruited into 'the secret organisation commonly known as the "Moonlights"'. On his induction he swore to be true and faithful to the Royal Irish Republic, to obey his superiors and to take up arms when required, and he was aware that death was the punishment for any violation of this oath. Connell's military training and army experience and, possibly, his insouciant disregard of authority distinguished him from the bulk of his comrades, and within a very short time he had become one of the society's leaders, its armourer and drill instructor. Sub-Inspector Starkie claimed that the oath sworn by Connell demonstrated that the Millstreet Moonlighters and their activities were simply a continuation of 'the old Fenian conspiracy'.[51] Connell substantiated Starkie's assertion in his evidence against forty-six Millstreet prisoners at their trial in late March 1882: 'I have been a member of a society the object of which is to incite the people to rebellion – to depose the queen, to overthrow the government and establish a republic. The proper name of the society is the Royal Irish Republic.'[52] Connell testified that the members frequently discussed the society's objectives and were fully committed to achieving them: 'They were talking about overthrowing the government of the realm and intimidating the landlords. The object of attacking houses was to aid and abet the Land League, and to supply ourselves with arms.'[53] There is no extant evidence to indicate when the society came into existence, but Connell's disclosures suggest that it was an active Fenian cell, substantially armed and drilled, whose members, numbering between 1,500 and 1,600 – although there is no independent corroboration of this estimate – engaged extensively in Moonlighting, particularly raiding for weapons, in mid and north-west Cork, and whose senior officers were linked to the leadership of the Millstreet Land League. If Connell's statements can be taken at face value – though caution is advised, given his approver status – the Royal Irish Republic was a practical manifestation of 'New Departure' realpolitik, a reflection of rural alignments at the height of the Land War.

Connell supplied the police with a substantial amount of information on the composition and structure of the Royal Irish Republic and similar clandestine associations. They were organised in battalions of 200 men, divided into half battalions, which in turn were subdivided into circles of 25 men each. There were thus eight circles to a battalion. A district generally contained from six to eight battalions, or about 1,500 sworn members, and each district was under the charge of a 'head' or 'captain'. Circles, bearing such names as 'Mountaineers', 'Chargers' or 'Irish Volunteers', convened each Sunday and there was a monthly meeting of all the circles in a district, at which resolutions were passed, rules made, and nocturnal punishments planned for those who disregarded the society's instructions or principles. Books recording the organisation's rules, members' names and details of the various outrages that had been committed were kept by the secretary, and these books, which bore the inscription 'The Irish Republic', were sent from Dublin. There was no connection between members in different districts, although the district captains were in contact with one another to coordinate 'united action in case of a general rising'. There was also a head over each county, and a head in Dublin over all the counties in Ireland in which the organisation had a presence.[54]

These networks emerged at the beginning of the land agitation, Starkie reported, and he was convinced that there were close local links between Moonlighters and the Land League, the former serving as the violent enforcers of the League's mandate. Starkie's assessment reflected the broader view of the RIC, the Irish administration and the Westminster government that the Land League was directly linked to agrarian outrage, and responsible for fomenting and financing violence in the Irish countryside.[55] In the Millstreet district, John Riordan was simultaneously secretary to the local Land League and captain of the clandestine Royal Irish Republic society prior to his arrest on 7 June 1881 under the PPP Act, and his brother Jeremiah succeeded him as captain or head of the society.[56] The Irish authorities believed that the Royal Irish Republic and similar organisations throughout the country aided the Land League by intimidating individuals who refused to subscribe to the League's manifesto and tactics, who interacted with boycotted persons, for example, or paid rent secretively, and the ultimate aim of these secret societies was to rise in open rebellion and establish an Irish republic when opportunity offered.

A combination of intimidation and inducement brokered allegiance and obedience to these associations. 'Moonlight detectives' provided district heads or captains with information on backsliders and other nonconformists, and the penalties for dissension were universally known and widely feared. Financial rewards were bestowed on members of secret societies who engaged in so-called acts of bravery or actions that promoted 'the cause' – a euphemism for intimidation, outrage and terrorism – and Connell, who suspected that the money originated with the Land League in Dublin, claimed to have received rewards amounting to £12, a considerable sum at the time.[57] A well-placed and trusted informant of John Mallon, the enterprising superintendent of G Division – the detective branch – of the Dublin Metropolitan Police (DMP), offered some corroboration of the Land League's financial involvement. He claimed that 'Land League money was freely spent in committing crime', and that the League had voted £10,000 'as a sop to the Fenians', who enforced the League's edicts in return, but, following a quarrel between the two organisations in mid-1881 over the disbursement of the money, the Fenians declined to act as heretofore, and the Land League was compelled to deploy 'the most reckless fellows in each locality to commit outrages'.[58]

The Parnell medal, which was made of silver and about the same size as a military medal, and which, according to Mallon, was struck in Paris, was another form of acknowledgement. Parnell's head, with an accompanying motto, which Connell thought might have been in Latin, adorned the obverse; 'The Irish Republic' was inscribed on the reverse, above a harp encircled with shamrocks and a crossed rifle and sword. The clasps attached to the medal bore the commendation 'For Bravery', or some such wording. Connell stated that these medals were supplied by 'the Fenian staff' and differed from those worn by Land League officers at meetings and processions. Connell provided the authorities with an illustration of the medal, whose inscription differed slightly from that outlined above.[59] According to Superintendent Mallon, the Land League

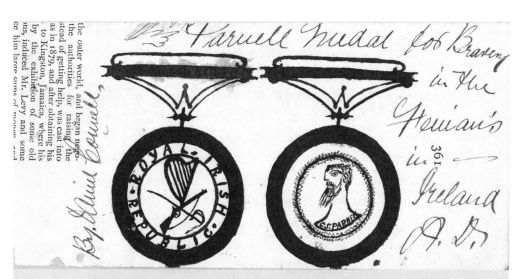

Fig. 6.1: 'Parnell Medal for Bravery' (Sketch by Daniel Connell), National Archives of Ireland, CSORP/1883/15390. IMAGE COURTESY OF THE NAI

Parnell medals were manufactured in Birmingham, in contrast to the Parisian origins of Connell's Fenian medals.[60]

Captain Charles P. Crane, who served as an RIC district inspector in Ireland's south-west during the period in which these medals featured, offered the following description of one: 'In size it was a little larger than a shilling and bore Parnell's head on one side and a shamrock-circled harp on the other, with the inscription "God Save Ireland". It was suspended by a little green ribbon, bearing a brass harp.' Crane observed that 'anyone who was of any consequence in the National League wore the medal pinned to his waistcoat'.[61] It thus appears that there were distinct Fenian and Land League Parnell medals in circulation, though they had common features – Parnell's representation and the shamrock and harp symbols; they also had a similar associative purpose – to promote and to identify publicly with the nationalist cause. The invocation 'God Save Ireland' derived from the title of T.D. Sullivan's ballad which was published in the *Nation* on 7 July 1867 as a lament for the Manchester Martyrs – Allen, Larkin and O'Brien, who were executed as part of the Fenian conspiracy – and which by the 1880s had become the de facto anthem of nationalist Ireland.[62] The differently cast and nuanced Parnell medals captured the zeitgeist of the 'New Departure', and

Parnell's political ascendancy, but the motifs in the Fenian medal – the inscription and the rifle and sword representation – served as a reminder of an older, more rudimentary force, ideology and methodology.

The Land League's modernity and sophistication, which scholars have noted, were further captured in the sale of branded matches and neck ties, merchandising that boosted consciousness and coffers alike. District Inspector Crane, on returning from a fruitless 'Moonlight' patrol in the disturbed Killarney district of County Kerry in which he was then stationed – fruitless because of the ease with which Moonlighters evaded such patrols – was struck by the incongruity of lighting a candle with matches that 'bore openly the name of an illegal organisation', and he was also conscious of the irony that they were the best and probably the only matches that could be procured locally.[63] The neck tie was made of green satin, and stamped with a gold harp and the words 'Land League'. Florence Arnold-Forster, the adopted daughter of the chief secretary for Ireland, W.E. Forster, who was shown one by a recipient, an Irish barrister in London, noted archly that if such appendages were being sent gratuitously to Irishmen in London who were unsympathetic to the Land League, the organisation must necessarily be in a strong financial position.[64] The depth of the Land League's coffers was a constant subject of debate in political circles, not least the possible allocation of the League's resources to fomenting agrarian crime and unrest in Ireland.

Sub-Inspector Starkie relayed further evidence to RIC headquarters – none of it conclusive – pointing to the links between the Land League and secret societies, at least some of which were affiliated to the broader Fenian conspiracy. He cited the retainer of 100 guineas which the Land League's solicitor paid to counsel to defend the Moonlight prisoners at the 1881 winter assizes at Cork as an indication of the connection between these organisations.[64] In subsequent House of Commons debates both the attorney general for Ireland and Prime Minister Gladstone drew upon this transaction as evidence that the Land League was centrally involved in orchestrating and funding the commission of crime and outrage in Ireland.[66] Irish nationalists rebutted these assertions, retorting that the government's coercive policy – the suppression of the Land League and imprisonment of its leaders – was responsible for the increase in agrarian crime in the winter and spring of 1881–2. Justin McCarthy, MP for Longford, argued that the government had been 'the direct cause of the revival of conspiracy and midnight outrage', not the Land League, and warned that if it persisted with its Irish policy the government would find that it had 'repressed agitation only to create conspiracy'.[67]

The tension between agitation and conspiracy was one of the defining themes of the Land War years. Sub-Inspector Starkie, adhering to the official RIC line, claimed in early 1882 that the symbiotic relationship between secret societies and the Land League was essential to the latter's success, as the League would have been powerless without the heft of its nocturnal enforcers: 'It would have been futile for the executive in Dublin to issue orders and manifestos to the people unless it had some instrument at its command for carrying out its decrees. The instrument was the Moonlight organisation and a very effective instrument it has proved itself to be.'[68]

He might have added that the secret societies appeared to possess a substantial stock of weapons, which suggests a purpose beyond the intimidation of non-compliant locals. According to Connell, the Millstreet Royal Irish Republic society had between 1,500 and 1,600 members, about 1,000 of whom were fully armed, although, again, there is no additional or objective evidence to support either assertion. In addition, Connell claimed that the cell possessed some 200 revolvers, a substantial amount of ammunition and a quantity of dynamite. John Sullivan, a butter merchant, was reputed to have brought some of the weapons to Millstreet from Cork. Seventy-five revolvers had been procured in May or June 1881, fifty from Dublin, the remainder from Cork, and Connell believed that the Land League had paid for them. The rest of the Millstreet arsenal originated with the Fenians of earlier decades, again suggesting links between the organisations, or had been acquired in house raids. Connell was not aware of the identities of the Dublin and Cork suppliers, nor did he know how the weapons were smuggled into the country.[69]

Connell's duplicity disrupted clandestine activity in north-west Cork, and his disclosures, which Hannah Reardon corroborated in some instances, produced a succession of arrests and committals, more than sixty in all, while many of their brethren, anticipating a similar fate, either went into hiding or fled the country. From the authorities' perspective such an outcome was often more favourable than attempting – and failing – to secure successful prosecutions. Sub-Inspector Starkie informed his superiors in Dublin that within two months of the first arrests on 9 January 1882 between 150 and 200 Moonlighters from Millstreet and Kanturk districts had decamped, mostly to America, their conspiracy dissolving with their departure.[70]

## The Millstreet Moonlight trials

Twenty-five-year-old James Twohig and his twenty-three-year-old brother Jeremiah, Ballinagree, County Cork, whose widowed mother Johanna farmed about 200 acres of mountain land, were the first of the Millstreet prisoners arrested on Approver Connell's evidence to come before the courts. They were charged with unlawful assembly and with attacking and breaking into the home of Catherine Fitzgerald on the night of 7 December 1881. The brothers, who were the only undisguised members of the raiding party, were identified by Andrew McCarthy, Fitzgerald's servant, who was in the house at the time of the attack, and his information accorded with Daniel Connell's. In his sworn testimony against the Twohigs, Connell admitted that he was a lieutenant in 'the Moonlights', second-in-command, and armourer for the Millstreet district, and had participated in about a dozen house raids. He claimed to have inducted several members and provided the police with a copy of the society's initiation oath: 'I swear to be true and faithful to the Irish Republic, to obey my superiors, to take up arms when required. Death to the traitor! So help me God!' The antipathy to renegades and turncoats expressed here was graphically captured in one version of the Ribbon oath: initiates pledged 'to shoot, hunt, destroy and pursue to death any former brother who may become [an] informer or traitor'.[71] Connell told the court, without a hint of irony, that 'a "Parnell medal" for bravery' was awarded to those whose Moonlight activities were considered worthy of particular distinction.[72] Defence counsel challenged Connell's evidence against his clients, questioned his credibility and integrity as a witness, and cast him before the jury as a 'double-dyed villain', a perjurer and deserter cashiered from the army. Despite counsel's dismissal of Connell's character and testimony, the jury found the two defendants guilty on all counts, and the judge sentenced each to seven years' penal servitude.[73]

Defence counsel offered similarly scathing assessments of Connell's moral probity at subsequent court hearings involving other Millstreet detainees. At the 1882 Munster summer assizes counsel argued that Connell was a 'degraded being', by his own admission 'a perjurer, a deserter, a gaol bird, a poacher, an informer and a spy'.[74] On another occasion, one of his defence colleagues was even more withering and dismissive, observing that Connell had lied on oath for the first time at the age of seventeen, and

> followed it up by perjury, ruffianism, and wound up his career as the hero and captain of the Moonlights ... His career was one dismal round of crime, outrage, faithlessness, perjury, treason, and treachery. God help the people if men like the prisoner were to have their liberties staked on the pledged oath of the perjured conscience of such men as Connell.[75]

Peter O'Brien, QC, who prosecuted the original case against the Twohig brothers on behalf of the crown, expressed a similar sentiment in his address to the jury, observing that the evidence of approvers like Connell 'ought to speak with trumpet tone to those unhappy people who form criminal confederacies. Such was the nature of the confederacies that there was no security for criminals, for the man who is a criminal today may be an approver tomorrow.'[76] O'Brien's reflection captured, albeit unintentionally, one of the more unsavoury aspects of Irish political activism and insurgency – the seeming ubiquity of informers, approvers and traitors.

Justice Fitzgerald, in charging the jury, stated that Connell's evidence and the oath he had sworn to the Irish Republic persuaded him that the trial concerned Fenianism rather than Moonlighting, with similar aspects to Fenian cases he had tried in the 1860s.[77] The oath was 'the old Fenian oath', the judge stated, and the Royal Irish Republic was a continuation of the Fenian conspiracy of earlier decades. The intrigue was as pervasive and malign as ever and as dangerous to society, and, Fitzgerald concluded, it was probably exploiting the Land League for its own ends.[78]

Florence Arnold-Forster, possibly reflecting Chief Secretary W.E. Forster's opinion, dissented from the trial judge's interpretation, claiming that the outrages perpetrated by the Royal Irish Republic were more closely associated with the Land League's current 'No Rent' policy than with Fenianism's declared objective of realising an Irish republic.[79] Her analysis, however, was marred by its partiality and its blindness to the complexities and subtleties of the case and the times. The Connell–Royal Irish Republic affair embodied the mutuality and commonality that linked nationalist associations in rural Ireland during the Land War, the nexus at local level between Fenians, Land Leaguers and members of agrarian secret societies. The Irish authorities acknowledged the fluidity of these relationships and were prepared to use all available means to negate their influence and effectiveness, including the enactment of draconian legislation, such as the suspension of habeas corpus which enabled the indefinite detention of prisoners without trial, and drastic sentences for those convicted of public order offences, notably the death penalty for capital crimes, as in the case of the 1882 Maamtrasna murders. Miscarriages of justice were an inevitable consequence of such policies, with the Maamtrasna case again serving as an example.[80]

Captain Thomas Plunkett, special resident magistrate for Kerry and Cork West Riding and a firm believer in the imposition of stern executive measures to suppress crime and outrage, predicted that the outcome of the judicial proceedings against the Millstreet Moonlighters at Cork would have a positive impact on midnight marauding and would restore confidence among the well-disposed but timid element of the community.[81] In late 1881 Chief Secretary Forster had appointed six special resident magistrates and entrusted them with responsibility for suppressing crime and outrage in the country's most troubled regions, one of which was Kerry and Cork West Riding.[82] From Plunkett's perspective, the Twohig convictions appeared to be a very positive beginning to his new posting and his task of restoring law and order to this disturbed district, but any optimism he may have felt proved premature. The trial of the remaining Millstreet prisoners, arrested for complicity in the Moonlight conspiracy and charged with treason-felony, dragged on for more than a year, deferred from one assizes to the next as the crown attempted to assemble additional evidence and strengthen its case against the accused.

Prior to the commencement of the Cork summer assizes in late July 1882 T.M. Healy, MP for Wexford, accused the crown in a House of Commons debate of delaying the progress of the trial of numerous individuals who were charged on Approver Connell's testimony. Healy claimed that the RIC were arresting and imprisoning the principal witnesses for the defence under the Protection of Person and Property (Ireland) Act, because they could disprove the charges against the defendants, and he informed the House that he would attend the assizes at Cork to keep a watching brief on proceedings.[83]

Two of the Millstreet prisoners, Timothy Moynihan and Michael Horgan, were indicted before Justice Barry at the Cork assizes on 31 July on a charge of treason-felony. Daniel Connell was the first witness examined and Hannah Reardon also testified. Barry reminded the jury that the prisoners were not charged with participating in outrages, Whiteboy offences, but with conspiracy to depose the queen and establish an Irish republic. In accordance with English law, the jury could convict on the evidence of an informer, but Barry advised that they should not do so without independent corroborative testimony. After a relatively short deliberation, the foreman reported that they were unable to agree on a verdict and the judge discharged the jury, remanding Moynihan and Horgan in custody. He released eleven of their fellow-accused on bail and another forty-one on their own recognisances, all to come up for trial at the next Cork assizes. The bailed prisoners included the brothers John and Jeremiah Riordan, each of whom had served as captain of the Royal Irish Republic, and the schoolmaster Thomas McCarthy, who had sworn Connell into the society, according to the latter's testimony.[84]

The crown secured a conviction against Moynihan at the Munster winter assizes in the following January, for a Whiteboy offence – involvement in a house raid in June 1881 – rather than on the more serious treason-felony charge, and Justice Barry sentenced him to seven years' penal servitude, the statutory minimum he could impose. Barry attributed the relative leniency of the sentence in part to Canon Griffin, the parish priest at Millstreet, who testified in court to Moynihan's previous good character. Griffin's was an unlikely intervention, given the hostility and opprobrium he had provoked among his parishioners for his support of the boycotted Jeremiah Hegarty.[85] The crown was less successful in relation to the remaining Millstreet Moonlighters, and in January 1883 abandoned all proceedings against them, having failed to secure a conviction against one of those arraigned for the attack on the Fitzgerald household more than thirteen months earlier, ironically William Twohig, a relative of the Twohig brothers who had been convicted and sentenced to lengthy prison terms for the same offence.[86]

William Verling Gregg, crown solicitor for Cork, blamed the collapse of the case on the composition of jury panels and fear of retribution, claiming that independent gentry were under-represented on such panels, which were composed mainly of farmers who were members of the Land League or under its influence, and this imbalance, coupled with intimidation – 'the dread of assassination or mutilation' – dissuaded jurors from returning what he called honest verdicts,[87] sentiments that chimed with Chief Secretary Forster's, as noted above. Similar fears convinced potential witnesses to remain silent and the crown often found it difficult to secure independent testimony, without which successful prosecutions were rarely achieved. Customarily, as we have seen, the Irish judiciary were reluctant to accept the uncorroborated evidence of an accomplice to a crime, and an approver's testimony, which was considered tainted, was insufficient to secure a conviction without independent affirmation.[88] Justice Barry was unambiguous in pronouncing on this matter at the 1883 Munster winter assizes: 'The merciful practice of the law in this country was that a judge always advised a jury not to act upon the uncorroborated testimony of an informer.'[89]

Notwithstanding the collapse and abandonment of the crown's case against the remanded Millstreet Moonlighters, the Irish authorities had effectively defused the threat they posed a year earlier. Connell's arrest and subsequent treachery resulted in the apprehension or flight of the principal leaders and many members of the organisation – the removal from unruly Millstreet and its environs of a troublesome cohort of active or potential Moonlighters, many of them linked to the Fenian movement. This reality was acknowledged by Justice Barry, crown prosecutor Peter O'Brien, QC, and Canon Griffin at the termination of the Munster winter assizes in January 1883. According to Griffin, who had himself been the victim of the prevailing lawlessness, and whose commitment to law and order and a reversion to the status quo ante was lauded by both Barry and O'Brien, the Millstreet district had previously been very disturbed, but during the previous five months things had 'quieted down very much'. He observed that the people were complying with the law of the land, returning to what he termed 'a sense of their religious and moral duties'.[90]

## Embroidering the truth?

After four months in Cork County jail Connell expressed dissatisfaction with his situation, complaining that he was obliged to wear prison clothing and that his diet was inferior to that supplied by the Land League to the prisoners against whom he was testifying.[91] Richard Cronin and his wife, of Finbarr's Quay, Cork were the conduits for the daily provisioning of the remanded Millstreet suspects, with funds provided by the Land League. Cronin, a shoemaker, was regarded as 'one of the most dangerous' Fenians in Cork and was under police surveillance. According to the Cork RIC, he had recently attached himself to the Land League and was a member of the 'Parnell election committee'.[92] The prison gatekeeper recalled Cronin's wife, who clearly shared her husband's political interests and allegiances, visiting the incarcerated Moonlighters two or three times a week, to monitor the prisoners' food supplies and to attend to their laundry and clothing requirements. He claimed that Jeremiah Riordan, 'being the most prominent of the prisoners', received better-quality food than the others,[93] which suggests that, even in jail, and among the brotherhood, a distinction was made between the organisation's officers and foot soldiers. The Ladies' Land League was another association that adopted the remanded suspects. At their weekly meeting on Sunday, 12 February 1882 the Millstreet Ladies' Land League acknowledged fulsomely the Cork branch's 'kindness' to the prisoners; their benevolence was unspecified but was necessarily of a practical nature.[94] The relationship between the prisoners, the Fenian-affiliated Cronins, the Land League and its sister organisation underlined once again the interconnected pan-nationalist political activism of this period. The involvement of Fenians and women from a different political background – and probably a socio-economic one also – suggests widespread empathy with the incarcerated Moonlighters, individuals who were in jail on the word of an approver, their one-time superior officer and fellow political activist.

Connell's treachery had drawn upon him the odium of a broad nationalist front: Land Leaguers, both male and female, Fenians, and, given the universal detestation of informers, it is reasonable to assume that popular sentiment was also arrayed against him. Connell had violated his own Moonlight oath, which proclaimed 'death to the traitor', and the Irish authorities had good reason for concern over his continued safety in Cork jail. Captain Plunkett, special resident magistrate for Kerry and Cork West Riding, proposed that Connell be discharged from custody and kept as an ordinary crown witness at the Ballybough witness protection depot near Clontarf RIC barracks in Dublin. The attorney general advised that he should be allowed to decide for himself whether he would feel more secure in Cork prison or in protective custody in the capital, but, ultimately, his safety might best be secured by removing him permanently from the country and resettling him in a crown colony. This was standard procedure, but it was a practice that disregarded colonial sensitivities, suggesting that these locations were little more than distant receptacles for the United Kingdom's problematic and unwanted.[95] The lord lieutenant concurred with his advisors' general sentiments, and instructed that Connell be protected and adequately provisioned.[96]

The prisoner opted to transfer from Cork jail and forwarded a petition to that effect to the lord lieutenant, in which he described his position as that of a crown prosecution witness against sixty individuals charged with membership of an unlawful and seditious conspiracy, the Royal Irish Republic, which, as the name suggests, aimed to sever the British connection entirely. He repeated the information he had earlier supplied to Sub-Inspector Starkie and claimed that since he had become a police approver in early January 1882 not a single outrage had been committed within twenty miles of Millstreet. He suggested that his release would encourage others to come forward with evidence, including information on the assassinations in the Phoenix Park, Dublin on 6 May, a mere three weeks earlier, of Lord Frederick Cavendish, newly arrived in Dublin as chief secretary for Ireland, and Thomas H. Burke, permanent under-secretary at Dublin Castle, which Paul Bew has described as 'the most traumatic political assassinations in nineteenth-century British political history'.[97] Connell described their deaths as 'brutal and cowardly', and their assassins as 'Fenian terrorists'. He pledged to give 'a full pedigree' of the Fenians and the Land League, including their plans, once he was transferred from Cork jail, intimating that he possessed information on these organisations that would be useful to the authorities. He appended the descriptor 'Fenian informer' to his signature.[98]

The lord lieutenant applied to the Home Office for a free pardon for Connell, and on 14 June 1882, while that process was underway, Connell was removed from Cork jail to Richmond prison in Dublin. On the following day he began a formal written account of the structure and activities of the secret society that operated in north-west Cork, of which he had been a key member, and of Fenianism more generally. The document, which was addressed to the lord lieutenant at Dublin Castle, was headed 'Royal Irish Republic, Fenian Brother-Hood, Moonlights', and signed 'Daniel Connell Fenian informer of Millstreet'. Connell compiled his declamatory and prolix, though surprisingly literate, record in three segments over a five-day period, 15–19 June 1882. If at times bombastic, and at others short on specifics, the document, with its illustrations of weapons, disguises and secret signs and signals, offers evidence of an artistic and talented individual, one who was not yet nineteen years of age.[99]

Fig. 6.2: Dot-dash code used by the Royal Irish Republic secret society (Sketch by Daniel Connell), National Archives of Ireland, CSORP/1883/15390. IMAGE COURTESY OF THE NAI

In the opening section, which focused on Fenian affairs, Connell claimed that several members of the organisation had gone to America within the past twelve months to train in the use of dynamite and firearms, and the Fenians in Ireland planned to rise in rebellion on their return. The Fenian officers communicated with one another in code, a ploy that was common to secret societies and other fraternities historically in Ireland and elsewhere. In the case of the Royal Irish Republic society, different combinations of dots and dashes, which Connell likened to musical notation, represented the letters of the alphabet.

Connell referred by name to several Fenians in Cork jail against whom he had provided evidence, including Pat Quinn, who, Connell claimed, changed his mind about becoming a crown prosecution witness following a visit, clearly intimidatory, from leading members of the Land League. Connell also named the Fenian 'head commander' in Dublin and several Fenian captains in Dublin and King's County (Offaly), information he had secretly obtained before his arrest from the captain of the Royal Irish Republic. Connell added that his own family in Millstreet were boycotted because of his actions, and in fear of their lives.

Connell incorporated a series of illustrations of the Moonlighters' disguises and weapons in the document's middle segment, specifically:

- a steel pike, about seven feet in length, with a sling attached (for night use – 'out by night')

- a home-made lance, which had a pennant or flag attached, and had been made by a blacksmith

- an 'old Fenian pattern sword'
- an 'American pattern, centre-fire, self-acting' pistol or revolver
- a 'new American pattern Martine-Henry repeating rifle', cocked, and with its lever open

Connell noted that the Moonlighters' remaining weapons were like the rifles and bayonets, swords, belts and ammunition pouches worn by the military, and did not require illustration. He sketched eight different disguises – variations of helmets and caps – and provided a short, written description of two – a false whisker and hair cap combination, and a disguise made from rabbit or other animal skin.

The final illustrations were of three armed and disguised men.

- The first wore a plumed hat with a logo, false whiskers, boots and spurs; a transverse belt (strapped across the figure's right shoulder) with revolver pouch attached; a whip across his other shoulder; the figure had a rifle in one hand and handcuffs in the other, with the appended comment: 'ready for handcuffing'.

- The second, in profile and standing on a chair, carried a sword in his left hand and wore a plumed helmet which sported a harp logo. Connell explained that the smaller men stood on chairs or other platforms behind a rank of their fellows to make them appear taller and thus render police identification more difficult.

- The third wore false whiskers and a plumed hat with a different harp logo to the one in the previous sketch; he was 'dressed in women's attire', armed with a revolver and rifle, and bore on his chest 'a medal for bravery as a Fenian'. His other accoutrements were 'sheers [sic] for cutting hair' and 'pinchers [sic] for extracting men's teeth who paid rent'.

Connell, formerly armourer, drill instructor and lieutenant or second-in-command of the Royal Irish Republic organisation at Millstreet, an individual with a militia and regular army background who had participated in numerous nocturnal house raids, observed that persons who were armed and disguised in such a manner were the very personification of

H.M. Male Prison Richmond (Dublin) — 16./6./82.

To His "Excellency, The Lord Lieutenant," — Dublin Castle

"I forward this deposition secondly as to the usual, disguises, etc
worn by the so called "Moonlights" when out by night, and day also, these
are the disguise Helmets, and caps, and Arms, — viz —"

"                                                                              "

(No.1.)   No.2.)   No.3.   No.4.   No.5.   No.6.

False whiskers
combined
and Hair Cap,
about 7ft long

with sling attached

No.7.   No.8   Rabbit skin   steel Pike out by night
                 or any Skin

old fenian Pattern Sword   Home made Lance, made by black   Smith,

Centre-fire
Self-acting   American
Pattern

Lever open
in full cock

New American Pattern Martine Henry Repeating Rifle

I need not draw the others out for they are the same as the
Military rifles, and bayonets, and swords, belts, Pouches, etc,
— These are men armed, and disguised, etc.

Ready for Handcuffing.)

"Please Governor forward to Dublin Castle,"

Rifle

whip

Handcuffs

All the Small men stands on a Chair or
any thing behind the tall men to make
them look tall men — say the time is by the
Land League that every man wears 6 pit-
in order to pretend it was a police party
his disguise — so it is impossible to identify them

Armed in

A revolver is attracting
their attention

A man is active armed
with Revolver and a similar rifle.

A pistol for cutting Hair

A pistol for Shaving a a fenian

Facing page: Fig. 6.3: Moonlighters' disguises and weapons (Sketch by Daniel Connell), National Archives of Ireland, CSORP/1883/15390. IMAGE COURTESY OF THE NAI

night-time terror, 'routing people out of their beds and ill using them in every possible manner using sheers [sic] and pinchers [sic] and small shot'. He claimed that the situation had deteriorated and it was now Captain Sunlight rather than Captain Moonlight who was responsible for such terrorism, implying daytime marauding and increased secret society activity, a reflection of the anarchy unleashed by the incarceration of Parnell and other political leaders in Kilmainham jail and possibly of heightened emotions and tensions following the Phoenix Park murders, but, he added, in an oblique reference to the significance of the information he possessed, soon it would be Captain Darknight, 'when all will be against these fellows'. Connell urged the constabulary to do everything in their power to suppress secret societies and their 'brutal doings', opining sanctimoniously that these miscreants had shed too much innocent blood. Irrespective of the sincerity or otherwise of his sentiments, the latter observation was one that resonated poignantly and powerfully in the wake of the recent political assassinations in the Phoenix Park. Connell claimed that the Parnell medals awarded for bravery were subversive, indicating as they did that 'the country was gained by Parnell's speeches, and Captain Moonlight's gun and sword, and the terrorists' dagger and revolver', but, he bragged, the conspirators had not yet achieved their aims, and their ambitions would be further curtailed once he had fully disclosed their plans and secrets to the authorities.

In the document's third and final section Connell recounted the details surrounding the Moonlight attack on Mrs Fitzgerald's boycotted household at Mushera, 5 miles from Millstreet in County Cork, on the night of 7 December 1881, following which he was arrested and charged. Connell was in command of the Moonlight party that 'visited' the house and assaulted Fitzgerald, although their real target may have been Andrew McCarthy, a farmer's son and former militia man currently employed by Fitzgerald, and also a crown prosecution witness at the Munster winter assizes which had commenced on the previous day.[100] McCarthy, who was part of the Millstreet conspiracy, had been arrested and charged with treason-felony, and, like Connell, had turned queen's evidence and was under police protection.[101] Connell stated that during the assault on the Fitzgerald household the Moonlighters were under the influence of whiskey purchased with Land League funds and were difficult to control, a claim that was not improbable given the frequent references to alcohol in evidence produced at Moonlight trials, which in turn raises the question about the role of alcohol in fomenting and fuelling secret society activity and the violence and excess associated with agrarian outrages.

The remainder of the document was taken up with a plea on his father's behalf. The latter was an ex-militia man, aged about fifty, who was employed as a handyman in the Millstreet workhouse. He was reduced to half-pay after his son became an approver and publicly reneged on his former associates. Connell's family became collateral victims of his perfidy, and their lives were disrupted in consequence. His actions had compromised his father's life and the welfare of his five younger siblings, though he regarded himself as entirely blameless, attributing the family's reduced and fearful circumstances solely to the climate engendered by Fenianism, boycotting, and what he claimed were Land League bribes. Connell concluded with the unctuous, self-serving assertion: 'I preserved the peace of Millstreet and the surrounding districts where over 200 houses were attacked and ransacked at midnight, and probably outrages would be in full bloom there still only for my information.' He signed the document 'Daniel Connell Fenian informer', as he had done in his petition to the lord lieutenant a few weeks earlier.[102]

## Camouflage and concealment

The types of disguises described and illustrated by Connell had many antecedents in Irish history, featuring among agrarian and other types of secret societies, insurrectionary conspiracies, and in more mundane criminal activities. Such disguises discharged several functions, the most important being identity concealment for the purpose of avoiding detection, prosecution, and the possibility of lengthy prison sentences.

Disguises were adopted to intimidate, to instil fear and thus compliance with the aims and activities of the obscured individual or gang. The fear and intimidation effect intensified when linked to nocturnal house raiding and punishment beatings. The adoption of disguises by Moonlighters and others engaged in illegal activities was devoid of any element of playfulness. The masquerade was ritualistically dark rather than ludic. Male to female cross-dressing as disguise and deflection was a common feature of agrarian secret society activity. The practice, which possibly had impulses other than simple identity concealment, may have had greater purchase in Ireland than elsewhere.[103]

The possibilities for personal concealment and identity protection were limited only by the human imagination, and the latter appears to have been particularly fecund and active in the anarchic period from autumn 1881 to early summer 1882, when much of the nationalist leadership was in prison and Parnell's prediction about Captain Moonlight's ascendancy in the Irish countryside was unfolding. Opportunistic tenants exploited the situation for their own ends, concocting nocturnal attacks on their homes as an excuse for non-payment of rent. One such group resided at Kingwilliamstown (now Ballydesmond), not far from Millstreet in north-west Cork. At the beginning of 1882, some months prior to Connell's disclosures to the lord lieutenant and while he was still imprisoned in Cork jail, the constabulary at Kingwilliamstown 'heard casually' that an armed and disguised nocturnal gang had 'visited' the homes of several tenant farmers whose rents were due and warned them not to pay. The tenants' subsequent statements to the police differed, as did the descriptions they offered of the raiders' appearances and disguises. One observed that the intruders 'wore feathers on their heads' and their faces were concealed; another stated that their faces were covered with long black veils, that they wore canvas overcoats, coloured white with blue stripes, and on their heads sported something resembling 'policemen's high hats, topped with the crowns of women's bonnets', and, he added, three of the group were armed. A third supposed victim informed the constabulary that a weapon was discharged through his kitchen window, that the invaders concealed their faces behind paper-like coverings, and that one had 'an old bag' thrown over him, though none had blue stripes on their clothing. Another of the farmers claimed that the trespassers did not have 'feathers or crowns of women's bonnets on their heads', and that they wore peaked caps and disguised their appearances with horsehair, not with black veils or other facial covering.[104]

The discrepancies in the tenants' stories convinced the police and the local resident magistrate, Heffernan F. Considine, that they had taken advantage of the prevailing lawlessness and the Land League's 'no-rent manifesto' to fabricate the Moonlight attacks on their homes, and had done so because they were under notice to pay their rents, some having been served with writs to that effect.[105] The government was aware of such opportunism, and Forster, the chief secretary, dismissed many home invasions as 'shams'.[106]

The Kingwilliamstown incident occurred during the tumultuous period that followed the proclamation of the Land League as an illegal organisation in October 1881, and the general lawlessness continued until the negotiation of the Kilmainham Treaty by Parnell and Gladstone in May 1882. The Kingwilliamstown tenant farmers had attempted to turn the prevailing sentiment to their advantage. Their general narratives and the descriptions they provided to the police of the raiders' actions and disguises were simply variations on a theme, and their concoction of the attacks on their homes suggests their own and the public's awareness of the Moonlighters' pervasiveness and *modus operandi*.

## Reaping the whirlwind?

The information that Connell supplied to the Irish authorities had both an immediate and localised impact – the dissolution of the Millstreet conspiracy – and a wider significance. According to Sub-Inspector Starkie, Connell's disclosures revealed 'the inner workings of a vast conspiracy' that extended over the greater part of the country, one that aimed to subvert law and order in the short term, and, ultimately, to overthrow British rule in Ireland.[107] Connell's revelations about the nature and extent of the Millstreet conspiracy alarmed the Irish authorities and prompted inquiries in the opening months of 1882 into the possible existence of similar societies in other parts of Cork and neighbouring County Limerick. The RIC inspector for County Cork responded that an 'organised system' like the one at Millstreet existed in the contiguous districts of Kanturk and Mallow, and that quantities of weapons had been secreted in Cork city, which, he claimed, was a 'hotbed of Fenianism and disloyalty'. There were Fenian cells and extensive caches of weapons in various parts of Limerick city and county, in Rathkeale, New Pallas and Kilfinane for instance. In Rathkeale, the members described themselves as 'Moonlights', and, like their Millstreet confrères, were sworn-in, armed and organised in circles. Four named shop assistants from Kilmallock collected money at chapels and public houses throughout the county for the purchase of weapons. The rifles and revolvers acquired by their and other conspirators' efforts were distributed among the Fenians in various ways, commonly by commercial travellers, or consigned singly or in small batches in goods despatched to shopkeepers – 'in boxes, sacks, chests and even in coffins in hearses', as one police report phrased it. These weapons were wrapped in blankets that had been steeped in paraffin oil to prevent rust and were concealed underground. The locations were known to a mere handful of individuals and were changed periodically to avoid detection.[108]

A similar situation existed in other parts of the country, in Athenry, County Galway, for instance, where the Fenian organisation had become 'irresistibly strong' by mid-June 1882, according to the local RIC inspector. He claimed that almost every man in the district had been sworn in as a member, that 'murder and outrage' were commonplace, and police intelligence suggested the possibility of dynamite attacks on constabulary barracks and the simultaneous targeting of landlords' residences.[109]

The assassination of the chief secretary for Ireland, Lord Frederick Cavendish, and the under-secretary, Thomas H. Burke, in Dublin's Phoenix Park on 6 May 1882 by seven knife-wielding members of the Irish National Invincibles, a shadowy and hitherto unknown secret society that had links to both the Land League and the Fenians, provoked horror and revulsion, and resulted in political and administrative changes: the appointment of a new chief secretary and under-secretary of necessity, and, on 25 May, less than three weeks after the assassinations, the establishment by Dublin Castle of a permanent secret service department, the Crime Special Branch, to coordinate the intelligence work of the RIC, the DMP and the special resident magistrates.[110] One of the Crime Special Branch's early tasks was to investigate the nature, extent and location of secret societies, and to assess the threat they posed to the political and social status quo.

The investigation focused on four movements: the Fenians, the Irish Republican Brotherhood (IRB), the Ribbon society, and the Moonlight society. The latter's profile was essentially compiled from the information provided to the Irish authorities by Daniel Connell; indeed, he was specifically referred to in the secret service memorandum as 'Connell (the informer)'. According to the report's author, the Moonlight society's close connections with the Land League, notably in its violent enforcement of the League's mandate, distinguished it from the other organisations. The Moonlight society existed prior to the formation of the Land League, but on the establishment of the latter a mutually advantageous connection was forged between the two, an observation that accorded with the view expressed by Sub-Inspector Starkie in his reports to the inspector general of the RIC on the Millstreet Moonlighters. According to the memorandum's compiler, the Land League availed itself of 'this more or less organised and armed body' to perpetrate outrages on individuals who opposed its doctrines, and in return provided the Moonlight society with money to purchase weapons and to develop its general organisation. The analyst noted that numerous arrests, fear of apprehension, convictions and imprisonment, attributable to police work and to Connell's disclosures, had rendered the Moonlight conspiracy defunct in the Macroom and Millstreet districts and in other places in the south of Ireland, but, he added, the conspiracy was still active in other parts of Munster, notably in the Killarney and Castleisland districts of County Kerry, and the report concluded by naming more than 120 Moonlighters in Castleisland and its environs.[111]

The police tended to differentiate between Ribbon and Whiteboy or Moonlight societies, although the difference was essentially one of geography: Ribbonism predominated in the midlands, in mid and north Leinster and south Ulster, while Moonlighting featured primarily in Cork,

Clare, Kerry and Limerick, and to some extent in the other counties in the south and west of the country. The Ribbon and Moonlight societies of this period shared a republican ideology, an antipathy to landlordism and its trappings, and, under the powerful slogan 'Ireland for the Irish', or the related mantra 'the land for the people', a determination that the ownership of Irish land should be vested in the Irish people. These sentiments were reflected in the two societies' initiation oaths, terse and succinct in that of the Moonlight society, more nakedly in the case of the Ribbon organisation. The latter's oath was overtly sectarian, gothic, and infinitely more elaborate than that sworn by other clandestine societies, defining features that can be traced to the Ribbon society's origins in Ulster's late eighteenth-century Defender movement.[112]

## Conclusion

The 1881 Munster winter assizes portrayed the nature and extent of agrarian lawlessness that prevailed in disturbed areas of the country at the height of the Land War, and the determination of the country's executive, police and judiciary to restore peace and tranquillity to the anarchic countryside, essentially by the vigorous pursuit and prosecution of the perpetrators of agrarian outrages – variously depicted as Whiteboys, Moonlighters, or, colloquially, in parts of Munster at least, as Moonlights – and the imposition of harsh prison sentences as a deterrent to potential recruits.

In their recent study of Ribbonism, Kyle Hughes and Donald M. MacRaild, drawing on the earlier work of Oliver MacDonagh, caution against perceiving the different strands of Irish nationalism as distinct and disconnected. 'Irish nationalism,' they note, 'was fluid and ever-changing. It could comprise elements of separatist and constitutional traditions simultaneously. Sometimes it was difficult to differentiate between the two.'[113] Such a reading captures the complexities and realities of the Land War period, the 'New Departure', and the composition, functioning and ideals of collectives such as the Royal Irish Republic. It is difficult to disentangle the demarcation between Fenianism,

Whiteboyism or Moonlighting, and Land League activism in Millstreet and its hinterland in the early 1880s, but from the Irish administration's perspective these overlapping allegiances, objectives and personnel collectively constituted the Fenian conspiracy to overthrow British rule in Ireland and establish an Irish republic. Analogous crossover networks with similar impulses and ideals were active in neighbouring County Kerry, particularly in the Castleisland district, and in other disturbed parts of Munster and Connacht.[114]

The information Connell supplied to the authorities contributed to the arrest, trial, remand, imprisonment and pre-emptive flight of as many as 250 individuals who were involved in dangerous clandestine activity in mid and north-west Cork, and the dismantling of a troublesome Fenian/Whiteboy network.[115] Connell's evidence and witness testimony were undoubtedly self-serving, his information coloured and tailored to enhance its significance and his importance. On that account alone, the historian needs to approach Connell's disclosures – to the constabulary at Millstreet, as witness at successive assizes at Cork, and to the lord lieutenant – with caution, indeed scepticism. Embellishment and exaggeration were probable, imaginative and resourceful fabrication possible, though unlikely given the detail involved in Connell's depositions, and the authorities' general acceptance of his testimony, some of which was corroborated by other approvers involved in the case. There remains, however, an unresolved and intriguing aspect of Connell's evidence that relates to the reliability and veracity of his statements and claims – the society's substantial arsenal which the police never discovered!

Fabrication or augmentation may also have been a feature of the name Connell assigned to the society – the Royal Irish Republic. The incongruity of the nomenclature, the oxymoron at its very core, is striking, and was the cause of some speculation among those involved with the Millstreet case. One trial judge, Justice Barry at the 1882 Cork summer assizes, commented on the absurdity of the organisation's name, its 'dynastic inconsistency' as he phrased it. The suggestion by Peter O'Brien, QC, who served as counsel for the crown, that the epithet royal was attached as an embellishment – 'giving a flash to it' – by individuals who did not properly understand the nuances of the word appears to be the most likely explanation. There is some internal support for O'Brien's contention. He noted, correctly, that the word royal did not appear in the oath initiates swore on joining the organisation – they simply pledged loyalty to the Irish Republic.[116] Additionally, the inscription 'The Irish Republic' adorned the books that recorded the society's membership details and operations.[117] The designation Royal Irish Republic may have been a figment of Daniel Connell's imagination – an individual capable and resourceful enough to give 'a flash' to any name – the epithet royal appearing to lend legitimacy, lineage and substance. What was not in doubt was the existence of an organisation, broadly conforming in outline and activity with the information Connell provided to the authorities and the courts, even if he concocted or enhanced its name, and possibly inflated the membership, to suit his own ends.

The Royal Irish Republic was a projection of lower-class Irish nationalism, a secretive illegal organisation within the Fenian conspiracy, one that shared that movement's political and social aspirations. The society's targets were not the elite landlord class, but parvenus like Jeremiah Hegarty who controlled access to land at local level; strong and middling farmers such as Thomas Cudmore who possessed wealth and weapons; and backsliders and transgressors like the widow Fitzgerald who broke faith and ranks with her local community. The Royal Irish Republic's redresser and enforcer operations, which were executed by groups of armed, masked and occasionally alcohol-fuelled young men, and which the Irish authorities categorised as Moonlighting – serious agrarian crime – featured reckless and unwonted brutality, a reality Justice Barry captured and deplored in his charge to the jury at the Cork summer assizes in early August 1882:

In no civilised country in the world would there be established on sworn testimony, unimpeached and not impeachable, such a state of things as had been proved to have existed in this Millstreet district. The houses of people fired into at the dead of night; men and women knocked down and beaten; a man made to run in his bare feet on stones, a couple of his ribs broken; naked men beaten with furze bushes.[118]

Connell's revelations enabled the Irish authorities to crush this conspiracy. His motivation was the avoidance of a lengthy prison sentence and in this he was successful, unlike the Twohig brothers and others whose conviction and imprisonment were secured by his perfidy, although his own freedom did come at considerable cost. In the eyes of the community, he was a collaborator and informer, and he and his family – innocent, but tainted by his transgressions – were exposed to social obloquy, ostracism and exile. His reward was a new, pseudonymous and, it appears, reluctant life in the Australian colonies, theirs, expatriation to Canada.

On 19 June 1882, the day he completed his extravagantly titled tripartite submission on Moonlighting and Fenianism to the lord lieutenant, Connell was granted a royal pardon and released from Richmond prison into protective custody at the Ballybough depot in Dublin, where he remained for several months. After the crown's case against the Millstreet remand prisoners collapsed in January 1883, Connell was no longer required as a witness, and the consensus among officials was that he should be provided with some financial assistance and removed to one of the colonies for his own safety. William Verling Gregg, crown solicitor for Cork, who was not one of Connell's admirers, opined that his support should not extend beyond the bare minimum to maintain him until he secured employment in his new location. Captain Plunkett, special resident magistrate for Kerry and Cork West Riding, was more sympathetic, contending that Connell's information had resulted in the conviction and lengthy imprisonment of four men for house raids in the Millstreet district, the detention and trial of between fifty and sixty more, and the flight of others from counties Cork and Kerry, effectively dismantling the conspiracy in what had been a seriously disturbed part of the country. Sub-Inspector Starkie and several crown law officers shared Plunkett's view, although some dissenting colleagues questioned the validity and value of Connell's disclosures. Plunkett believed that Connell deserved protection and a gratuity for his contribution, and he argued for £100, the maximum that could be awarded. The chief secretary demurred, finally sanctioning £55, plus £23 2s. 6d. to cover Connell's passage and expenses.[119]

Connell indicated a preference for Sydney in New South Wales, and he departed from Dublin for Gravesend, the port of embarkation, on Monday, 9 July 1883, accompanied by a police constable who was to see him safely on board. This precaution was proposed by a senior RIC officer who claimed that Connell was an unstable character, and supported by Connell's police liaison officer in Dublin who believed that he was likely to change his mind and refuse to go without such encouragement.[120] Connell, who travelled under the name Robert Davis, appears on the ship's manifest as a 23-year-old labourer of English nationality. He arrived in Sydney in early September 1883, but attempts to locate him in the Australian colonies, under his own name or his new identity, have proved fruitless to date.[121]

The volume's next and final chapter develops the Moonlighting theme – the activities of agrarian clandestine organisations in Irish society. It explores the topic from a literary perspective, George Fitzmaurice's little-known and seldom-performed 1914 drama *The Moonlighter*, and posits a connection between historical reality and literary creativity.

CHAPTER 7

# Moonlighting and Playwriting: The 1881 Scrahan outrage and George Fitzmaurice's *The Moonlighter* (1914)

Sure, but for the Moonlighters, where would ourselves and our children be at the mercy of landlords and grabbers?

George Fitzmaurice, *The Moonlighter*, in George Fitzmaurice, *Five Plays* (London and Dublin: Maunsell & Co., 1914), p. 108

## Prologue

In his foreword to Fiona Brennan's biography of the Kerry-born playwright George Fitzmaurice, Fintan O'Toole, theatre critic and *Irish Times* columnist among other accomplishments, described her subject as 'the great lost soul of twentieth-century Irish theatre',[1] a pithy assessment that captures the views of earlier biographers and commentators on Fitzmaurice's work.[2] The playwright's soul remained lost to the contributors and editors of a major compendium of modern Irish theatre that was published in late 2016 – there is only a single, passing reference to Fitzmaurice in the book's 41 chapters and 764 pages.[3] Well might O'Toole, in an otherwise overwhelmingly positive review in *The Irish Times*, bemoan Fitzmaurice's absence from the volume, casting him as 'the unjustly neglected Kerry surrealist'.[4]

This chapter's focus is on the real rather than surreal in Fitzmaurice's work, on his imaginative reconstruction of social realities and rituals in late nineteenth-century north Kerry – his intimate exploration of life in the Irish countryside, as he himself phrased it.[5] The chapter's core is a Whiteboy or Moonlighting incident, the so-called Scrahan outrage, which occurred during Fitzmaurice's childhood, involved his father, and may have inspired or influenced *The Moonlighter*, Fitzmaurice's realistic drama that was published in 1914. An essential part of the analysis is the historical context in which Moonlighting occurred and the forces that shaped this type of rural social protest in late nineteenth-century Ireland. As Fitzmaurice never wrote a preface to *The Moonlighter* or any of his other plays, and in the absence of further defining or supporting evidence, the hypothesis offered for the play's origins is necessarily speculative. This essay concerns itself less with the drama, the action of the play, than with the dramatis personae, and the ways in which their characters, personal motivation, and the motifs and themes they embody reflected contemporary political and social realities.

The playwright was named after his father, Rev. George Fitzmaurice, who was born on 20 May 1821 at the ancestral home, Springmount, Duagh, Listowel, County Kerry. George senior graduated from Trinity College Dublin in 1844 and served as a Church of Ireland clergyman in counties Kildare and Limerick, before abandoning active ministry sometime in the 1850s. He lived in the gate lodge of Bedford House, near Listowel, whose owners, the Batemans, were connected to the Fitzmaurice family by marriage. In her rather excited and overwrought reconstruction of Rev. Fitzmaurice's life and circumstances, Brennan speculates that the Batemans had presented the lodge to the clergyman as a gift, and that Fitzmaurice subsequently abused their hospitality, occupying Bedford House without the family's consent following the death of the incumbent leaseholder, Dr Samuel Raymond, in 1859, and remaining there until his own death thirty-two years later. Throughout this period, Fitzmaurice resisted all attempts by the Batemans to remove him from Bedford House, projecting himself locally as the owner of the property, though he was neither owner nor lessor and paid only nominal rent to the Batemans.[6] Following Fitzmaurice's death in 1891, his wife, Winifred O'Connor, a Catholic who was twenty years her husband's junior, moved with her children, including fourteen-year-old George, to a house and farm at Kilcara Beg, near Duagh village, 5 miles south-east of Listowel and close to Abbeyfeale in County Limerick. There the future playwright lived until he went to work in Cork in 1900, relocating to Dublin in the following year.

Locations in North Kerry, featuring Duagh area

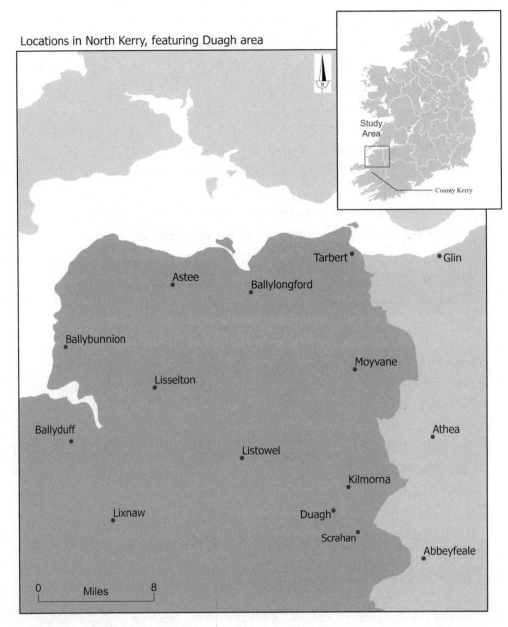

Map 7.1: North Kerry.
IMAGE COURTESY OF MIKE MURPHY, DEPARTMENT OF GEOGRAPHY, UCC

## The drama

Rev. George Fitzmaurice was centrally involved in one of the Moonlight or Whiteboy cases tried at the Munster winter assizes in 1881, the

Scrahan outrage which had been perpetrated in the parish of Duagh. In August of that year Fitzmaurice summoned Cornelius McAuliffe and the brothers Daniel and Michael Galvin for malicious damage to the gate at the entrance to the driveway to Bedford House. Their motive remains hidden, no further details having emerged, but Rev. Fitzmaurice must have offended the trio in some way, or the rural community among whom they worked and lived. The case was heard on 27 August at Listowel petty sessions, where the defendants were found guilty, largely on the testimony of a local woman, Bridget Lennane, and each was ordered to pay £3 compensation and costs of 8s. 6d., which was a considerable imposition on poorly paid agricultural labourers, the occupation of the three offenders. They refused to pay the fine, and in default each was sentenced to two months' imprisonment with hard labour in Tralee jail.[7]

On the night of 25 November 1881, about a month after the prisoners had completed their sentences, a party of eighteen men, disguised, armed, and fuelled by the alcohol they had consumed at a local funeral earlier in the day, broke into Lennane's house at Scrahan, close to Duagh village, and assaulted and beat her. One of the intruders discharged a firearm, wounding Lennane superficially and her daughter more seriously. On Lennane's information, the Royal Irish Constabulary arrested seven men: Patrick Cronin, Bartholomew Nolan, James Quinlan, Maurice Molony, and the trio she had previously helped to convict – Daniel Galvin, Michael Galvin and Cornelius McAuliffe. On the following Monday, 28 November, Captain R.A. Massy, resident magistrate, conducted a preliminary investigation at Listowel, at which Lennane identified the seven individuals, and her son and niece, who were present in the house during the attack, corroborated her evidence against Cronin. Massy remanded the accused to Tralee jail to await their trial at the Munster winter assizes at Cork early in the following month.[8]

Massy informed the Dublin Castle authorities that the attack on Lennane's home and person was punishment for the evidence she had given at Listowel petty sessions in the previous August – she admitted at the magisterial inquiry that she had 'proved the charge' on that occasion. The resident magistrate described her as a woman of 'immoral character', an unmarried mother of three children, two girls and a boy. He speculated further that the shot that wounded Lennane and her daughter was not intended for them but for Lennane's son, Robert, who recognised Patrick Cronin and inadvertently blurted out his name during the Moonlight invasion of the family home. Massy added that the injured child had received little or no religious instruction, and, as she did not understand the nature of an oath, it was inappropriate for her to make a deposition. As crown witnesses, Lennane, her three children and her niece were maintained under police protection in lodgings at Listowel until the commencement of the trial, the resident magistrate and the RIC county inspector anticipating attempts to intimidate them.[9]

The Scrahan seven appeared before Justice John David Fitzgerald at the Munster winter assizes on Saturday, 10 December 1881. The charge against the defendants was that two weeks earlier, on 25 November, at Scrahan, Duagh, County Kerry, they

> assembled with firearms and other weapons, with their faces blackened and covered with cloths and otherwise disguised, and did then and there unlawfully assemble and make a riot, and did assault and break into the dwelling of Bridget Lennane, and did carry away the sum of 14s and a petticoat, the property of Ellen Hennessy.

The motive assigned for the violation of Lennane's home was the evidence she gave at Listowel petty sessions in the previous August, which resulted in the imprisonment of some of the defendants.[10]

Ellen Hennessy was Lennane's niece and lived with her and her three children – Robert Buckley, Johanna Stack and Mary Dillane – in the house that Lennane had occupied for the previous eleven years. Lennane, who made her living by labouring and sewing, acknowledged that she had never married and that her three children were 'called after their several fathers'. Counsel for the defence informed the court that a local priest had previously denounced her 'immorality' from the altar.[11] Her perceived lack of moral probity prompted the unchristian comment from the editor of one Kerry newspaper that Lennane was clearly 'not Caesar's wife', and he urged his readers to keep a close watch on developments in the case.[12]

Lennane's evidence at the trial was essentially a repetition of that which she had presented at the preliminary investigation some weeks earlier, albeit delivered more colourfully and with greater elan. She deposed that a party of eighteen men, some armed and all disguised, broke into her house around midnight; three of the intruders pressed their guns to her breast and subsequently struck her on the back and head with their weapons. One asked if she was 'the devil that swore on those decent boys and put them into gaol'. The raiders forced her to kneel and, in a parody of the oath taken by members of secret societies, compelled her to swear on a powder flask or shot pouch and subsequently on a half-pint bottle of whiskey that she would never again give evidence against any person, nor report that night's proceedings to the RIC. After the 'officer' of the gang, whom she identified as Bartholomew Nolan, threatened to shoot her, Lennane's younger daughter, Mary Dillane, grasped her and implored melodramatically: 'Mamma, let us lie down and die together.' Lennane recognised seven of the eighteen intruders, despite their disguises of soot-blackened faces and whitened eyebrows, claiming that some of them were neighbours whom she had known for varying periods. When her seventeen-year-old son disclosed Cronin's name, a gang member doused the lamp, and a single shot was discharged, for which Cronin was subsequently held responsible. The child Mary Dillane was wounded in both legs and Lennane received a minor injury. The intruders made further threats against Lennane, gave her a week to leave the district, and then departed. While they were assembling outside, she overheard a discussion about whether they should hang her or shoot the entire household, and a voice she recognised as McAuliffe's rebutting both suggestions. They then marched off in military formation in the direction of Duagh village. Lennane heard a dog barking sometime later and identified the animal as Nolan's. Subsequently she saw both Nolan and Molony pass by on their way to their respective homes. On the following morning Lennane informed the constabulary of the night's occurrences and they arrested the defendants.[13]

Robert Buckley corroborated his mother's evidence and identified several of the intruders, including Cronin. Buckley's cousin, Ellen Hennessy, also testified to Cronin's presence in the house. Ulysses

Fitzmaurice, Rev. George Fitzmaurice's sibling, was the doctor at Listowel who attended Lennane and her daughter Mary Dillane, and he informed the court that the latter's wounds were serious, though not life-threatening. In response to a question from defence counsel, Fitzmaurice stated that he knew Nolan personally and the families of the other prisoners, testifying that 'they were most respectable, quiet people', which elicited the cynical response from one of the prosecuting barristers that it was always respectable, quiet people whom the crown had in the dock in Kerry.[14]

Witnesses for the defence – 'a vast number', according to the *Cork Constitution* newspaper, and 'all related to the prisoners as fathers, mothers, brothers, or sisters' – swore that the prisoners could not possibly have been engaged in the outrage as they were asleep in their beds at the time and did not leave their respective homes. Crown counsel Peter O'Brien, QC, ridiculed the alibis provided by the defence witnesses, and while he did not accuse them directly of perjury the implication was clear.[15] Bartholomew Dillane, despite a blood relationship with two of the accused, was an unlikely witness for the defence, though his testimony was as questionable as that of the defendants' families. He was employed by Rev. George Fitzmaurice as a caretaker or land bailiff, and he, along with Bridget Lennane, had given evidence at the Listowel petty sessions in August that resulted in the conviction and imprisonment of three of the defendants. His house was situated a short distance from Lennane's, and it may have been entirely coincidental that he and one of her children bore the same surname. According to Dillane's uncorroborated testimony, the Moonlighters who violated her home broke into his house earlier the same evening, stole his gun, beat him, and for 'the cause of Ireland' subjected him to an oath-swearing farrago like that recounted by Lennane. He testified that the men involved were strangers, disguised and unknown to him, which would not have been the case had they been locals, evidence that contradicted and challenged Lennane's. Dillane informed her after the violation of their respective homes that her prosecution of the young men had caused 'a great deal of aggravation among the people', and he told the court that she and her neighbours were on 'very bad terms'.[16]

The outcome of the trial turned on the question of identity. The charge against six of the seven accused rested entirely on Bridget Lennane's evidence, and counsel for the defence attempted to undermine her testimony by impugning her integrity and credibility. Counsel argued that Lennane harboured 'the most malignant feelings towards the prisoners', which originated in her lowly standing in the community. He referred to her three illegitimate children, each by a different father and bearing a different surname. Counsel claimed that Lennane's immorality had excluded her from the fellowship of a community where chastity was the defining feature of a woman's life. He attributed her rancour and ill-feeling towards her neighbours to her social rejection and isolation, and he denounced her as 'an immoral and vindictive woman' who hoped 'to blast the reputation' of the defendants' families by securing a conviction and criminalising the accused. Moral probity was the essence of counsel's case. He argued that Lennane's disreputable character and behaviour discredited her testimony, but, as one juror interjected during counsel's cross-examination, her morals and lifestyle were not on trial and were irrelevant to the proceedings.[17]

The presiding judge concurred with the juror's assessment. In his charge to the jury Fitzgerald stated that the motive for the attacks on the Lennane and Dillane households was revenge, retribution for the evidence they had given at Listowel petty sessions some months earlier. He claimed that

in the unfortunate state of public opinion amongst a certain class in the community – and the most numerous class too – giving evidence in a court of justice in such a matter was not a popular act. It begot no favour for the party giving evidence, and often begot feelings of revenge.

The judge described the actions of the midnight marauders as 'atrocious', and he condemned the violation of Lennane's home as 'the greatest disgrace', observing that 'this country was the only part of the civilised world in which a transaction of the kind could take place'. Fitzgerald was inured to the moral obloquy in which Lennane was held locally, depicting her as 'that helpless woman living on the mountainside, some eight or nine miles from the police station, where the unfortunate woman could hope for no help'. He informed the jury that the intruders 'wanted to revenge themselves on this woman and frighten her out of the district, as she might be an impediment to them in their course of crime by becoming a witness'. He added that the outrage was committed by some of Lennane's neighbours who had taken 'some little refreshment' at a funeral they had attended on the day in question, and all that was required of the jury was the identity of these individuals. Fitzgerald concluded that it was an all-important case for 'the public peace, and for the district in which it occurred'.[18]

After deliberating for some forty minutes the jury returned a guilty verdict against the seven accused. In passing sentence Fitzgerald returned to the sentiments he had expressed in his charge to the jury. He stated that several outrages were committed on 'the defenceless woman and her family. She was alone and unprotected, the only male in the house being a boy of about sixteen years of age – a poor, feeble boy.' Fitzgerald denounced the intrusion as 'a cowardly and a dastardly outrage', typical of the wanton violence that currently disgraced the south of Ireland. The sentence he was about to impose, he said, was a deterrent rather than an act of vengeance, a proclamation to the people of the country that peace would be restored and maintained. The judge observed that it was the poor in their desolate cabins, rather than the comfortable classes, who were subjected to the 'odious and horrible tyranny' that prevailed, and it was his duty to impose some limitations upon it. Fitzgerald was convinced of Cronin's more serious involvement and culpability – 'the evidence is clear that it was you fired the shot and you alone' – and he sentenced him to ten years' penal servitude, a sentence that caused a sensation in court. Bartholomew Nolan pleaded for leniency, stating that he had eight young children and an eighty-year-old mother to support. He was in his early forties, had no previous convictions, and was prepared to swear that he was not a participant in the attack on the Lennane household. His pleas were unavailing and Justice Fitzgerald, who displayed little judicial impartiality during the proceedings, sentenced Nolan and each of the other five accused to five years' penal servitude.[19]

The crown, through its judicial representative, John David Fitzgerald, was determined to make an example of the defendants, to punish the individuals concerned in the hope of deterring potential Whiteboy activists in disturbed districts from engaging in similar nocturnal activities, a proposition that will be further explored in a later section of this chapter.

## Crown and defence witnesses

Individuals who testified in court on behalf of the crown revealed themselves as collaborators and informers in the eyes of the majority nationalist community, and exposed themselves and their families to social obloquy, ostracism and physical punishment, which occasionally resulted in fatalities. Bridget Lennane did it twice, relatively harmlessly in the first instance, far more seriously in the second, the so-called 'Scrahan outrage', her testimony resulting in the imposition of lengthy prison sentences on seven individuals, some of whom were her neighbours. She never revealed her motive, but, regardless of the reason, she endangered her own life and the lives of her children and her niece. She was maintained under police protection while the trial was in progress, and it appears that the authorities had made some arrangement, 'suitable provision' according to Captain Massy, RM, for her continued safety and that of her children after the trial was over.[20] No other details have emerged, but her own and her family's security would have necessitated their removal from Scrahan, possibly to another location in Ireland, or, as in Daniel Connell's case in the previous chapter, to the Australian colonies, or Canada, where Connell's family were sent. Such removals were usually executed surreptitiously for obvious reasons, but when discovered or suspected caused deep annoyance to the authorities in these jurisdictions.

Captain Massy was unhappy with Rev. George Fitzmaurice's role in the Scrahan affair, and he informed his superiors in Dublin Castle after the nocturnal house attacks on 25 November 1881 that Fitzmaurice's arms licence should be revoked. It transpired that Fitzmaurice, as Bartholomew Dillane's employer, had provided him with the firearm that was taken during the raid on the latter's home. Massy had previously refused a licence for the gun, on the grounds that an armed Dillane would be a potential target for individuals or subversive organisations intent on acquiring weapons. Fitzmaurice ignored the magistrate's action, which prompted Massy's call for the revocation of the clergyman's licence. In the magistrate's estimation Fitzmaurice had shown himself 'unworthy of being entrusted with arms'. Fitzmaurice applied for a licence to carry a revolver following the trial and conviction of the Scrahan seven, which suggests that he feared for his safety following the verdict. Massy again objected, reiterating his call for the cancellation of Fitzmaurice's arms licence, a stance reinforced by the appearance of Fitzmaurice's caretaker, Dillane, as a witness for the defence at the Scrahan trial. The magistrate believed that Dillane had perjured himself – he was 'not entitled to credit on oath' – a view substantiated by the jury's verdict.[21] The discrepancy between Dillane's and Bridget Lennane's testimony in court, his sworn statement that the intruders were strangers and hers that some of them were their neighbours, suggests that he had connived in the attack on his own home, if indeed there had been any such incident. His actions reflected poorly on his employer, whose own behaviour appears to have been less than exemplary, though in keeping with Fitzmaurice's character and his contemptuous disregard of public opinion.

Massy was more favourably disposed to another of the actors in the Scrahan drama, the Listowel lodging-housekeeper who accommodated Lennane and her family prior to the assizes, thereby risking communal ire and endangering both himself and his business. The individual concerned was a publican and army pensioner, and Massy recommended that the crown should provide him with 'a special secret reward of £20' in recognition of his 'loyalty and courage' and the 'public odium' he had incurred. The issue of the reward was referred to Alexander Morphy, crown solicitor for Kerry, to the solicitor general, and the under-secretary at Dublin Castle. The latter decided that £20 was 'extremely large' and that £10 would be a more appropriate reward. Massy demurred, claiming that the 'courageous services' of the individual concerned deserved the larger amount, but deferred, under protest, to the under-secretary's higher authority.[22]

The crown, despite its curmudgeonly response to the innkeeper's defiance of popular opinion, had secured the desired judicial result – the conviction and lengthy imprisonment of the seven accused, which the authorities hoped would act as a deterrent to similar Moonlighting activity. Justice Fitzgerald acknowledged at the conclusion of the Munster winter assizes some weeks later that he had imposed 'some very serious sentences', specifically in the Scrahan case, and in that of the Twohig brothers whom we encountered in the previous chapter. Fitzgerald added that the government would be willing to reconsider these verdicts once peace and respect for the law had been restored, and he expressed his willingness to be involved in the review process.[23] The judge's statement reflected his reservations and uncertainty regarding the Moonlight cases tried at the assizes, and suggests that the sentences were in some way conditional, which must have offered a degree of hope to the prisoners, their families and friends.

Doubts about the safety of the Scrahan convictions surfaced immediately, prompted in part by Fitzgerald's comments. An editorial in the *Cork Examiner* on the morning after he delivered his verdict drew attention to the severity of the sentences, while acknowledging that they were not excessive given the nature of the offences for which they were imposed. The writer claimed that the injuries inflicted on 'the wretched woman' and her daughter constituted 'a hideous piece of brutality', but, he added, there was a strong possibility that some, if not all, of the accused had been wrongly convicted. One of the defendants – Nolan – had been particularly vehement in protesting his innocence, which prompted the editorial writer to suggest that the testimony on which he was convicted was such as 'to make a revision of the sentence by the authorities desirable'. The implication was clear – the crown's anxiety to make an example of the accused had resulted in a miscarriage of justice.[24]

The reservations about the Scrahan verdict and sentencing revolved around the nature and reliability of the evidence on which the convictions were secured. Six of the defendants were convicted solely on Bridget Lennane's evidence, and each received a lengthy custodial sentence with hard labour. As we saw in the previous chapter, it was unusual for the Irish judiciary to convict on such testimony, and Justice

John David Fitzgerald shared in the general disquiet, as his subsequent equivocation demonstrated. There was a tendency to differentiate between Patrick Cronin's case and those of the other defendants. The various officials involved with the trial were convinced of Cronin's guilt, which was reflected and measured in the severity of his sentence – ten years' penal servitude. He was convicted on Lennane's witness testimony, supported by that of her son and niece. Justice Fitzgerald, Captain Thomas Plunkett, special resident magistrate (later divisional magistrate), Alexander Morphy, crown solicitor, and the RIC believed that Cronin had discharged the gun that wounded Lennane and her daughter, and they were unanimous that there should be no leniency in his case.

The defence argued that the testimony of the morally suspect Lennane was tainted and unreliable, as was that of her illegitimate son and her niece by association. Additionally, the defence claimed that some of the accused were victims of mistaken identity, their alibis supported by members of their families, whose unblemished character contrasted with Lennane's. The alibis offered by the defendants were in turn ridiculed by the prosecution, a tactic that was also a feature of the other Moonlight cases tried at the 1881 Munster winter assizes, and which raises questions about the probity of such witnesses and the reliability of their evidence.

## The prisoners, their families, and the appeals process[25]

Bartholomew Nolan differed from the other Scrahan prisoners in several respects, being older, less educated, and married with eight dependent children. He was aged forty-four on conviction, the others, who were single, ranged in age from seventeen to twenty-three: one was twenty, another twenty-one, and two were twenty-two. They were educated to the extent that they could read and write, while Nolan was illiterate. The seven prisoners had one feature in common, their Roman Catholic religion. Patrick Cronin's and Maurice Molony's prison records describe them as farmers, suggesting that they were destined to inherit their respective family holdings. Nolan was a labourer who worked for the Cronin family; the other four were also recorded as labourers, though they might equally have been categorised as farmers' sons, younger siblings without a claim on the family farm. The health of all seven was recorded as good on their committal to Mountjoy jail in late December 1881, but each was to endure health problems while incarcerated, and each would be transferred for a period to Spike Island prison in Cork Harbour, either to prevent incipient illness or to recuperate. They were hospitalised for varying conditions and periods while serving their sentences. Patrick Cronin, the most severely penalised of the Scrahan seven, spent time in hospital on Spike Island and while in Mountjoy jail for various conditions – pleurodynia, bronchitis, pleuritis, and dyspepsia – and was treated for a range of minor ailments throughout his imprisonment.[26]

The lord lieutenant of Ireland or viceroy, and he alone, had the right to exercise the royal prerogative in Ireland, and it was customary for prisoners convicted of Whiteboy offences and their families to petition him for clemency. Once an appeal was received at Dublin Castle, the under-secretary normally consulted the prison governor and the prison doctor regarding the prisoner's behaviour and health while in custody. He also sought the views of the local police and magistracy on the peace or otherwise of the district in which the crime had been committed. Justice Fitzgerald, who presided over the 1881 Munster winter assizes, was consulted in relation to memorials submitted on behalf of individuals convicted at the assizes, including the Scrahan seven, and he was informed of any developments in their appeals. In the official documentation, they were referred to as 'Lord Fitzgerald's cases', Fitzgerald having been appointed a lord of appeal with a life peerage in June 1882, some months after the conclusion of the Munster assizes.[27] The responses of various officials to prisoners' petitions, which were mediated through the under-secretary, influenced, and often determined, the lord lieutenant's decision to grant or reject a clemency appeal.

Bartholomew Nolan's conviction was the weakest link in the Scrahan case, reflected in the trial judge's avowed sympathy with his family circumstances, and the reservations expressed editorially in at least one newspaper. Catherine Nolan petitioned the lord lieutenant on her husband's behalf on 22 December 1881, a week after the conclusion of the case, and based her appeal on the judge's comments at the termination of the trial. Rev. George Fitzmaurice and his older brother, Maurice, Duagh House, Listowel, were among those who supported her petition. Justice Fitzgerald's response to the appeal was that the gravity of Nolan's offence warranted a severe custodial sentence, one that would serve as a deterrent to others, but the prisoner's mitigating family circumstances prompted him to propose that the verdict be reconsidered after Nolan had served one year of his sentence, and that Catherine Nolan be informed of this decision.[28] The lord lieutenant duly reviewed Nolan's case and those of the other Scrahan prisoners with the exception of Cronin after each had been in prison for a year, but refused to remit any of their sentences, resorting to the standard refrain in all such rejections: 'Let the law take its course.'

The Scrahan prisoners and their families worked the system adroitly and assiduously over the following years, lodging appeal after rejected appeal, and recruiting influential members of the community – nationalist MPs, Catholic clergymen, landowners, Poor Law guardians, magistrates and county grand jurors – to lend moral weight and authority to their clemency pleas to the lord lieutenant. The appellants and their families were clearly in receipt of legal advice and guidance, and were well coached in the appeals process, though the agency and funding of the assistance afforded is unclear. The appeals themselves – and there were many stretching over a period of years – took the form of formulaic petitions or memorials, and featured several recurring themes, notably the law-abiding and peaceful state of the Duagh district where the offence occurred, which the Scrahan families and their supporters insisted would not be threatened by the prisoners' early release from jail. Other tropes included:

- family circumstances and difficulties, leavened with a dollop of late Victorian sentimentality;

- Bridget Lennane's uncorroborated evidence, which was compromised by her moral impropriety;

- the prisoners' alibis and (in contrast to Lennane) the moral rectitude of those who supported them on oath, usually the victims' families and friends;

- the prisoners' physical and/or mental health problems;
- mistaken identity (in Patrick Cronin's case), resulting in a miscarriage of justice.

Two of the prisoners secured early release on health grounds, eighteen-year-old Daniel Galvin in May 1883, and Bartholomew Nolan two years later. An emaciated Galvin was seriously ill with liver disease and died from his condition less than two years after his discharge.[29] Nolan was released in early June 1885, having spent the previous sixteen months in Maryborough (Portlaoise) invalid prison in Queen's County (Laois), where his mental and physical health had deteriorated. His discharge had tragic consequences. Within a month he killed his wife, Catherine, who had campaigned tirelessly for his freedom, by cutting her throat. At the coroner's inquest on 9 July 1885 the jury concluded that Catherine Nolan's death was caused by injuries inflicted by her husband who was insane at the time, and in a rider reprimanded the authorities for discharging a mentally ill person from prison. In the House of Commons, the chief secretary for Ireland denied that Nolan was released because he was mentally or physically unfit, which provoked scepticism among politicians, the press and the public, as Nolan had clearly been delusional for some time.[30]

Under Irish prison regulations, Cornelius McAuliffe, Maurice Molony, Michael Galvin and James Quinlan were each entitled to one year's remission in their sentence, provided they did not violate prison rules during their incarceration. Accordingly, all four were eligible for release on licence by early December 1885. Six months later, in response to a parliamentary question on their continued detention, the chief secretary, John Morley, explained that the crown exercised its statutory powers to delay releasing convicts on licence before the expiration of their sentence if it had 'special reasons' for doing so, which, in the Scrahan case, was the disturbed state of Duagh district. However, he thought the time had come when he could recommend the four prisoners' conditional release to the lord lieutenant, and they were discharged in early June 1886.[31] Patrick Cronin, who had been sentenced to ten years' penal servitude, was now the only imprisoned member of the original

Scrahan seven. His resourceful parents, Johana and James, mounted a sustained campaign for his release, which involved variously the princess of Wales, the parish priest of Duagh, the justice of the peace and the grand jurors of north Kerry, nationalist MPs, and questions in the House of Commons. Cronin was finally released on licence on 5 August 1889, having served almost eight years of his controversial ten-year sentence, and he returned to his parents' holding in north Kerry, his health severely compromised by his long incarceration.[32]

## The crown apparatus

The different agencies involved in securing convictions against the Scrahan seven and other perpetrators of outrages were propelled by the need to combat the activities of agrarian secret societies – whether they were designated Moonlighters, Whiteboys, Ribbonmen or other – and to restore peace to disturbed districts. The methods employed to realise these aims did not always fall within the parameters of the ordinary law, and, as we have seen, concerns about the integrity and safety of the Scrahan convictions were reflected in the trial judge's comments when he was passing sentence on the seven accused. The only certainty in the judge's mind was Patrick Cronin's guilt – he had fired the shot that wounded Bridget Lennane and her daughter – and that he fully deserved his sentence of ten years' imprisonment with hard labour. This was an inordinately harsh penalty, one that had a double purpose: to punish the perpetrator of violence, Patrick Cronin, and to discourage other individuals – enrolled or potential Moonlighters – from engaging in similar activities.

Justice Fitzgerald, who was then in his mid-sixties, was an experienced law officer and trial judge, having served as a justice of the Court of Queen's Bench in Ireland since February 1860, prior to which he was Liberal MP for Ennis, solicitor general for Ireland during Lord Palmerston's first ministry, and attorney general for Ireland for two terms. Within six months of the conclusion of the Scrahan trial he was appointed a lord of appeal and elevated to the House of Lords.[33] Despite his partiality during the trial, the conviction of six of the seven accused on uncorroborated witness testimony bothered him, suggesting that he was cleft between the needs of the crown and the integrity of the law. There were several factors that were problematic in Nolan's case, including his age and family circumstances. He was an atypical Moonlighter – activists were mostly single men in their late teens or early to mid-twenties; Nolan was twice the average age, married with eight children and supporting an aged mother on an agricultural labourer's wage. He was employed in that capacity by Patrick Cronin's family and possibly felt pressurised into engaging in Moonlighting activities. After the trial, Bridget Lennane informed Alexander Morphy, crown solicitor, that Nolan 'was virtually helpless', as he would have lost his employment if he chose to disobey Patrick Cronin's orders to join the Moonlighters.[34] Lennane's suggestion appears at odds with the evidence she gave at the Scrahan trial, wherein she identified Nolan as the 'officer' commanding the Moonlight party that attacked her home,[35] a discrepancy that raises further questions about the reliability of her evidence and the security of the convictions that rested on it alone. Nolan, who was illiterate, and who may have had latent mental health issues, was an unlikely leader of men. Ultimately, he was convicted on Bridget Lennane's sworn testimony that he was a participant in the violation of her home, but during his trial he denied vehemently that he was present on the occasion, offering to 'confess' – to swear – to that effect before God and Justice Fitzgerald.[36]

Fitzgerald's unease over Nolan's conviction prompted him within weeks of the trial's conclusion to suggest to the Dublin Castle authorities that the prisoner might be released on licence after he had served one year of his sentence, and Fitzgerald subsequently proposed a similar arrangement for the other Scrahan prisoners, Cronin excepted.[37] In July 1883, two months after Daniel Galvin's discharge from prison on health grounds, the lord lieutenant, Earl Spencer, met Fitzgerald in London to discuss the cases of fourteen prisoners whom the latter had convicted of Whiteboy offences at the 1881 Munster winter assizes.[38] Following that consultation the lord lieutenant decided to amend some of the sentences but to leave unaltered those of the seven Scrahan prisoners.[39] Fitzgerald's continuing disquiet about their convictions was captured in a private memorandum he compiled on Christmas Day 1883, in which he reaffirmed Cronin's guilt – he 'fired the shot which wounded the child' – but for the first time conceded that there were mitigating circumstances, most significantly the unpremeditated nature of Cronin's action. Fitzgerald noted that the Moonlighters' apparent objective was to frighten Lennane into leaving the neighbourhood, not intentionally to shoot her, but the disturbed state of the country at the time obliged him to impose punitive sentences as an example and a warning to others. The key issue, and the cause of his unease, was the lack of corroborative evidence in establishing the identity of the perpetrators. All but one of the Scrahan prisoners had been arrested, charged and convicted solely on Lennane's sworn information, a situation Fitzgerald regarded as unsatisfactory. He concluded his Christmas Day reappraisal – his conscience clearly bothered – by proposing that five of the Scrahan prisoners, having served two years of their five-year jail term, should be released on licence, and that a similar concession be made in Cronin's case on 5 December 1886, after he had completed half of his ten-year sentence.[40]

The authorities disregarded Fitzgerald's recommendations, but the submission of a clemency appeal by Cornelius McAuliffe in early February 1884 prompted another review of the prisoners' cases. Alexander Morphy, crown solicitor, stated that comparatively little agrarian crime occurred at any time in the Duagh district, and, as far as he was aware, there had been no reported incident since the original outrage in late November 1881. He claimed that the speed with which the legal process was executed on that occasion – arrest, trial, conviction and sentence – had 'a remarkable effect' on the district. Morphy stated that Cronin 'was the organiser' and he suggested that a distinction be made between Cronin and the others, but he was convinced that the return of any of the prisoners to their homeplace would not have a negative impact on 'its peaceable condition'. Captain Plunkett, divisional magistrate, concurred with Morphy's assessment of the satisfactory state of the district in the early months of 1884, attributing it partly to the crown's resolute response to the Scrahan outrage, but he argued that any concession to the prisoners would be counterproductive: 'It would be very detrimental to the interests of the district if they were again let loose on society before their sentences expire.'[41]

The lord lieutenant rejected McAuliffe's appeal but ordered another review of the Scrahan case files in August 1884. On that occasion, Plunkett, 'having regard to the present condition of the country', signalled his strong opposition to any remission in the prisoners' sentences.[42] Their cases were further considered on 1 February and again on 1 April 1885, but the redoubtable Plunkett was as uncompromising as ever: 'The state of this district is still unsettled and far from satisfactory.'[43] In November 1885 the General Prisons Board reported to the Dublin Castle authorities that McAuliffe, Galvin, Molony and Quinlan were eligible for parole under normal prison regulations and recommended their release on licence. Plunkett's response was a terse one-liner: 'The state of this district is worse than when my last report was made.'[44]

Divisional Magistrate Plunkett's intervention was once again decisive and the lord lieutenant refused to release the four prisoners, though they were successful when their case was next reviewed in June 1886. Each received a gratuity on release and payment of their fares to their hometown. McAuliffe chose to remain in Dublin. Two months later he informed the General Prisons Board of his desire to emigrate to the United States and requested the board to provide the passage money, or in default recommend him to the Prisoners' Aid Society. He justified his request by claiming: 'Were it not for being detained in prison seven months longer than ordinary prisoners of same sentence I need not solicit this aid.'[45] McAuliffe's stance indicated an awareness among those convicted of Moonlighting offences that they were more harshly punished than common criminals, that there was a political dimension to their prison treatment.[46] They were the casualties of the Irish authorities' deployment of the convict prison system as an instrument in the campaign against agrarian anarchy and terrorism.

Captain Thomas Plunkett was the authoritarian rock on which a succession of clemency appeals foundered. The Spike Island prison doctor, trial judge Fitzgerald and crown solicitor Morphy were prepared to make concessions to the Scrahan prisoners, even in Cronin's case eventually, and the relevant lord lieutenant might have given his imprimatur had he been so advised. Plunkett, however, was adamant that none of the Scrahan sentences should be commuted. As divisional magistrate he was charged with restoring and maintaining law and order in the south-west of the country, and he was unwavering in his stance that the Scrahan prisoners serve their full term as an example and a caution to others, thereby discouraging any return to the social anarchy of the early 1880s. Plunkett prolonged the prison ordeal of six of the seven Scrahan prisoners, the exception being the youthful Daniel Galvin who received an early discharge because of his poor health, the gravity of which was reflected in his death within two years of his release. Plunkett's intransigence was largely responsible for a succession of viceroys resorting to the formulaic response to prisoners' clemency appeals: 'Let the law take its course.'

## George Fitzmaurice, *The Moonlighter*

The Scrahan outrage and subsequent trial featured many of the elements of nineteenth-century melodrama, and occasionally farce: the victims – a defenceless mother and her children; the shooting of her youngest child, and her own (superficial) injury; the powder-flask and whiskey bottle imitation of secret society oath-taking; the dog that barked in the night; identity misdirection and questionable alibis; and, above all, the bravura performance of the leading actor, the unconventional Bridget Lennane, who discharged her role with consummate artistry and skill.

George Fitzmaurice captured many of these features and tensions, not least the centrality of identity and alibis, in his early twentieth-century drama *The Moonlighter*:

> ... A man is as safe in the moonlighters as out of them. And if the choice fell on a man to do a bad deed itself, 'tisn't him might be hung at all but someone as free of the crime as Jesus Christ himself, if he hadn't his alibi correct or was about the vicinity. The peelers don't care a devil but to make a case; the judge don't give a whack but to choke you for an example, and a jury of Cork Scotchmen would swing the nation on circumstantial evidence.[47]

Fitzmaurice was only a child at the time of the Scrahan outrage, but the involvement of his father and at least two of his uncles in the subsequent court case and its aftermath may have become part of family history and storytelling. The future playwright lived in the locality throughout the 1880s, the period of the Scrahan seven's imprisonment and their families' attempts to secure their release, supported variously by nationalist MPs, Catholic clergy and respectable and responsible members of the local community. It is inconceivable that the young George Fitzmaurice was unaware of the affair, filtered as it must have been through a process of family and social osmosis.

*The Moonlighter*, a four-act tragedy set in Kerry and Fitzmaurice's longest work, was first performed by the Earlsfort Players at the Peacock Theatre, Dublin in September 1948, more than three decades after its publication, and rarely thereafter. Internal evidence sets the play in 1888–9, the time of the Plan of Campaign agrarian agitation when Kerry and other parts of the country were again seriously disturbed. The drama revolves around a band of Moonlighters led by Morgan Synan, their twenty-five-year-old captain. The two central characters are Eugene Guerin and his friend and fellow activist Tom Driscoll. Eugene's father, Peter, was a Fenian at the time of the 1867 rebellion but subsequently renounced the cause and was strongly opposed to Eugene's Moonlighting activities. Eugene is a strawman, vainglorious, full of bluster and bombast, and, as the play reveals on more than one occasion, essentially a coward – a 'gammy Moonlighter' in the estimation of two of his fellow conspirators. He may have projected himself as 'a national man', devoted passionately to the cause of Dark Rosaleen, and his mother may have perceived him as 'mad with nationality', but Eugene's patriotic sentiment was of the vocal rather than active variety. Tom Driscoll is Eugene's antithesis, an accidental Moonlighter, sworn into the conspiracy one night after taking 'a share of porter', but one who was courageous and steadfast to the end.

The first three acts take place over a two-day period, during which the Moonlighters prepare for and execute an arms raid on the local 'Great House', which results in several deaths. A year passes between these sanguinary events and the play's resolution in the fourth act, wherein the differences in character, personality and nationalist sentiment of the leading players, not least those distinguishing Tom Driscoll and Eugene Guerin, are exposed.

Eviction is one of the play's tropes, and the drama begins with one, that of the Widow Casey of Carlevoye, which was witnessed by Eugene, Tom and many others who were drawn to the scene by the blowing of horns, the standard signal for assembly and social protest in nineteenth-century rural Ireland. Eugene, who was one of the horn-blowers, exclaimed: 'It's a grand day's work for Ireland this horn is after doing, and it calling to her children from far and near to do battle against those devils from hell, the police and bailiffs.' A band of musicians – another regular feature of evictions – attended and played the nationalist anthem 'God Save Ireland' as they marched home, Eugene and Tom singing along:

> ... God save Ireland, cried the heroes,
> God save Ireland, cried they all,
> And whether upon the scaffold high,
> Or in the battlefield we die –
> Sure no matter when for Erin dear we fall.[48]

Eugene was subsequently sworn into the Moonlight conspiracy – as 'a soldier in the army of the night' – symbolically kissing a bauble held by Captain Synan, a parody of swearing on and kissing the bible. While some of the Moonlighters were engaged in Eugene's initiation ceremony Synan reminded Tom and others of their cause, their Moonlighting purpose and intent:

> Grand is our work surely, but small the glory that has ever come to us since we first rose up under another name a long while ago. But 'tisn't glory is troubling us, for there's a fierce thing makes us go out battling in the night – a fierce thing since the first of us rose up out of the ground that is scorched with the salt tears of the generations and with the tears of blood of the generations, and the churchyards full of the helpless innocent that were wronged and murdered by tyrants.[49]

Synan was passionately committed to 'the Cause', half-mad with hatred, which was starkly demonstrated in his casual disclosure that he had committed three murders. He had, additionally, raided for weapons –

a key feature of Moonlight, or secret society, activity during the later nineteenth century – spiked meadows, posted threatening notices, and endured imprisonment for intimidating landlords, 'emergency men' employed by landlords to execute evictions, and land grabbers. Synan made these potentially damning admissions to demonstrate the sincerity of his nationalist beliefs and commitment, and to refute any suggestion of ulterior motives for his Moonlight activism. He did acknowledge, however, that while the raid on the Great House was primarily for arms, he had 'a little private affair' of his own to settle, to avenge himself on Sylvester Cook, the recently returned scion of the Great House, for the 'long ago' seduction of Synan's sister Mage, whom Cook begot with child – 'the bye-child' – and his sister's subsequent suicide by drowning.[50]

The play reveals tensions, dissensions and personal agendas at work among the Moonlighters: one arrived drunk at their gathering, not for the first time, and was reprimanded by Synan; another felt slighted that the captain had chosen Tom and Eugene to assist him in the raid on the Great House over more seasoned recruits; a third, Morisheen Lucy, was preoccupied with the declared intention of a land grabber named Pringle to acquire possession of the Lucy family's evicted holding on the following day, and he wished to draw lots to determine which of the Moonlighters should confront and punish the offender.

Big William Cantillon, Eugene's maternal uncle, was another who lusted after the Lucys' farm: 'I was fit to eat my fill of that lovely earth and that lovely grass', he rhapsodised as he sought the purchase price from his brother Malachi, a money lender – 'the genius of a gombeen man', as he described himself – and Big William expressed his determination to thwart Pringle's ambition and to acquire the evicted property for himself.[51] Morisheen Lucy's denunciation of Cantillon as 'that hound of hell' captured and expressed the popular attitude to land grabbers, who were perceived as usurpers, violators of the moral rights of others, and he outlined graphically the punishment he would inflict on Cantillon – and, by extension, that which grabbers generally could expect:

If I could only have these fingers around the grabber's throat, around his throat choking him, murdering him! Ah, wouldn't it be the handsome sight to see his face swelling red and blue, and the big eyeballs lepping out of the sockets! May Jesus send him in my way till I'll batter the dirty life out of him on the stones, to be screeching with joy and I dancing a jig on his dirty bloody corpse![52]

Lucy despatched Cantillon eventually with a knife rather than by strangulation or battery, but he may yet have screeched with joy and danced a jig on his bloodied remains.

The fourth act reveals the outcome of the raid on the Great House: the deaths of Synan and a fellow Moonlighter, and that of Sylvester Cook at the hand of Tom Driscoll. The latter was subsequently betrayed by Michaeleen Cosdee, one of his erstwhile Moonlight associates, which obliged him to flee from the police and 'the law that has no mercy'. Eugene was another who fled but returned a year later to the family home and holding, determined to live a quiet, low-key and politically inactive farmer's life. In the play's denouement, and in contrast to Eugene's self-exculpation and supine acceptance of the political and social status quo, Tom Driscoll and Peter Guerin – Moonlighter and Fenian man, representatives of different generations of political activism – fell to the peelers' guns for 'Erin dear'. The closing scene bestows a sanction or legitimacy on their actions, which may have chimed with the rising nationalist sentiment of the years in which the play was conceived and executed. Even Malachi Cantillon, the selfish and usurious gombeen man, was forced to acknowledge: 'It's now I know, and maybe I knew it a long time, that all who rose up and fought for Ireland, howsoever they rose up and fought for Ireland, were the great-hearted and the kind.' Breda Carmody, once Tom's betrothed, added her lamentation:

He is gone now, and I'm too late to tell him my heart throbbed only for him ... Ah, what signifies it now what anyone did or didn't, since he is dead? But it is for him and the like of him that the flowers smile, and always smiled, in the green soil of Ireland. But he is dead.[53]

# Epilogue

Farmers' and agricultural labourers' sons, young men in their late teens or early to mid-twenties, with limited education, skills and expectations were the heartbeat of agrarian secret societies. They joined for a variety of reasons:

- idealism – a genuine commitment to Irish freedom and social justice;

- boredom and frustration arising from rural restrictions and limited employment opportunities and prospects;

- fraternity, sociability, adventure and excitement – possibly lubricated by alcohol, which appears to have been a pervasive presence and influence.

Captain Synan embodied some of this motivational complexity, this compound of idealism and personal reasons: he was genuinely devoted to the Irish cause and raiding the Great House for arms to liberate the country was part of that process, but he was also driven by a consuming passion to avenge his sister's defilement and subsequent suicide.

Members of agrarian secret societies bound themselves under oath to protect, protest and punish, to safeguard and enforce communal aspirations and solidarity, and to sanction those who threatened their aims and ambitions. The features of these societies included initiation ceremonies, primarily swearing an oath of fealty; disguises, which were often elaborate and imaginative; military exercises and formation; nocturnal activity – 'the army of the night' – which intensified fear and encouraged compliance; house raids; weapons theft; punishment beatings; and the ubiquitous and reviled informer or approver, represented by Michaeleen Cosdee in *The Moonlighter*.

Fitzmaurice's drama portrays many of the features and attitudes of late nineteenth-century Irish rural life, and it offers an accurate representation of agrarian secret societies and their activities. Mercenary landlords and their retinues, including the emergency men whom they employed to execute and enforce evictions, were frequently ostracised or boycotted by nationalist society and targeted by Moonlighters and other social enforcement agencies. Landlords and many of their supporting cast attracted attention also as possessors of wealth and weapons, and arms raids were a key feature of Moonlight activity during the later nineteenth century, the period in which the play is set.

Big William Cantillon and his brother Malachi, land grabber and gombeen man respectively, represent the unsavoury side of Irish rural society. Such individuals preyed and prospered on the misfortunes of others, one by opportunistic acquisition of evicted holdings, the other by usurious money lending, and such exploiters were equally feared and reviled. Land grabbers, or simply grabbers, took over farms and property from which others had been evicted, generally for non-payment of rent, and eviction, which was a powerful inciting and recruiting force for late nineteenth-century Irish nationalism, is another of the play's themes. Although the Widow Casey's eviction occurs backstage rather than in the foreground, its trappings and the choreography of ejectment proceedings generally are well portrayed, including the presence of a protesting crowd, assembled by the blowing of horns; the attendance of a marching band; and the playing and singing of T.D. Sullivan's rousing anthem 'God Save Ireland'. The various strands of such protests had the same associative purpose – to secure 'the land of Ireland for the people of Ireland' and, ultimately, to achieve the country's political independence.

# NOTES

## Introduction

1. For an assessment of the work that remains to be done on the Irish Land War see Fergus Campbell, 'The Unreaped Harvest', in Fergus Campbell and Tony Varley (eds), *Land Questions in Modern Ireland* (Manchester: Manchester University Press, 2013), pp. xxvi–viii. For an assured and polished overview of Irish land and its issues in the late nineteenth and early twentieth centuries see Terence Dooley, 'Irish Land Questions, 1879-1923', in Thomas Bartlett (ed.), *The Cambridge History of Ireland. Volume IV: 1880 to the present* (Cambridge: Cambridge University Press, 2018), pp. 117-44.

2. The 1879-80 famine has attracted scholarly attention, albeit limited and selective, and there remains the need for a comprehensive analysis. See Gerard Moran, 'Famine and the Land War: Relief and distress in Mayo, 1879-1881', *Cathair na Mart: Journal of the Westport Historical Society*, vol. 5, no. 1, 1985, pp. 54-66; vol. 6, no. 1, 1986, pp. 111-27; idem, '"Near Famine": The crisis in the west of Ireland, 1879-82', *Irish Studies Review*, vol. 5, no. 18, Spring 1997, pp. 14-21; idem, '"Near Famine": The Roman Catholic Church and the subsistence crisis of 1879-82', *Studia Hibernica*, vol. 32, 2002-3, pp. 155-77; Norman Dunbar Palmer, *The Irish Land League Crisis* (New Haven: Yale University Press, 1940), pp. 67-105; Merle Curti, *American Philanthropy Abroad* (New Brunswick, NJ: Rutgers University Press, 1963), pp. 81-98. For a selection of documentary source material see Christine Kinealy and Gerard Moran (eds), *The History of the Irish Famine: 'Fallen leaves of humanity'. Famine in Ireland before and after the Great Famine* (Abingdon, Oxon: Routledge, 2018), part 8, 'The "Forgotten Famine", 1879-81'; see also *The Irish Crisis of 1879-80. Proceedings of the Dublin Mansion House Relief Committee, 1880* (Dublin: Browne & Nolan, 1881). For the voluminous correspondence and other records relating to this committee's appeal see 'Mansion House Fund for the Relief of Distress in Ireland 1880', Dublin City Library & Archive, 138-44 Pearse Street, Dublin 2.

3. For a survey of the historiography see Maura Cronin, *Agrarian Protest in Ireland, 1750-1960*, Studies in Irish Economic and Social History, vol. 11 (Dundalk, 2012).

4. See, for example, Michael Davitt, *The Fall of Feudalism in Ireland or the Story of the Land League Revolution* (London and New York: Harper & Brothers, 1904); John E. Pomfret, *The Struggle for Land in Ireland, 1800-1923* (Princeton: Princeton University Press, 1930); Palmer, *The Irish Land League Crisis*.

5. Gearóid Ó Tuathaigh, 'Irish Land Questions in the State of the Union', in Campbell and Varley (eds), *Land Questions in Modern Ireland*, pp. 3-24, at p. 10. The author argues for the plural, land questions, rather than the singular, claiming: 'There never was a single "Irish land question", but a dense matrix of interlocking issues and questions relating to the story of land in Ireland', p. 16.

6. There is an extensive historiography on the causes of the Irish Land War and the forces that shaped it. See, inter alia, Paul Bew, *Land and the National Question in Ireland, 1858–82* (Dublin: Gill & Macmillan, 1978); Samuel Clark, *Social Origins of the Irish Land War* (Princeton, NJ: Princeton University Press, 1979); idem, 'Strange Bedfellows? The Land League alliances', in Campbell and Varley (eds), *Land Questions in Modern Ireland*, pp. 87–116; Samuel Clark and James S. Donnelly, Jr (eds), *Irish Peasants: Violence and political unrest, 1780–1914* (Manchester: Manchester University Press, 1983); R.V. Comerford, 'The Land War and the Politics of Distress, 1877–82', in W.E. Vaughan (ed.), *A New History of Ireland. Volume 6: Ireland Under the Union, II: 1870–1921* (Oxford: Clarendon Press, 1996), pp. 26–52; L.P. Curtis, Jr, 'On Class and Class Conflict in the Land War', *Irish Economic and Social History*, vol. 8, 1981, pp. 86–94; James S. Donnelly, Jr, *The Land and the People of Nineteenth-century Cork: The rural economy and the land question* (London and Boston: Routledge & Kegan Paul, 1975); David Fitzpatrick, 'Class, Family and Rural Unrest in Nineteenth-century Ireland', in P.J. Drudy (ed.), *Irish Studies, 2. Ireland: Land, politics and people* (Cambridge: Cambridge University Press, 1982), pp. 37–75; Donald E. Jordan, Jr, *Land and Popular Politics in Ireland: County Mayo from the plantation to the Land War* (Cambridge: Cambridge University Press, 1982); T.W. Moody, *Davitt and Irish Revolution, 1846–82* (Oxford: Oxford University Press, 1994); Barbara L. Solow, *The Land Question and the Irish Economy, 1870–1903* (Cambridge, MA: Harvard University Press, 1971); W.E. Vaughan, *Landlords and Tenants in Mid-Victorian Ireland* (Oxford: Clarendon Press, 1994). For Parnell see particularly F.S.L. Lyons, *Charles Stewart Parnell* (London: Collins, 1977); Paul Bew, *Enigma: A new life of Charles Stewart Parnell* (Dublin: Gill & Macmillan, 2011).

7. Clark, *Social Origins of the Irish Land War*, pp. 225–32; Moody, *Davitt and Irish Revolution*, pp. 328–34; Vaughan, *Landlords and Tenants in Mid-Victorian Ireland*, pp. 208–16.

8. Bew, *Land and the National Question in Ireland*, p. 5. Ó Tuathaigh's and Dooley's more recent assessments chime with Bew's: Ó Tuathaigh, 'Irish Land Questions in the State of the Union', in Campbell and Varley (eds), *Land Questions in Modern Ireland*, pp. 3–24; Dooley, 'Irish Land Questions, 1879–1923', in Bartlett (ed.), *The Cambridge History of Ireland*, vol. IV, p. 123.

9. See n. 6 above.

10. See particularly, though not exclusively, Donnacha Seán Lucey, *Land, Popular Politics and Agrarian Violence in Ireland: The case of County Kerry, 1872–86* (Dublin: UCD Press, 2011); Breandán Mac Suibhne, *The End of Outrage: Post-Famine adjustment in rural Ireland* (Oxford: Oxford University Press, 2017); Margaret Kelleher, *The Maamtrasna Murders: Language, life and death in nineteenth-century Ireland* (Dublin: UCD Press, 2018); Kyle Hughes and Donald M. MacRaild (eds), *Crime, Violence and the Irish in the Nineteenth Century* (Liverpool: Liverpool University Press, 2017); Kyle Hughes and Donald M. MacRaild, *Ribbon Societies in Nineteenth-century Ireland and Its Diaspora: The persistence of tradition* (Liverpool: Liverpool University Press, 2018).

11. Kelleher, *The Maamtrasna Murders*; Mac Suibhne, *The End of Outrage*.

12. Kelleher, *The Maamtrasna Murders*, p. 20.


## Chapter 1: 'Little Short of Death by Slow Starvation'

1. *Standard* (London), cited in *The Irish Crisis of 1879–80. Proceedings of the Dublin Mansion House Relief Committee, 1880* (Dublin: Browne & Nolan, 1881), p. 49.

2. Paul Bew, 'A Vision to the Dispossessed? Popular piety and revolutionary politics in the Irish Land War, 1879-82', in Judith Devlin and Ronan Fanning (eds), *Religion and Rebellion: Papers read before the 22nd Irish conference of historians, held at University College Dublin, 18–22 May 1995 (Historical studies XX)* (Dublin: UCD Press, 1997), pp. 137-51, at p. 137; Sheridan Gilley, *Tablet*, 18 September 1979, 'The Background to Knock'.

3. E. Margaret Crawford, 'Indian Meal and Pellagra in Nineteenth-century Ireland', in J.M. Goldstrom and L.A. Clarkson (eds), *Irish Population, Economy, and Society: Essays in honour of the late K.H. Connell* (Oxford: Clarendon Press, 1981), pp. 113-33, at p. 131, n. 38.

4. James S. Donnelly, Jr, 'The Marian Shrine of Knock: The first decade', *Éire-Ireland*, vol. 28, no. 2, 1993, pp. 54-99, at p. 57.

5. Eugene Hynes, *Knock: The Virgin's apparition in nineteenth-century Ireland* (Cork: Cork University Press, 2008), pp. 137-9.

6. Christine Kinealy and Gerard Moran (eds), *The History of the Irish Famine:* 'Fallen leaves of humanity'. *Famine in Ireland before and after the Great Famine* (Abingdon, Oxon: Routledge, 2018), pp. 1, 16-17, 195-6.

7. Annual Report of the Local Government Board for Ireland, Being the Eighth Report Under 'The Local Government Board (Ireland) Act', 35 & 36 Vic., c. 69, HC 1880 [c. 2603, c. 2603-1], xxviii. 1, 39, p. 7.

8. Ibid., pp. 7-11, Appendix A, 111.1, pp. 53-5, Report from the Local Government Board to His Grace the Lord Lieutenant, 28 October 1879; Correspondence Relative to Measures for the Relief of Distress in Ireland, 1879-1880, HC 1880 [c. 2483, c. 2506], lxii. 157, 187, pp. 159-60, 166; Agricultural Statistics of Ireland, 1885, HC 1886 [c. 4802], lxxi. 1, p. 12, table viii.

9. Annual Report of the Local Government Board for Ireland, Being the Eighth Report Under 'The Local Government Board (Ireland) Act', 35 & 36 Vic., c. 69, pp. 70-2.

10. Ibid., pp. 105-6.

11. Ibid., p. 83.

12. Ibid., pp. 77, 103, 108, 121.

13. Ibid., pp. 118-19, 130, 134-5. Robinson did note the enterprise displayed by the peasantry; the seaweed that was no longer saleable for kelp was disposed of for manure along the Galway and Clare coastal belt and as far inland as Athlone, p. 135.

14. Ibid., p. 63.

15. Ibid., pp. 84-5.

16. Ibid., pp. 7-11, Appendix A, 111.i, pp. 53-5, Report from the Local Government Board to His Grace the Lord Lieutenant, 28 October 1879; Correspondence Relative to Measures for the Relief of Distress in Ireland, 1879-1880, HC 1880 [c. 2483, c. 2506], lxii, 157, 187, pp. 159-60, 166; Agricultural Statistics of Ireland, 1885, HC 1886 [c. 4802], lxxi. 1, p. 12, table viii.

17. The Irish Crisis of 1879-80, pp. 178-80, Bishop Laurence Gillooly to the Mansion House relief committee, 8 January 1880.

18. Ibid., pp. 15, 34-43, 222-94.

19. Ibid., p. 39.

20. Ibid., p. 35; Sally Warwick-Haller, William O'Brien and the Irish Land War (Dublin: Irish Academic Press, 1990), pp. 40-2. O'Brien had similarly investigated conditions on Nathaniel Buckley's Galtee Mountain property in the winter of 1877-8 for the Freeman's Journal. [William O'Brien], Christmas on the Galtees: An inquiry into the conditions of the tenantry of Mr Nathaniel Buckley, by the special correspondent of the Freeman's Journal (Dublin: The Central Tenants' Defence Association, 1878); Warwick-Haller, William O'Brien, pp. 29-34.

21. Standard (London), 26 January 1880, cited in The Irish Crisis of 1879-80, pp. 36, 49.

22. James Redpath, Talks about Ireland (New York: P.J. Kenedy, 1881), pp. 29-30.

23. Anne Hardy, 'Relapsing Fever', and Victoria A. Harden, 'Typhus, Epidemic', in Kenneth F. Kiple (ed.), The Cambridge World History of Human Disease (Cambridge: Cambridge University Press, 1993), pp. 967-70, 1080-4; William P. MacArthur, 'Medical History of the Famine', in R. Dudley Edwards and T. Desmond Williams (eds), The Great Famine: Studies in Irish history, 1845-52 (Dublin: Browne & Nolan, 1956), pp. 265-8; John D. Post, Food Shortage, Climatic Variability, and Epidemic Disease in Pre-Industrial Europe: The mortality peak in the early 1740s (Ithaca and London: Cornell University Press, 1985), pp. 26-7, 228-33, 270-4.

24. Cork Examiner, 1 November 1879; West Cork Eagle and County Advertiser, 1, 8, 22 November 1879; The Irish Crisis of 1879-80, pp. 123, 237.

25. National Archives of Ireland (Hereafter NAI), CSORP/1880/7872; CSORP/1880/7869.

26. NAI, CSORP/1880/7620.

27. The Irish Crisis of 1879-80, pp. 234-5.

28. Ibid., pp. 60, 123–4.

29. Ibid., pp. 257–8, Michael J. Doherty, Charlestown relief committee, County Mayo to the Dublin Mansion House relief committee, 18 June 1880. See also *Connaught Telegraph*, 'Outbreak of Famine Fever', 26 June 1880, p. 5. According to the report, the onset of fever had provoked 'great alarm' throughout the Charlestown district.

30. *Freeman's Journal*, 28, 29 June 1880. See also ibid., 9 July 1880.

31. Ibid., 29 June 1880.

32. Ibid., 28, 29 June 1880.

33. Ibid., 19 July 1880. This type of social reaction to the presence of communicable diseases like 'fever' and cholera, ascribable generally to pre-scientific medical ignorance, fear of the unknown, and empirical awareness of the potentially devastating consequences of disease epidemics, had long been a feature of Irish society. For some context, see Laurence M. Geary, *Medicine and Charity in Ireland, 1715–1851* (Dublin: UCD Press, 2004), Chapter 4, 'Fever Hospitals' and Chapter 8, 'Medical Relief During the Great Famine'.

34. *Freeman's Journal*, 6 July 1880, F.J. McCormack, bishop of Achonry, Ballaghadereen, to T.W. Croke, archbishop of Cashel, 5 July 1880.

35. *The Irish Crisis of 1879–80*, p. 234.

36. Ibid., pp. 247–8. See also comments by the chairman of the Moylough relief committee in County Galway, ibid., p. 248.

37. See, for instance, a series of articles by William O'Brien which appeared in the *Freeman's Journal* in January and early February 1880, variously entitled 'The Distress in the West', and 'Famine in the West', Warwick-Haller, *William O'Brien*, pp. 40–2. See also, inter alia, *Standard* (London), 14, 20, 26 January 1880; *Daily Telegraph*, 6, 12 January 1880; Michael de Nie, *The Eternal Paddy: Irish identity and the British press, 1798–1882* (Madison, WI: The University of Wisconsin Press, 2004), p. 204.

38. *The Irish Crisis of 1879–80*, pp. 189–94.

39. *Distress in Ireland: Extracts from correspondence published by the Central Relief Committee of the Society of Friends, no. 1* (Dublin, 1847), pp. 35–40, at p. 40.

40. Annual Report of the Local Government Board for Ireland, Being the Eighth Report Under 'The Local Government Board (Ireland) Act', 35 & 36 Vic., c. 69, p. 13; 43 Vic., c. 4, 'An Act to Render Valid Certain Proceedings Taken for the Relief of Distress in Ireland, and to Make Further Provision for Such Relief; and for Other Purposes', 15 March 1880.

41. Virginia Crossman, '"With the Experience of 1846 and 1847 Before Them": The politics of emergency relief, 1879–84', in Peter Gray (ed.), *Victoria's Ireland? Irishness and Britishness, 1837–1901* (Dublin: Four Courts Press, 2004), pp. 167–81, at p. 171.

42. Ibid., p. 175; Virginia Crossman, *Politics, Pauperism and Power in Late Nineteenth-century Ireland* (Manchester and New York: Manchester University Press, 2006), pp. 109-16, at p. 110; idem, 'Writing for Relief in Late Nineteenth-century Dublin: Personal applications to the Mansion House Fund in 1880', *Cultural and Social History*, vol. 14, no. 5, 2017, pp. 583-98, at p. 585; Mel Cousins, *Poor Relief in Ireland, 1851-1914* (Oxford: Peter Lang, 2011), pp. 114-16; Donnacha Seán Lucey, 'Power, Politics and Poor Relief During the Irish Land War, 1879-82', *Irish Historical Studies*, vol. 37, November 2011, pp. 584-98, at pp. 592-3.

43. *The Times*, 18 December 1879, duchess of Marlborough to the editor, 16 December 1879; R.F. Foster, 'To the Northern Counties Station: Lord Randolph Churchill and the prelude to the orange card', in F.S.L. Lyons and R.A.J. Hawkins (eds), *Ireland Under the Union: Varieties of tension. Essays in honour of T.W. Moody* (Oxford: Clarendon Press, 1980), pp. 237-87, at pp. 248-50; Norman Dunbar Palmer, *The Irish Land League Crisis* (New Haven: Yale University Press, 1940), pp. 84-90.

44. R.V. Comerford, 'The Land War and the Politics of Distress, 1877-82', in W.E. Vaughan (ed.), *A New History of Ireland. Vol. 6: Ireland Under the Union, II: 1870-1921* (Oxford: Clarendon Press, 1996), pp. 26-52, at p. 37. Two weeks after the duchess of Marlborough launched her appeal a west of Ireland Catholic clergyman affirmed her humanitarianism in one of Ireland's leading nationalist publications, asserting that her hand and purse were 'always open to works of charity and benevolence', *Nation*, 10 January 1880, p. 11, Rev. Patrick Grealy, Carna, Recess, County Galway, to the editor, 29 December 1879.

45. *The Irish Crisis of 1879-80*, p. 337.

46. *Freeman's Journal*, 26 December 1879, 3 January 1880; *The Irish Crisis of 1879-80*, pp. 13-15, 177-8.

47. Annual Report of the Local Government Board for Ireland, Being the Ninth Report Under 'The Local Government Board (Ireland) Act', 35 & 36 Vic., c. 69, HC 1881 [c. 2926, c. 2926-1], xlvii. 269, 305, p. 8.

48. *Freeman's Journal*, 6 July 1880.

49. C.J. Nixon, 'The Epidemic of Fever in Swineford [sic] Union (County Mayo)', *Lancet*, 14 August 1880, pp. 256-8.

50. Annual Report of the Local Government Board for Ireland, Being the Ninth Report Under 'The Local Government Board (Ireland) Act', 35 & 36 Vic., c. 69, Appendix A, p. 41.

51. These domestic realities were captured in a newspaper depiction of west of Ireland cabins as 'crooked, battered, semi-roofless outside, wretched to the last degree and comfortless within', *Freeman's Journal*, 10 July 1880.

52. Local Government Board (Ireland). Further reports, dated respectively 9 and 15 July 1880, made to the Local Government Board in Ireland by Dr C.J. Nixon, temporary

medical inspector, relative to an outbreak of fever in the Swineford [sic] union, County Mayo, HC 1880 (277) (277-1), lxii. 271, p. 275; *The Irish Crisis of 1879-80*, p. 153.

53. Nixon, 'The Epidemic of Fever in Swineford [sic] Union', pp. 256-8. See, also, Annual Report of the Local Government Board for Ireland, Being the Ninth Report Under 'The Local Government Board (Ireland) Act', 35 & 36 Vic., c. 69, Appendix A, pp. 31-8.

54. Nixon, 'The Epidemic of Fever in Swineford [sic] Union', pp. 256-8.

55. Laurence M. Geary, 'A Psychological and Sociological Analysis of the Great Famine in Ireland', in Robert Dare (ed.), *Food, Power and Community* (Adelaide: Wakefield Press, 1999), p. 183.

56. Nixon, 'The Epidemic of Fever in Swineford [sic] Union', pp. 256-8.

57. *Lancet*, 14 August 1880, p. 267.

58. James McGeachie, 'Science, Politics and the Irish Literary Revival: Reassessing "Dr Sigerson" as polymath and public intellectual', in Catherine Cox and Maria Luddy (eds), *Cultures of Care in Irish Medical History, 1750-1970* (London: Palgrave Macmillan, 2010), pp. 113-40; David Murphy, 'Kenny, Joseph Edward', in James McGuire and James Quinn (eds), *Dictionary of Irish Biography* (Cambridge: Cambridge University Press, 2009), https://www.dib.ie/biography/kenny-joseph-edward-a4503

59. This was certainly the stance taken by conservative newspapers such as *The Irish Times*. See, for instance, the report by its special correspondent on 10 July 1880: 'Neglect, dirt and misery seem the three features of the place [Charlestown district], and where they exist it is not difficult even without the intensifying influence of distress to imagine concomitant disease ... In this locality it seems as if an experiment had been tried to ascertain how long a non-observance of the rules of health might be practised with impunity.'

60. The Mansion House relief committee reported regularly to the government on fever outbreaks. See, for instance, NAI, CSORP/1880/16157, V.B. Dillon, honorary secretary, Mansion House relief committee, to W.E. Forster, 30 June 1880, on the appearance of fever in Loughrea, Manorhamilton and Carrick-on-Shannon Poor Law unions and in Kilbaha and Carrigaholt districts in County Clare; NAI, CSORP/1880/16693, Dillon to Forster, 7 July 1880. Dillon forwarded a letter from Canon McDermott, PP, Kilmovee, County Mayo, stating that Kilmovee was one of the largest parishes in the county, that 1,300 of the 1,400 families in the parish required relief and that 'fever induced by privation had broken out in some parts'. See also NAI, CSORP/1880/17543, Dillon to Forster, 21 July 1880, on resolutions passed by the Mansion House relief committee following the submission of Sigerson and Kenny's report.

61. *The Irish Crisis of 1879-80*, pp. 132-6.

62. Ibid., p. 143.

63. Ibid., p. 145.

64. Ibid., p. 149.

65. Ibid., pp. 155-7.

66. Ibid., pp. 151-2.

67. Ibid., pp. 152-4.

68. Ibid., pp. 61-4, 129-31, 161, 163-4.

69. Ibid., pp. 164-6. Dr Stewart Woodhouse, who was appointed by the LGB to investigate almost 200 cases of fever in the parishes of Kilglass and Castleconnor, County Sligo, over an eight-month period from the beginning of November 1879, arrived at a similar conclusion. He claimed that most of the cases were typhoid or simple fever, with five of typhus and none of relapsing fever, and that the people's diet during the period of the inquiry had been a powerful predisposing cause. In almost all the fever cases, the staple food was Indian meal stirabout, which about one-half of the individuals concerned were obliged to consume without milk, whereas in previous years the peasantry would have lived on 'potatoes, bakers' bread, home-made bread, vegetables, tea and occasionally a little bacon', Annual Report of the Local Government Board for Ireland, Being the Ninth Report Under 'The Local Government Board (Ireland) Act', 35 & 36 Vic., c. 69, Appendix A, pp. 27-31, at p. 31. The *Freeman's Journal*, 17 July 1880, claimed editorially that Nixon's and Woodhouse's reports to the LGB conveyed political and social truths. The writer stated that 'the most frightful calamities' had been averted solely by the efforts of the different relief committees, that it behoved the government to intervene directly to address the fever epidemic that still threatened the west of Ireland, and that statements in the House of Commons that the prevailing distress was imaginary were shown to be 'cruel, false and wicked in the last degree'.

70. *The Irish Crisis of 1879-80*, pp. 166-7.

71. Annual Report of the Local Government Board for Ireland, Being the Eighth Report Under 'The Local Government Board (Ireland) Act', 35 & 36 Vic., c. 69, p. 27; *The Irish Crisis of 1879-80*, pp. 168-70.

72. Joseph Robins, *The Miasma: Epidemic and panic in nineteenth-century Ireland* (Dublin: Institute of Public Administration, 1995), pp. 70-1.

73. Annual Report of the Local Government Board for Ireland, Being the Eighth Report Under 'The Local Government Board (Ireland) Act', 35 & 36 Vic., c. 69, p. 27. The board claimed that the practice of waking the dead helped to spread infection.

74. *The Irish Crisis of 1879-80*, pp. 168-70.

75. Ibid., pp. 171-4.

76. *Medical Press and Circular*, 4 August 1880, pp. 96-7, 'The Fever in the West of Ireland'.

77. *The Irish Crisis of 1879–80*, pp. 66–7, 199–203, 213–14.

78. Ibid., pp. 210–11.

79. Ibid., pp. 71–2.

## Chapter 2: The Australasian Response to the 1879–80 Famine in Ireland

1. *Freeman's Journal* (Dublin), 6 May 1880, p. 5.

2. *Freeman's Journal* (Sydney), 3 January 1880, editorial, pp. 12–13. John McEncroe, a Tipperary-born, Maynooth-educated priest, established the paper in June 1850, Malcolm Campbell, *Ireland's New Worlds: Immigrants, politics, and society in the United States and Australia, 1815–1922* (Madison, WI: The University of Wisconsin Press, 2008), p. 57.

3. *South Australian Register*, 27 December 1879, supplement, p. 3.

4. *Express and Telegraph* (Adelaide), 9 December 1879, p. 3, Clare to the editor. Her letter was also published, through a proxy, in the American press, *New York Herald*, 16 December 1879, p. 4, Lady Blanche Murphy, North Conway, NH, to the editor, 10 December 1879. Clare reissued her appeal, with minor changes, in the Australian Catholic press early in the following month, *Advocate* (Melbourne), 3 January 1880; *Freeman's Journal* (Sydney), 10 January 1880.

5. Maria Luddy, Introduction, *The Nun of Kenmare: An autobiography* (London: Routledge/Thoemmes Press, 1998), pp. v–xiv; Margaret Mac Curtain, 'Cusack, Margaret Anne [name in religion Mary Francis Clare; called the Nun of Kenmare] (1829–1899), founder of the Sisters of St Joseph of Peace and writer', *Oxford Dictionary of National Biography* (Oxford: Oxford University Press, 2004), https://www.oxforddnb.com/view/10.1093/ref:odnb/9780198614128.001.0001/odnb-9780198614128-e-45792

6. *Express and Telegraph*, 9 December 1879, p. 2. Sister Mary Francis Clare's letter and the *Express and Telegraph*'s editorial encomium were reproduced in the weekly *South Australian Chronicle and Weekly Mail*, 13 December 1879, pp. 4, 13.

7. *Express and Telegraph*, 15 December 1879, p. 3, Montgomery to the editor, 13 December 1879.

8. *South Australian Register*, 27 December 1879, supplement, p. 3. See also *South Australian Advertiser*, 27 December 1879, p. 13, and *The Irish Crisis of 1879–80. Proceedings of the Dublin Mansion House Relief Committee, 1880* (Dublin: Browne & Nolan, 1881), p. 332.

9. *Brisbane Courier*, 25, 27, 31 December 1879, 1 January 1880. See Laurence M. Geary, 'Sir Arthur Kennedy, Australian Colonial Governor, and the Great Famine in Ireland', in Tadhg Foley and Fiona Bateman (eds), *Irish-Australian Studies: Papers delivered at the ninth Irish-Australian conference* (Sydney: Crossings Press, 2000), pp. 78–92.

10. *Advocate*, 15 May 1880, p. 16; *Sydney Morning Herald*, 6 January 1880, p. 6.

11. *South Australian Register*, 15 January 1880, p. 4.

12. For exhortatory editorials see, for instance, *Newcastle Morning Herald and Miner's Advocate*, 2 January 1880; *Maitland Mercury*, 10, 15 January 1880; *Age* (Melbourne), 3 January 1880; *Bendigo Advertiser*, 9 January 1880; *Ballarat Courier*, 6 January 1880; *Ararat and Pleasant Creek Advertiser*, 13 January 1880; *Tasmanian Mail*, 10 January 1880; *South Australian Register*, 15 January 1880; *Brisbane Courier*, 7 January 1880; for cartoons see *Melbourne Punch*, 15 January 1880; *Australian Sketcher*, 14 February 1880; for verse see Anon., 'Help for Ireland', *Melbourne Punch*, 15 January 1880; J. Brunton Stephens, 'The Famine in Ireland', *Brisbane Courier*, 28 January 1880; T.W., 'The Irish Famine', *Bulletin*, 13 March 1880; J.E.H., 'A Lament for Ireland', *Gippsland Times*, 23 January 1880.

13. *Melbourne Punch*, 15 January 1880, p. 5, 'Help for Ireland', http://nla.gov.au/nla.news-article174556052; *Advocate*, 17 January 1880, p. 9, '"Punch" on Irish Distress'.

14. *Sydney Morning Herald*, 2, 7, 9, 14 January 1880.

15. *Freeman's Journal* (Sydney), 10 January 1880, p. 13.

16. See, for instance, *Argus* (Melbourne), 29 January 1880, p. 5.

17. See, for instance, *South Australian Register*, 15 January, 2 March, 11 October 1880; *Maitland Mercury*, 15 January 1880; *Advocate*, 21 February 1880.

18. *Brisbane Courier*, 8 January 1880, p. 3; *Age*, 10 January 1880, p. 6; *Sydney Morning Herald*, 13 January 1880, p. 7.

19. *Age*, 10 January 1880; *Advocate*, 17 January 1880; *Australian Dictionary of Biography* (Canberra: National Centre of Biography, Australian National University), *passim*.

20. *Melbourne Punch*, 15 January 1880, p. 6, 'One Good at Any Rate'.

21. *The Irish Crisis of 1879–80*, p. 333. For Montgomery and his role in the South Australian relief effort, see Stephanie James, 'Distress in Ireland 1879–80: The activation of the South Australian community', in Philip Payton and Andrekos Varnava (eds), *Australia, Migration and Empire: Immigrants in a globalised world* (Basingstoke: Palgrave Macmillan, 2019), pp. 119–50.

22. *Brisbane Courier*, 8 January 1880; *The Irish Crisis of 1879–80*, p. 332.

23. *Tasmanian Mail*, 31 January 1880.

24. *Ballarat Courier*, 15 January 1880.

25. *Sydney Morning Herald*, 13 January 1880.

26. *Age*, 10 January 1880.

27. *Ararat and Pleasant Creek Advertiser*, 13 January 1880.

28. *Tasmanian Mail*, 10 January 1880.

29. *South Australian Register*, 10 January 1880.

30. See, for instance, *South Australian Register*, 10 January 1880; *Express and Telegraph*, 9 December 1879, p. 2.

31. *Maitland Mercury*, 17 January 1880.

32. *South Australian Register*, 27 December 1879, supplement, p. 3; *South Australian Advertiser*, 27 December 1879, p. 13.

33. *Gippsland Times*, 14 January 1880; *Maitland Mercury*, 17 January 1880; *Bendigo Advertiser*, 9 January 1880; *Border Post*, 4 February 1880; *Brisbane Courier*, 8 January 1880; *Sydney Morning Herald*, 13 January 1880.

34. *Brisbane Courier*, 8 January 1880.

35. Father English, Maitland, NSW, who claimed that corn was dumped in the sea while 3 million perished, was an exception, *Maitland Mercury*, 17 January 1880, p. 6.

36. *Age*, 17 January 1880, p. 7.

37. *Sydney Morning Herald*, 13 January 1880, p. 7.

38. *Echo* (Sydney), 15 January 1880.

39. *Freeman's Journal* (Sydney), 7 February 1880, p. 13. See also *Mercury*, 23 February 1880; *Age*, 27 January 1880; *Bendigo Advertiser*, 9 January 1880; *Warwick Argus*, 20 January 1880; *Kyneton Guardian*, 14 January 1880.

40. *Mercury*, 27 January, 23 February 1880.

41. *Advocate*, 10 January 1880, p. 14.

42. Ibid. See also *Kyneton Guardian*, 14 January 1880, editorial, and 28 January 1880, Martin McKenna, JP, to the editor; *Gippsland Times*, 14 January 1880.

43. See, for instance, *Sydney Morning Herald*, 13 January 1880 (William Bede Dalley and Sir John Hay); *Mercury*, 27 January 1880 (Sir Frederick A. Weld).

44. *Melbourne Punch*, 15 January 1880.

45. *Warwick Argus*, 24 January 1880, 'Australis' to the editor.

46. *Kyneton Guardian*, 24 January 1880, 'Cerberus' to the editor.

47. *Bendigo Advertiser*, 28 January 1880 (Rev. E.A. Thomas).

48. See, for instance, *Age*, 9 January 1880.

49. *Jewish Herald*, 9 January 1880.

50. *Advocate*, 17 January 1880, p. 10, 'The Distress in Ireland'.

51. *Freeman's Journal* (Sydney), 21 February 1880, p. 18. 'If we have sown spiritual good among you, is it too much if we reap your material benefits?' (1 Corinthians 9:11).

52. *Advocate*, 3 January 1880; *Freeman's Journal* (Sydney), 10 January 1880.

53. *Advocate*, 3 January 1880.

54. Ibid., 10 January 1880.

55. *Sydney Morning Herald*, 20 January 1880.

56. *The Irish Crisis of 1879–80*, p. 333.

57. *Advocate*, 31 January 1880; *South Australian Advertiser*, 24 January 1880; *South Australian Register*, 16 January 1880; *Age*, 27 January 1880.

58. *South Australian Advertiser*, 24 January 1880.

59. *Mercury*, 13, 16 February 1880.

60. *Sydney Morning Herald*, 28 January 1880.

61. Ibid., also 13 February 1880.

62. *South Australian Register*, 31 January 1880.

63. *Mercury*, 14 February 1880.

64. *Brisbane Courier*, 16 January 1880.

65. Ibid., 15, 16 January 1880.

66. *Bendigo Advertiser*, 21, 23, 24 February 1880.

67. *The Irish Crisis of 1879–80*, p. 83. On 31 December 1879 Victoria's estimated population was 841,757; New South Wales, 708,666; Queensland, 205,220; South Australia, 265,055; Tasmania, 112,506; Western Australia, 29,139: C.M.H. Clark (ed.), *Select Documents in Australian History, 1851–1900* (Sydney: Angus & Robertson, 1955), pp. 664–5.

68. Donald Harman Akenson, *Half the World from Home: Perspectives on the Irish in New Zealand 1860–1950* (Wellington: Victoria University Press, 1990), p. 63.

69. *The Irish Crisis of 1879–80*, pp. 339–40.

70. *Grey River Argus*, 24 January 1880.

71. *The Irish Crisis of 1879–80*, p. 338. See also *New Zealand Tablet*, 6 February 1880, p. 16.

72. *New Zealand Tablet*, 23 January 1880, pp. 17–18.

73. *The Irish Crisis of 1879–80*, p. 344.

74. Ibid., pp. 338–40, 343.

75. Ibid., pp. 339–40. See also *New Zealand Tablet*, 19 March 1880, p. 16.

76. *The Irish Crisis of 1879–80*, p. 338.

77. Caroline Gray, Dublin's lady mayoress, was possessed of 'great personal beauty and singularly fascinating manners', according to the Irish correspondent of the *New Zealand Tablet*, 20 February 1880. For her mother, Caroline Chisholm, see Judith Iltis, 'Chisholm, Caroline (1808–1877)', *Australian Dictionary of Biography*, http://adb.anu.edu.au/biography/chisholm-caroline-1894/text2231

78. *The Irish Crisis of 1879–80*, pp. 336–7.

79. *Freeman's Journal* (Dublin), 28 January 1880, p. 4.

80. Ibid., 14 May 1880, p. 2. For Smyth see D.J. O'Donoghue and Brigitte Anton, 'Smyth, Patrick James (c. 1823–1885), Politician and Journalist', *Oxford Dictionary of National Biography* (Oxford: Oxford University Press, 2004), https://www.oxforddnb.com/view/10.1093/ref:odnb/9780198614128.001.0001/odnb-9780198614128-e-25956

81. *The Irish Crisis of 1879–80*, pp. 24–7.

82. *Goulburn Herald*, 21 January 1880.

## Chapter 3: North America

1. See, for instance, *South Australian Register*, 10 January 1880, p. 5.

2. *The Irish Crisis of 1879–80. Proceedings of the Dublin Mansion House Relief Committee, 1880* (Dublin: Browne & Nolan, 1881), p. 337.

3. T.W. Moody, *Davitt and Irish Revolution 1846–82* (Oxford: Oxford University Press, 1981), pp. 355–8; F.S.L. Lyons, *Charles Stewart Parnell* (London: Collins, 1977), pp. 106–15; idem, *John Dillon: A biography* (Chicago: Chicago University Press, 1968), pp. 34–6.

4. R.F. Foster, *Charles Stewart Parnell: The man and his family* (Hassocks, Sussex: Harvester Press, 1976, 1979); Norman Dunbar Palmer, *The Irish Land League Crisis* (New Haven: Yale University Press, 1940), pp. 83–105; Merle Curti, *American Philanthropy Abroad* (New Brunswick, NJ: Rutgers University Press, 1963), pp. 81–98; Ely M. Janis, *A Greater Ireland: The Land League and transatlantic nationalism in Gilded Age America* (Madison: University of Wisconsin Press, 2015), pp. 17–49.

5. Janis, *A Greater Ireland*, pp. 34–6, 41–2.

6. *Cork Examiner*, 22 December 1879, p. 3.

7. *Weekly Irish Times*, 10 January 1880, p. 5; Michael Davitt, *The Fall of Feudalism in Ireland or the Story of the Land League Revolution* (London and New York: Harper & Brothers, 1904), p. 193. Davitt's chapter on the American mission (pp. 193–210) is informed by Parnell's rough diary of the trip.

8. Paul Bew, *Land and the National Question in Ireland, 1858–82* (Dublin: Gill & Macmillan, 1978), pp. 75–7. McCloskey's view is captured succinctly in 'Mr Parnell and

Cardinal McCloskey', *Weekly Irish Times*, 31 January 1880, p. 3. For a similar perspective, and an extremely negative American appraisal of Parnell's mission generally, see *New York Journal of Commerce*, reproduced in the *Weekly Irish Times*, 31 January 1880, p. 5. Another New York journal announced that 'Ireland can get money, all she wants, for her hungry people, but active political sympathy is out of the question. The people of the United States will never hold up the flag of the Fenian revolution. They leave each nation to make its own history', *New York Zeitung*, 12 February 1880, cited in the *Weekly Irish Times*, 23 February 1880, p. 5. See also Janis, *A Greater Ireland*, pp. 41–6, 'Criticism of Parnell in the United States'; Curti, *American Philanthropy Abroad*, pp. 86–8.

9. For Nast see L. Perry Curtis, Jr, *Apes and Angels: The Irishman in Victorian caricature* (Newton Abbot: David & Charles, 1971), pp. 58–9.

10. *New York Herald*, 17 December 1879, p. 6. See also editorials on 3, 5, 9, 23 December.

11. Davitt, *The Fall of Feudalism in Ireland*, pp. 193–4; Janis, *A Greater Ireland*, pp. 31–2; *Weekly Irish Times*, 24 January 1880, p. 5. Parnell appeared to distinguish Irish Americans from other American residents, and to have different expectations of each constituency. In an interview with a *New York Tribune* correspondent, he stated that Irish Americans were expected to support the land movement financially, whereas the only onus on Americans was to contribute towards the relief of distress in Ireland, *Weekly Irish Times*, 24 January 1880, p. 5.

12. *Weekly Irish Times*, 24 January 1880, p. 5; Janis, *A Greater Ireland*, pp. 31–2; Donal McCartney, 'Parnell and the American Connection', in Donal McCartney and Pauric Travers, *The Ivy Leaf: The Parnells remembered* (Dublin: UCD Press, 2006), pp. 50–3.

13. *Weekly Irish Times*, 24 January 1880, p. 5; Janis, *A Greater Ireland*, pp. 34–5.

14. *Weekly Irish Times*, 17 January 1880, p. 5; Davitt, *The Fall of Feudalism in Ireland*, p. 194; Bew, *Land and the National Question in Ireland*, pp. 77–8.

15. Janis, *A Greater Ireland*, pp. 32, 46–7. In the late 1870s Anna, Fanny and Theodosia Parnell lived with their American-born mother, Delia Tudor Stewart Parnell, in the Stewarts' family home at Bordentown, New Jersey, which Delia had inherited. At the conclusion of Parnell's fund-raising mission in March 1880, all except Fanny returned with him to Europe, he to contest a general election, Theodosia to wed Claude Paget, an English naval officer, in Paris some months later, her mother and sister (and Charles) to attend her nuptials, Foster, *Charles Stewart Parnell*, pp. 217–18, 225–6; McCartney, 'Parnell's Women', in McCartney and Travers, *The Ivy Leaf*, pp. 72–3; T.M. Healy, *Letters and Leaders of My Day*, 2 vols (London: Thornton Butterworth, 1928), vol. I, p. 87.

16. Fanny Parnell stated, as an indication of Dillon's disorganised nature, that he 'left his slippers in one hotel, and his night-shirt in another', Healy, *Letters and Leaders of My Day*, vol. I, p. 81.

17. Ibid., p. 87. See also Foster, *Charles Stewart Parnell*, pp. 244–5.

18. *New York Herald*, 3 December 1879, p. 6. These strictures attracted favourable editorial comment and support from the London *Times*, 5 December 1879, and from elements of the conservative and religious press in Ireland. The *Irish Ecclesiastical Gazette*, organ of the recently disestablished Church of Ireland, whose sympathies were avowedly conservative and landed, offered an equally partisan perspective on what it termed Ireland's 'recurring famine scares', positing that 'a chronic agitation which keeps capital out of the country, improvidence, superficial and dirty tillage, drinking habits, and a strange unwillingness to relieve the excess of population through the natural outlet of emigration have much more to say to our miseries than an inclement sky or an unkind soil', 31 February 1880, pp. 156–7. The *Irish Ecclesiastical Gazette* was written and read by lay and clerical members of the Church of Ireland. Its editor from 1871–93 was the Rev. James Anderson Carr, vicar of Whitechurch in the diocese of Dublin.

19. *New York Herald*, 5 December 1879, p. 5, Anna Parnell, Trenton, NJ, to the editor, 3 December 1879; reproduced in *New Zealand Tablet*, 19 March 1880, p. 17.

20. Ibid., Fanny Parnell, Bordentown, NJ, to the editor, 3 December 1879. A short time previously, Fanny had dismissed as 'an impudent falsehood and libel' an editorial claim in a New York newspaper that her brother Charles condoned the murder of Irish landlords, *New York Tribune*, 22 November 1879, p. 4, 'The Irish Agitation'; 24 November 1879, p. 5, 'A Sisterly Defence', F. Parnell, New York City, to the editor, 22 November 1879; Jane McL. Coté, *Fanny and Anna Parnell: Ireland's patriot sisters* (Houndmills: Macmillan, 1991), pp. 108–9.

21. *Pilot*, 6 September 1879, pp. 4, 6, Irishwoman [Fanny Parnell] to the editor, 25 August 1879; *Nation*, 20 September 1879, p. 12; Ely M. Janis, 'Petticoat Revolutionaries: Gender, ethnic nationalism, and the Irish Ladies' Land League in the United States', *Journal of American Ethnic History*, vol. 27, no. 2, 2008, pp. 5–27, at p. 9.

22. *Weekly Irish Times*, 7 February 1880, p. 6.

23. Ibid.; *Irish Canadian*, 11 February 1880, p. 5: Peter O'Leary, Toronto, to the editor, 9 February 1880.

24. *New York Herald*, 28 January 1880, p. 7, 'The Nun's Petition', Clare to Fanny Parnell, 4 January 1880; 'An Appeal from Kerry', Fanny Parnell, New York Hotel, to the editor, 23 January 1880.

25. Healy, *Letters and Leaders of My Day*, vol. I, pp. 79–87; C.S. Parnell, 'The Irish Land Question', *North American Review*, vol. CXXX, no. 1, April 1880, pp. 388–406. According to Healy, Parnell did not write a word of this article, it was entirely Fanny's handiwork, *Letters and Leaders of My Day*, vol. I, p. 87. Healy's biographer speculates that during his time in America Healy may have harboured 'an unrequited passion' for Fanny Parnell, who was six years his senior. Frank Callanan, *T.M. Healy* (Cork: Cork University Press, 1996), 'With Parnell in America', pp. 32–8, at p. 36.

26. Fanny Parnell, *The Hovels of Ireland* (New York: Thomas Kelly, 1880), pp. i–iii, 3, 55–6, 61–2, 65; McL. Coté, *Fanny and Anna Parnell*, pp. 111–15. Fanny Parnell's pamphlet was promoted in the *Pilot*, 31 January 1880, p. 8, the *Irish World*, and the *Irish Canadian*, 18 February 1880, p. 5. There was a short notice in the following week's *Irish Canadian*, p. 5, in which Fanny Parnell was not referred to by name, but as 'a sister of Mr Charles Stewart Parnell', and as 'the fair author': 'Her book is thoughtful, well written, clever. It breathes with Christian sympathy on Irish patriotism.' The pamphlet was mentioned in the editorial columns of *Ave Maria*, a Catholic weekly magazine published at Notre Dame, Indiana, vol. 16, 28 February 1880, pp. 176–7. On 4 March 1880, Portland's *Catholic Sentinel* commended Fanny Parnell's pamphlet for upholding 'the cause of Ireland's rights against landlord oppression', observing that her arguments were both 'truthful and convincing', p. 1. For a consideration of Fanny Parnell's political opinions see Foster, *Charles Stewart Parnell*, pp. 246–50.

27. Lyons, *Parnell*, p. 107.

28. Davitt, *The Fall of Feudalism in Ireland*, pp. 193–4.

29. See, for example, *Weekly Irish Times*, 7 February 1880, p. 6, in which Parnell described the members of the Mansion House relief committee as 'flunkeys, Castle-hacks, and men belonging to the narrowest landlord interest'. See also *New York Herald*, 29 January 1880, p. 4, Parnell, Rochester, NY, 27 January 1880, to the editor, in which he claimed that American money sent to the Mansion House committee 'will be indirectly used for political purposes in bolstering up an expiring and tyrannical land system, and that all aid from it [Mansion House committee] will be refused to those of the starving peasantry who have actively participated in the present agrarian movement'; and Parnell at Richmond, Virginia, 6 February 1880, *New York Herald*, 7 February 1880, p. 5.

30. *Freeman's Journal*, 25 February 1880, p. 4, editorial; *Nation*, 28 February 1880, p. 4.

31. See Davitt, *The Fall of Feudalism in Ireland*, p. 217.

32. Lyons, *Parnell*, pp. 93–5.

33. *Freeman's Journal*, 25 February 1880, p. 4.

34. *New York Tribune*, 5 February 1880, p. 4, editorial, 'The Collapse of Mr Parnell'.

35. *Irish Ecclesiastical Gazette*, 31 January 1880, p. 94, and issues for 17, 24 January 1880, pp. 51, 73, and for 28 February 1880, p. 178, P.D., 'A New Ingredient in Ireland's Cup of Woe', a partial, splenetic reaction to Parnell's address to the US House of Representatives, an event that will be considered below. See also *Tablet*, 28 February 1880, pp. 259–60 for an English Catholic perspective on Parnell's vilification of the rival relief committees.

36. *Nation*, 28 February 1880, p. 8.

37. *New York Herald*, 7 February 1880, p. 5, Anna Parnell, New York, to the editor, 4 February 1880.

38. *Catholic Sentinel*, 1 July 1880, p. 5, Redpath, New York, to the editor, 21 June 1880. The communication appeared under the heading: 'The Famine in Ireland. Scathing reply to the lord mayor's appeal, by James Redpath. Appalling facts and figures for reflecting contributors in America.' There is a copy in the John Devoy Papers, National Library of Ireland, Ms 18011/2. Elsewhere, in an equally powerful philippic, Redpath denounced Irish landlords and the British government as the 'infidel Saracens of the nineteenth century', James Redpath, *Talks about Ireland* (New York: P.J. Kenedy, 1881), p. 23. Such sentiments explain the inclusion of Redpath's portrait, alongside those of Michael Davitt, T.D. Sullivan, A.J. Kettle, Thomas Brennan, and Patrick Egan, in *The Land League Song Book*, which an enterprising Dublin publisher brought out in mid-1881, *Nation*, 11 June 1881, p. 4.

39. Dublin Diocesan Archives (DDA), Papers of Edward McCabe, 1880, 346/4/111, Relief of Distress, Gray to McCabe, 30 January 1880.

40. *Freeman's Journal*, 4 February 1880, p. 6. See also *Tablet*, 7 February 1880, pp. 161-2, 'The Irish Bishops and the Mansion House Committee'.

41. *Freeman's Journal*, 4 February 1880, p. 4.

42. *Pilot*, early January 1880, reproduced in *New Zealand Tablet*, 20 February 1880, p. 19.

43. *Weekly Irish Times*, 7 February 1880, p. 6.

44. Ibid., 31 January 1880, p. 5; 14 February 1880, p. 6.

45. Ibid., 17 January 1880, p. 5.

46. *Catholic Sentinel*, 1 April 1880, p. 1. The author, Margaret F. Sullivan (née Buchanan), was a prominent Irish-American journalist and former schoolteacher. She was married to Alexander Sullivan of Chicago, a leading member of the dominant Irish-American nationalist organisation Clan na Gael. Sullivan became the first president of the Irish National League of America in 1883: William O'Brien and Desmond Ryan (eds), *Devoy's Post Bag, 1871–1928* (Dublin: Fallon, 1948), vol. 1, pp. 497-8, Alexander Sullivan to John Devoy, 5 March 1880.

47. Davitt, *The Fall of Feudalism in Ireland*, pp. 208-9.

48. For an assessment of what Parnell said to the various constituencies he addressed see McCartney, 'Parnell and the American Connection', in McCartney and Travers, *The Ivy Leaf*, pp. 48-53.

49. *Weekly Irish Times*, 31 January 1880, p. 5; 14 February 1880, p. 6; Janis, *A Greater Ireland*, p. 36.

50. *Weekly Irish Times*, 31 January 1880, p. 5; *Pilot*, 7 February 1880, p. 3.

51. *New York Herald*, 29 January 1880, p. 4, Parnell to the editor, 27 January 1880; *Weekly Irish Times*, 7 February 1880, p. 6.

52. *Weekly Irish Times*, 31 January 1880, p. 5.

53. Lyons, *Parnell*, pp. 111–13; Davitt, *The Fall of Feudalism* in Ireland, p. 204; Moody, *Davitt and Irish Revolution*, p. 357; Bew, *Land and the National Question in Ireland*, pp. 79–80.

54. *Weekly Irish Times*, 17 January 1880, p. 5; 24 January 1880, p. 5; Davitt, *The Fall of Feudalism in Ireland*, pp. 194–6; Janis, *A Greater Ireland*, pp. 39–40.

55. *Weekly Irish Times*, 31 January 1880, p. 5; 20 March 1880, p. 3; *Irish Canadian*, 10 March 1880, p. 3; Davitt, *The Fall of Feudalism in Ireland*, pp. 197, 203–5.

56. *Weekly Irish Times*, 7 February 1880, p. 6. Parnell's address is reproduced in its entirety in Davitt, *The Fall of Feudalism in Ireland*, pp. 197–203.

57. The sentiment was encapsulated in a line from 'An Appeal to the Irish Race in America', verses written to mark the occasion of a meeting of the Hudson County Land League, Hoboken, New Jersey: Ireland, 'A beggar among the nations, and a slave among the free', *Connaught Telegraph*, 1 January 1881, p. 2.

58. *Weekly Irish Times*, 20 March 1880, p. 3. Egan had previously discharged the same role for the Irish Republican Brotherhood, and he was also a member of that organisation's supreme council.

59. Ibid.

60. *Irish Canadian*, 4 February 1880, p. 2, Parnell and Dillon, New York City, to the people of the dominion of Canada, 26 January 1880; *Pilot*, 7 February 1880, p. 3.

61. *Irish Canadian*, 3 March 1880, p. 4. For Boyle see Mark McGowan, 'Boyle, Patrick', in *Dictionary of Canadian Biography*, vol. 13, University of Toronto/Université Laval, 2003, http://www.biographi.ca/en/bio/boyle_patrick_13E.html

62. *Irish Canadian*, 10 March 1880, p. 5.

63. *Cork Examiner*, 22 March 1880, p. 2. The IRB in Cork was more restrained in its welcome. In an address to Parnell, P.N. Fitzgerald, the IRB's local leader, announced the organisation's support for the Land League, but indicated an abstentionist policy in the pending election, neither approving, supporting or rejecting Parnell's candidature: Owen McGee, *The IRB: The Irish Republican Brotherhood, from the Land League to Sinn Féin* (Dublin: Four Courts Press, 2005), pp. 69–70. For a congratulatory illuminated address which the Land League presented to Parnell on his return to Ireland see William J. Smyth, 'Conflict, Reaction and Control in Nineteenth-century Ireland: The archaeology of revolution', in John Crowley, Donal Ó Drisceoil and Mike Murphy (eds), *Atlas of the Irish Revolution* (Cork: Cork University Press, 2017), pp. 21–55, at p. 36.

64. *Cork Examiner*, 22 March 1880, p. 2.

65. Lyons, *Parnell*, p. 108.

66. *The Irish Crisis of 1879–80*, pp. 22–3, 73. Confusingly, the Mansion House

committee reported that it received contributions amounting to £11,245 from the United States, and £26,876 from America! pp, 23, 27.

67. *South Australian Advertiser*, 3 April 1880, p. 4, editorial.

68. *Advocate* (Melbourne), 21 February 1880, p. 10, 'Mr Parnell'. The rumour of Parnell's intended visit to Australia was contradicted shortly afterwards, *Tablet*, 28 February 1880, p. 259.

69. See, for instance, *Freeman's Journal*, 19 April 1880, p. 2, T.P. Fallon to Gray, 5 March 1880.

70. Malcolm Campbell, *Ireland's New Worlds: Immigrants, politics and society in the United States and Australia, 1815–1922* (Madison: University of Wisconsin Press, 2008), pp. xii, 146.

71. Ibid., pp. xi–xii, 104–5, 111–16, 125–31. For the assassination attempt on Prince Alfred see Keith Amos, *The Fenians in Australia, 1865–1880* (Sydney: University of New South Wales Press, 1987), pp. 45–7; Robert Travers, *The Phantom Fenians of New South Wales* (Sydney: Kangaroo Press, 1986), pp. 63–79.

72. McCartney, 'Parnell and the American Connection', in McCartney and Travers, *The Ivy Leaf*, pp. 54–5.

73. Janis, *A Greater Ireland*, pp. 11, 18, 49.

74. Curti, *American Philanthropy Abroad*, pp. 81–92. For the American charitable response to the Great Famine, 1845–52, see Christine Kinealy, *Charity and the Great Hunger in Ireland: The kindness of strangers* (London: Bloomsbury, 2013), Chapter 4, '"An ocean of benevolence": The General Relief Committee of New York', pp. 85–106.

75. *New York Herald*, 4 March 1880, p. 3.

76. Ibid., 4 February 1880, p. 3; 7 February 1880, p. 5, Anna Parnell to the editor, 4 February 1880.

77. Ibid., 4 February 1880, p. 6; Curti, *American Philanthropy Abroad*, p. 89; Susan Hayes Ward, *George H. Hepworth: Preacher, journalist, friend of the people. The story of his life* (New York: E.P. Dutton, 1903), pp. 193–5.

78. Curti, *American Philanthropy Abroad*, pp. 89–90.

79. *Puck*, vol. 6, no. 153, 11 February 1880, p. 792. The cartoonist was American-born James Albert Wales, who was also responsible for Fig. 3.4. For *Puck*, Keppler and Wales see Curtis, *Apes and Angels*, pp. 59–62.

80. *Nation*, 7 February 1880, p. 14

81. Ibid., 14 February 1880, pp. 8–9.

82. *Weekly Irish Times*, 7 February 1880, p. 6.

83. *New York Herald*, 7 February 1880, p. 5, Parnell at Richmond, Virginia.

84. *Irish Canadian*, 10 March 1880, p. 3; Curti, *American Philanthropy Abroad*, pp. 92–3. On the same occasion, Peoria, Illinois, 3 March 1880, Parnell provided a detailed account of the origins of the *New York Herald* relief committee and his proposed role on it.

85. Curti, *American Philanthropy Abroad*, p. 92; Ward, *Hepworth*, pp. 193–5. In mid-May, by which time the *Herald* had almost completely abandoned its coverage of the Irish famine and associated philanthropic efforts, the paper listed total cash receipts of $332,360, *New York Herald*, 15 May 1880, p. 7.

86. Curti, *American Philanthropy Abroad*, p. 93; Ward, *Hepworth*, pp. 199–201. Shaw, King-Harman and McCabe were also members of the Dublin Mansion House relief committee.

87. *Irish Canadian*, 25 February 1880, p. 1; William M. Baker, 'Anglin, Timothy Warren', in *Dictionary of Canadian Biography*, vol. 12, University of Toronto/Université Laval, 2003, http://www.biographi.ca/en/bio/anglin_timothy_warren_12E.html

88. Relief Funds (Ireland). Report of the joint committee selected from the committees of the duchess of Marlborough relief fund and the Dublin Mansion House fund for relief of distress in Ireland, to administer the sum of 100,000 dollars voted by the parliament of the domain of Canada towards the relief of distress in Ireland, HC 1881 (326), lxxv. 859, pp. 3–6. The Marlborough committee was represented by the duchess of Marlborough (succeeded by Viscount Monck), Lieutenant-Colonel G.R. Dease and Dr T.W. Grimshaw; the Mansion House committee by E. Dwyer Gray, Thomas Pim, Jr and V.B. Dillon, Jr.

89. Relief Funds (Ireland), pp. 15–16, 20–2; Appendix 1, pp. 23–7; appendices 2 and 3, pp. 27–9; Appendix 4, p. 30.

90. Curti, *American Philanthropy Abroad*, pp. 97–8.

## Chapter 4: The Catholic Church

1. Gerard Moran, '"Near Famine": The Roman Catholic Church and the subsistence crisis of 1879–82', *Studia Hibernica*, vol. 32, 2002–3, pp. 155–77.

2. Ibid., pp. 168–71. For the international reach and influence of the nineteenth-century Irish Catholic Church, Ireland's spiritual empire, see, inter alia, Sheridan Gilley, 'The Roman Catholic Church and the Nineteenth-century Irish Diaspora', *Journal of Ecclesiastical History*, vol. 35, no. 2, 1984, pp. 188–207; Colin Barr, '"Imperium in Imperio": Irish episcopal imperialism in the nineteenth century', *English Historical Review*, vol. 502, 2008, pp. 611–50; idem, *Ireland's Empire: The Roman Catholic Church in the English-speaking world, 1829–1914* (Cambridge: Cambridge University Press, 2019); Sarah Roddy, 'Spiritual Imperialism and the Mission of the Irish Race: The Catholic Church and emigration from nineteenth-century Ireland', *Irish Historical Studies*, vol. 38, no. 152, November 2013, pp. 600–19.

3. *Nation*, 6 December 1879, pp. 1, 7.

4. *Ave Maria: A journal devoted to the honor of the Blessed Virgin* (Notre Dame, Indiana), vol. 15, 29 November 1879, p. 958.

5. James J. Green, 'American Catholics and the Irish Land League, 1879–1882', *Catholic Historical Review*, vol. 35, no. 1, April 1949, pp. 19–42, at pp. 19–20.

6. Merle Curti, *American Philanthropy Abroad* (New Brunswick, NJ: Rutgers University Press, 1963), p. 84.

7. Dublin Diocesan Archives (DDA), Papers of Edward McCabe, 1880, 346/4/111, Relief of Distress; Moran, 'Near Famine', pp. 168–71.

8. DDA, Papers of Edward McCabe, Relief of Distress; see, for instance, Denis M. Bradley, chancellor, diocese of Portland, Maine, to McCabe, 9 February 1880; William George McCloskey, bishop of Louisville, Kentucky, to McCabe, 25 February 1880; John Macdonald, bishop of Aberdeen, to McCabe, 26 February 1880.

9. Moran, 'Near Famine', p. 171.

10. *Connaught Telegraph*, 6 March 1880, p. 2, Irish Relief Society, Richmond, VA, to McCabe and Trench, 16 February 1880; Moran, 'Near Famine', p. 171.

11. DDA, Papers of Edward McCabe, Relief of Distress, Corrigan to McCabe, 4 February 1880.

12. *Tablet*, 14 February 1880, pp. 215–16.

13. *Nation*, 29 November 1879, p. 11.

14. Michael Davitt, *The Fall of Feudalism in Ireland or the Story of the Land League Revolution* (London and New York: Harper & Brothers, 1904), pp. 189–90.

15. *Tablet*, 14 February 1880, pp. 215–16; *Nation*, 14 February 1880, p. 2.

16. Ibid.

17. Ibid.

18. DDA, Papers of Edward McCabe, Relief of Distress, Duggan to McCabe, 12 March 1880.

19. *Tablet*, 14 February 1880, pp. 215–16; *Nation*, 14 February 1880, p. 2.

20. *Kerry Sentinel*, 4 May 1880, p. 3, McCarthy to Redpath, 19 March 1880.

21. Philanthropy and virtue were prominent features of the society's ritual and principles: 'The object of Forestry is to unite the virtuous and good in all sects and denominations of man in the sacred bonds of brotherhood so that while wandering through the forest of this world they may render mutual aid and assistance to each other.' See, generally, Anthony D. Buckley, '"On the Club": Friendly societies in Ireland', *Irish Economic and Social History*, vol. 14, 1987, pp. 39–58; Joe Fodey, 'The

Creation of the Irish National Foresters Benefit Society, 1877', *History Ireland*, vol. 27, no. 2, March–April 2019, pp. 24–6.

22. DDA, Papers of Edward McCabe, Relief of Distress, E. Jones Smallhorne and James Collins to McCabe, 9 March 1880; Moran, 'Near Famine', p. 170. The Ancient Order of Foresters had responded to an earlier subsistence crisis in Ireland, subscribing £100 to a relief appeal in 1863, *Report of the Central Committee for Relief of Distress in Ireland, with Appendices* (Dublin: Browne & Nolan, 1864), p. 69, also Appendix C, list of subscriptions, p. 86.

23. See, for instance, *Nation*, 10 January 1880, p. 11, Rev. Patrick Grealy, Carna, Recess, County Galway, to the editor, 29 December 1879, 'It is a rare thing to find a person here able to read, write, or even to speak the English language.'

24. [William O'Brien], *Christmas on the Galtees: An inquiry into the conditions of the tenantry of Mr Nathaniel Buckley, by the special correspondent of the Freeman's Journal* (Dublin: The Central Tenants' Defence Association, 1878). See Sally Warwick Haller, *William O'Brien and the Irish Land War* (Dublin: Irish Academic Press, 1990), pp. 29–34.

25. DDA, Papers of Edward McCabe, Relief of Distress, Fahey to Dr Dannell, 30 January 1880. John Macdonald, bishop of Aberdeen, informed McCabe that he had received two similar direct appeals from Ireland, including one from the Convent of Mercy, Oranmore, County Galway, ibid., Macdonald to McCabe, 26 February 1880.

26. *Tablet*, 31 January 1880, p. 150, Fahey to editor (ND).

27. DDA, Papers of Edward McCabe, Relief of Distress, Duggan to McCabe, 12 March 1880. For similar apprehensions among the Ballina relief committee see *Tablet*, 17 January 1880, p. 86, Hugh Conway, bishop of Killala, to the editor.

28. *The Irish Crisis of 1879–80. Proceedings of the Dublin Mansion House Relief Committee, 1880* (Dublin: Browne & Nolan, 1881), pp. 74–5.

29. Ibid., p. 75.

30. Laurence M. Geary, '"The Whole Country Was in Motion": Mendicancy and vagrancy in pre-Famine Ireland', in Jacqueline Hill and Colm Lennon (eds), *Luxury and Austerity: Historical studies XXI* (Dublin: UCD Press, 1999), pp. 121–36; idem, 'The Medical Profession, Health Care and the Poor Law in Nineteenth-century Ireland', in Virginia Crossman and Peter Gray (eds), *Poverty and Welfare in Ireland, 1838–1948* (Dublin: Irish Academic Press, 2011), pp. 189–206, at pp. 198–9.

31. DDA, Papers of Edward McCabe, Relief of Distress, Fahey to Dr Dannell, 30 January 1880.

32. *Nation*, 10 January 1880, p. 11, Rev. Patrick Grealy, Carna, Recess, County Galway, to the editor, 29 December 1879.

33. Ibid., 22 November 1879, p. 2.

34. Barr, *Ireland's Empire*, pp. 478–9.

35. *Advocate* (Melbourne), 24 April 1880, p. 16, McDermott to the editor, 12 February 1880. For similar international clerical appeals on behalf of their parishioners, from Fr Michael O'Friel, Kilteevogue, Stranorlar, County Donegal, and Fr James McFadden, Gweedore, County Donegal, see *Tablet*, 24 January, 28 February, 20 March 1880, pp. 97–8, 279, 373, and from Fr Patrick Lavelle, Cong, County Mayo, vice-chairman of Cong relief committee, see *Irish Canadian*, 4 February 1880, p. 5. Lavelle and McFadden were particularly well known and influential, indeed notorious, members of the Irish parochial clergy during the later nineteenth century.

36. *Freeman's Journal* (Sydney), 24 April 1880, p. 19, Fr John Molony to the editor, 15 February 1880.

37. Thomas Bracken, who was born in County Meath, was the first in New Zealand to publish Molony's appeal, in the *Saturday Advertiser*, which he launched as a weekly in July 1875. See also *North Otago Times*, 1 May 1880; *Southland Times*, 4 May 1880. For background on the *Saturday Advertiser*, see Papers Past, Newspapers, Collection, National Library of New Zealand. Molony, through a friend in the United States, issued a similar appeal to American Catholics on behalf of his parishioners, *Ave Maria*, vol. 16, 29 May 1880, p. 433.

38. *Freeman's Journal* (Sydney), 6 December 1879, p. 6; *Express and Telegraph*, 15 December 1879, p. 3, M.T. Montgomery to the editor, 13 December 1879.

39. *New Zealand Tablet*, 20 February 1880, pp. 5–7. County Wicklow-born Patrick Moran, the first Catholic bishop of Dunedin, established the journal in 1873 and edited it until 1881.

40. Religious sisters had intervened in similar subsistence crises in the past, in the early 1860s for example, when seventy convents received funding to support charitable relief work among the children attending their schools. The convents were mainly in the west and south of Ireland, though there were several in Dublin, and one in Hampstead, London, that of the Sisters of Our Lady of Charity, *Report of the Central Committee for Relief of Distress in Ireland*, Appendix F, list of allocations, pp. 102–3. For their relief efforts during the Great Famine see Christine Kinealy, *Charity and the Great Hunger in Ireland: The kindness of strangers* (London: Bloomsbury, 2013), pp. 154–6.

41. In November 1879 Sister Mary Francis Clare, the Nun of Kenmare, appealed to English Catholics through a proxy in London, Katherine Mary Stone, for 'parcels of clothing, blankets, knitted goods and any help in kind', noting in particular that 'spare yarns and wools of any length, colour, or quality, for knitting, old railway rugs and warm coverings of any description will be especially useful in view of the coming winter and failure of fuel', *Tablet*, 2 November 1879, p. 654, Stone to the editor, ND.

42. *Express and Telegraph* (Adelaide), 17 December 1879, p. 3; *South Australian Advertiser*, 17 December 1879, p. 6; *South Australian Chronicle and Weekly Mail*, 20 December 1879,

p. 9. There were historical links between women religious in Ireland and Australia. From the late 1830s Irish religious sisters travelled to Australia, where they established networks of convents, schools and hospitals. Many of these women had familial links to bishops and priests already settled in Australia and New Zealand: Barr, *Ireland's Empire*, pp. 352-8.

43. *Advocate*, 24 April 1880, p. 16, McCarthy to the editor, 5 March 1880.

44. Ibid.

45. *Tablet*, 20 March, 29 May 1880, Sister M. Aloysius Doyle to the editor, 16 March, 26 May 1880, pp. 373, 695. For Doyle see M. de Lourdes Fahy, 'Mother M. Aloysius Doyle (1820-1908)', *Journal of the Galway Archaeological and Historical Society*, vol. 36, 1977-8, pp. 70-7.

46. *Catholic Sentinel*, 25 March 1880, p. 4.

47. *New York Herald*, 14 March 1880, p. 7.

48. *Nation* (Dublin), 29 November 1879, p. 11, MacManus to the editor, 23 November 1879. During the subsistence crisis of the early 1860s, a member of the Clifden relief committee praised the Sisters of Mercy in the town in similar fashion. He observed that the mother superior, Esmonde White, was better informed about the circumstances of the local poor than the committee itself and that her awareness and greater knowledge enabled her to select 'the most fitting objects of relief' and to assist them systematically and effectively, *Report of the Central Committee for Relief of Distress in Ireland*, pp. 70-1. MacManus was also involved in the early 1860s relief effort, *Cork Examiner*, 22 November 1861, p. 4, public meeting, Clifden, 17 November 1861; *Freeman's Journal*, 15 January 1862, p. 3, MacManus to the editor, 13 January 1862; 14 January 1863, pp. 2-3, MacManus to the editor, 12 January 1863; 29 January 1863, p. 3, MacManus to the editor, 26 January 1863.

49. Laurence M. Geary, 'A Psychological and Sociological Analysis of the Great Famine in Ireland', in Robert Dare (ed.), *Food, Power and Community: Essays in the history of food and drink* (Adelaide: Wakefield Press, 1999), pp. 181-92; idem, 'What People Died of During the Famine', in Cormac Ó Gráda (ed.), *Famine 150. Commemorative lecture series* (Dublin: Teagasc/UCD, 1997), pp. 95-111.

50. *New York Herald*, 5 March 1880, p. 3, Fr McCartie, chaplain of the Academy of the Sisters of Charity, Madison, New Jersey (the addressee of the Skibbereen Sisters appeal), to the editor.

51. Green, 'American Catholics and the Irish Land League', p. 21; *Ave Maria*, vol. 16, 1880, pp. 413, 517, 535, 618, 673, 694, 755. I am grateful to Aedín Ní Bhróithe Clements, Irish Studies Librarian and Curator of Irish Studies Collections, University of Notre Dame, Indiana, for assistance with this source.

52. *New Zealand Tablet*, 5 December 1879, p. 11, E. O'Connor to the editor. For context, in relation to proselytism, children and education in nineteenth-century Ireland,

see Maria Luddy, *Women and Philanthropy in Nineteenth-Century Ireland* (Cambridge: Cambridge University Press, 1995), especially Chapter 3, 'Saving the Child', pp. 68–96.

53. Moran was mistaken in his claim: proselytists were active in the west and south-west of Ireland long before the Great Famine.

54. *New Zealand Tablet*, 5 December 1879, 'Famine in Ireland', pp. 2–3. For Moran, see Hugh Laracy, 'Moran, Patrick', Dictionary of New Zealand Biography, first published in 1993. Te Ara – The Encyclopedia of New Zealand, https://teara.govt.nz/en/biographies/2m55/moran-patrick; Ciara Breathnach, 'Irish Catholic Identity in 1870s Otago, New Zealand', *Immigrants & Minorities*, vol. 31, no. 1, 2013, pp. 1–26, at pp. 13–14; Barr, *Ireland's Empire*, pp. 43–59.

55. Desmond Bowen, *The Protestant Crusade in Ireland, 1800–1870: A study of Protestant–Catholic relations between the Act of Union and Disestablishment* (Dublin: Gill & Macmillan, 1978); Irene Whelan, 'The Stigma of Souperism', in Cathal Póirtéir (ed.), *The Great Irish Famine* (Cork: Mercier Press, 1995), pp. 135–54; Miriam Moffitt, *Soupers and Jumpers: The Protestant mission in Connemara, 1848–1937* (Dublin: Nonsuch, 2008); Kinealy, *Charity and the Great Hunger in Ireland*, pp. 257–76; Niall R. Branach, 'Edward Nangle and the Achill Island Mission', *History Ireland*, vol. 8, no. 3, 2000, pp. 35–8; David Fitzpatrick, *'Solitary and Wild': Frederick MacNeice and the salvation of Ireland* (Dublin: Lilliput Press, 2012), pp. 15–51; Tom Kelley, Linde Lunney, 'Nangle, Edward Walter', in James McGuire and James Quinn (eds), *Dictionary of Irish Biography* (Cambridge: Cambridge University Press, 2013), https://www.dib.ie/biography/nangle-edward-walter-a6133. For Archbishop McCabe's pastoral concerns about proselytists targeting Dublin's poor, including children, in the opening months of 1881 see *Freeman's Journal*, 12 March 1881, p. 2.

56. *Ave Maria*, vol. 16, 10 April 1880, p. 295, Fullerton, Ayrfield, Bournemouth, England, to the editor, 14 March 1880; 3 July 1880, p. 535, Fullerton, Park Lane, London, to the editor, 4 June 1880. Fullerton, the third of four children of Lord Granville Leverson-Gower, later 1st Earl Granville, and his wife, Lady Henrietta Elizabeth, daughter of William Cavendish, 5th duke of Devonshire, was an unlikely champion of the Irish poor, and of their religion. She converted to Catholicism in 1846, after her father's death. She and her County Antrim-born husband, also a Catholic convert, were committed philanthropists and supporters of numerous charitable organisations. Fullerton had an international profile as novelist, poet and biographer, and her publications, which were infused with Catholic religious sentiment, were produced primarily to raise money for charity. Solveig C. Robinson, 'Fullerton [née Leveson-Gower], Lady Georgiana Charlotte (1812–1885), novelist and philanthropist', *Oxford Dictionary of National Biography* (Oxford: Oxford University Press, 2004), https://www.oxforddnb.com/view/10.1093/ref:odnb/9780198614128.001.0001/odnb-9780198614128-e-10242.

57. Ibid., vol. 16, 3 July 1880, pp. 527–8, 535, Fullerton, Park Lane, London, to the editor, 4 June 1880.

58. *Catholic Sentinel*, 20 May 1880, p. 1. For similar acknowledgements see ibid., 10 June 1880, p. 1, Laurence Gillooly, bishop of Elphin, to Archbishop Seghers, Portland, Oregon, 2 May 1880; John MacHale, archbishop of Tuam, to Seghers, 30 April 1880; John MacEvilly, coadjutor archbishop of Tuam, to the editor, 1 May 1880.

59. Ibid., 6 May 1880, p. 5.

60. *Express and Telegraph*, 13 December 1879, p. 3, Byrne to the editor, 12 December 1879.

61. Ibid., Prendergast to the editor, 12 December 1879.

62. Ibid., 13 December 1879, p. 3.

63. Ibid., 15 December 1879, p. 3, Montgomery to the editor, 13 December 1879; 16 December 1879, p. 3, for Prendergast's and Byrne's responses.

64. Ibid., 17 December 1879, p. 2. This editorial and the foregoing correspondence arising from Clare's appeal appeared also in the *South Australian Chronicle and Weekly Mail*, 20 December 1879, p. 9. See also *South Australian Advertiser*, 13 December 1879, p. 6; 15 December, p. 6.

65. *Catholic Sentinel*, 13 November 1879, p. 5.

66. *New Zealand Tablet*, 2 January 1880, p. 19.

67. Kevin Molloy, 'Victorians, Historians and Irish History: A reading of the *New Zealand Tablet*, 1873-1903', in Brad Patterson (ed.), *The Irish in New Zealand: Historical contexts and perspectives* (Wellington: Stout Research Centre for New Zealand Studies, Victoria University of Wellington, 2002), pp. 153-70, at p. 154.

68. Ibid., p. 154; Breathnach, 'Irish Catholic Identity in 1870s Otago', p. 20.

69. *Catholic Sentinel*, 18 December 1879, p. 1.

70. Ibid.

71. *Irish Canadian*, 3 December 1879, pp. 3, 4, Clare to the editor, ND.

72. Ibid., 19 November 1879, p. 1, O'Leary, London, to the editor, 29 October 1879. O'Leary acknowledged his acquaintanceship with the editor, Patrick Boyle.

73. *Catholic Sentinel*, 22 January 1880, p. 5, O'Leary to editor, Montreal, 30 December 1879.

74. *Irish Canadian*, 17 December 1879, p. 2.

75. Ibid., 21 January 1880, p. 5: O'Leary, Toronto, to the editor, 17 January 1880.

76. Ibid., 11 February 1880, p. 5: O'Leary, Toronto, to the editor, 9 February 1880. In the previous chapter we noted Clare's efforts to garner Fanny Parnell's support, and her request for a share of the relief funding generated by her brother Charles, Chapter 3, at n. 23.

77. *New Zealand Tablet*, 14 May 1880, p. 9, Clare to the editor, 16 March 1880. Under the heading 'Starving Kerry', Clare, through a proxy, published a lengthy appeal in the *New York Herald*, 16 December 1879, p. 4, Lady Blanche Murphy, North Conway, NH, to the editor, 10 December 1879; *Pilot*, 7 February 1880, p. 3.

78. *Catholic Sentinel*, 11 December 1879, p. 5. See also ibid., 22 April 1880, p. 4.

79. Ibid., 18 December 1879, p. 1. Clare was born on 6 May 1829, not 1830 as stated in the biographical sketch. The latter was published alongside Bishop McCarthy's letter, buttressing her charitable appeal, which had appeared a fortnight earlier in the *Irish Canadian*. Clare's biographical detail was reproduced in the *New Zealand Tablet*, 27 February 1880, p. 7, and in the *Irish Canadian*, 21 April 1880, p. 1, further evidence of the links between Catholic publications throughout the English-speaking world.

80. Reproduced in *New York Herald*, 16 February 1880, p. 3.

81. *Connaught Telegraph*, 1 January 1881, p. 2. The interview was dated 30 August 1880 and was probably reproduced from the *New York Tribune*.

82. Some later commentators have persisted with this less than critical appraisal of Clare's life and achievements, one authority on religious sisters and convent life describing her as 'surely the most independent and daring religious woman of the nineteenth century': Mary Peckham Magray, *The Transforming Power of the Nuns: Women, religion, and cultural change in Ireland, 1750–1900* (New York and Oxford: Oxford University Press, 1998), p. 130. Others, including this writer, would argue for a more contested legacy.

83. *Catholic Sentinel*, 11 December 1879, p. 5, 'Friends of the Nun of Kenmare' to the editor, 6 December 1879. Their anonymity was subsequently breached, which provoked a furious editorial response from the *Catholic Sentinel*, the writer distinguishing between the spirit of true charity displayed by anonymous Catholic donors and 'the Protestant fashion' of parading their names before the world, 'of giving 50c. to God and asking a dollar's worth of glory from the world therefor', ibid., 22 April 1880, p. 4.

84. See, for example, ibid., 11 March 1880, p. 5; 6 May 1880, p. 5, Laurence Gillooly, bishop of Elphin, to the editor, 7 April 1880. Some subscribers to the *Catholic Sentinel*'s Irish famine fund specified that their contributions were intended for the Land League's relief fund, or Parnell's fund as it was called, which Parnell and Dillon were then promoting in North America.

85. *Tablet*, 10 January 1880, pp. 37–8.

86. Ibid., 30 March 1880, pp. 372–3, Clare to the editor, ND.

87. Ibid., advertisement, p. 377. The *Cork Examiner* promoted the bazaar in its edition of 26 April 1880, p. 2: 'We would decidedly ask all, without exception, to cooperate in this benevolent undertaking, and lend the Nun of Kenmare any and every form of assistance in her charitable work.'

88. *Tablet*, 15 May 1880, pp. 630-2, Clare to the editor, 'Feast of St Michael'.

89. Sister Mary Francis Clare, *The Apparition at Knock, with the Depositions of the Witnesses Examined by the Ecclesiastical Commission Appointed by His Grace the Archbishop of Tuam; and the Conversion of a Young Protestant Lady by a Visit of the Blessed Virgin* (London: Burns & Oates, 1880). The preface was reproduced in *Cork Examiner*, 24 April 1880, supplement, p. 5.

90. Clare, *The Apparition at Knock*, pp. 114-18; *Autobiography*, p. 91. The Knock pamphlet also featured the bazaar and lottery which was advertised in the *Tablet*, both publications dating from around the same time, Easter 1880, although there are minor differences in the two versions of the bazaar notice.

91. *Catholic Sentinel*, 23 September 1880, p. 4, Clare to the editor, 29 August 1880.

92. Ibid., 21 October 1880, p. 1, Clare to the editor, 19 September 1880.

93. Philomena McCarthy, *The Nun of Kenmare: The true facts* (Kenmare: St Clare's Convent, 1989), p. 36.

94. *Catholic Sentinel*, 10 June 1880, p. 1, Raphael to the editor, 29 April 1880.

95. Ibid., 17 June 1880, p. 5, Clare to the editor, 2 May 1880.

96. *Weekly Irish Times*, 7 February 1880, p. 6.

97. *Catholic Sentinel*, 17 June 1880, p. 5, Clare to the editor, 20 May 1880.

98. Clare had an extremely poor opinion of Indian meal, or 'yallow male' as it was called in the vernacular. She described it as a compound of sawdust and bad flour which was doled out to the Irish poor in times of famine and food shortages, a substitute food that was hardly fit for pigs. *The Nun of Kenmare: An autobiography* (Boston: Ticknor & Company, 1889), p. 88.

99. *New Zealand Tablet*, 14 May 1880, p. 9, Clare to the editor, 16 March 1880.

100. *Catholic Sentinel*, 15 April 1880, p. 4, Clare to the editor, 19 March 1880.

101. Ibid., 24 June 1880, p. 5, Clare to the editor, ND.

102. *The Nun of Kenmare: An autobiography*, pp. 118, 122; Maria Luddy (ed.), *The Nun of Kenmare: An autobiography* (London: Routledge/Thoemmes Press, 1998), p. ix; Norman Dunbar Palmer, *The Irish Land League Crisis* (New Haven: Yale University Press, 1940), p. 102; Jane McL. Coté, *Fanny and Anna Parnell: Ireland's patriot sisters* (Houndmills: Macmillan, 1991), pp. 122-4.

103. John White, 'The Cusack Papers: New evidence on the Knock apparition', *History Ireland*, vol. 4, no. 4, 1996, pp. 39-44.

104. *Kerry Sentinel*, 10 December 1880; *The Nun of Kenmare: An autobiography*, pp. 101-22.

105. See, for instance, *The Nun of Kenmare: An autobiography*, pp. 9-100, 122-7; *Tablet*, 20 March 1880, pp. 372-3; *New Zealand Tablet*, 14 May 1880, p. 9.

106. *Freeman's Journal*, J. Sullivan, Kenmare, to the editor, cited in *The Nun of Kenmare: An autobiography*, pp. 89–90.

107. *The Nun of Kenmare: An autobiography*, p. 86.

108. *Connaught Telegraph*, 1 January 1881, p. 2.

109. For the status and cultural authority of Irish religious sisters see Magray, *The Transforming Power of the Nuns*, pp. 74–86.

110. *The Irish Crisis of 1879–80*, p. 74.

111. Gearóid Ó Tuathaigh, 'Introduction: Ireland 1800–2016: Negotiating sovereignty and freedom', in Thomas Bartlett (ed.), *The Cambridge History of Ireland. Volume IV: 1880 to the Present* (Cambridge: Cambridge University Press, 2018), pp. 1–29, at p. 2.

## Chapter 5: Distribution of International Aid

1. *The Irish Crisis of 1879–80. Proceedings of the Dublin Mansion House Relief Committee, 1880* (Dublin: Browne & Nolan, 1881), pp. 16–27, 73; *Freeman's Journal*, 23 April 1880, duchess of Marlborough to the Irish people, 21 April 1880.

2. The money was expended as follows: food and relief works, £82,144; seed, including seed potatoes, £36,983; clothing and blankets, £10,091; migration and emigration, £1,458; general expenses, £1,950. The balance was used to facilitate the emigration of families from distressed areas of the country: Norman Dunbar Palmer, *The Irish Land League Crisis* (New Haven: Yale University Press, 1940), pp. 88–90. See also R.F. Foster, 'To the Northern Counties Station: Lord Randolph Churchill and the prelude to the orange card', in F.S.L. Lyons and R.A.J. Hawkins (eds), *Ireland Under the Union: Varieties of tension. Essays in honour of T.W. Moody* (Oxford: Clarendon Press, 1980), pp. 238–87, at p. 249, n. 5. Foster described the Marlborough famine appeal as 'a prodigy of organisation and financial productivity'. It did, however, attract criticism from political and religious ideologues, and the committee's authority was further eroded by an embezzling secretary, prone to drink and remorse.

3. *The Irish Crisis of 1879–80*, pp. 72–3.

4. Ibid., p. 328, J.H. Connor to Gray, 20 January 1880.

5. *Advocate* (Melbourne), 17 January 1880, p. 7.

6. *The Irish Crisis of 1879–80*, p. 330, Samuel Evans Burgess to Gray, 1 May 1880.

7. See Chapter 3, ns 18 and 19.

8. *The Irish Crisis of 1879–80*, pp. 222–60.

9. Ibid., pp. 234, 247–8.

10. Ibid., pp. 254–5.

11. Ibid., p. 260.

12. Ibid., p. 28.

13. See Miriam Moffitt, *Society for Irish Church Missions to the Roman Catholics* (Manchester and New York: Manchester University Press, 2010). Connemara and the Erris peninsula in County Mayo witnessed similar dissension and a lack of inter-denominational co-operation during the Great Famine, with charges of proselytism, 'souperism', levelled at evangelical clergymen in these regions. See Chapter 4, n. 55.

14. *The Irish Crisis of 1879–80*, p. 29.

15. Ibid., pp. 1, 27-33.

16. Ibid.

17. James H. Tuke, *Irish Distress and Its Remedies: The land question. A visit to Donegal and Connaught in the spring of 1880* (London: W. Ridgway, 1880), p. 2.

18. Merle Curti, *American Philanthropy Abroad* (New Brunswick, NJ: Rutgers University Press, 1963), pp. 94-6.

19. *Cork Examiner*, 26 April 1880, p. 4; Palmer, *The Irish Land League Crisis*, pp. 99-100.

20. *New York Times*, 28 March 1880, p. 12; 'Letter from the Secretary of the Navy, Transmitting Report of the Commander of the Relief Ship Constellation, 15 June 1880', 46th Congress, 2nd session, Senate, ex. doc., no. 215, pp. 1-2, E.E. Potter to R.W. Thompson, secretary of the navy, Washington, DC, 20 April 1880.

21. *Cork Examiner*, 21 April 1880, p. 3.

22. *New York Times*, 26 March 1880, p. 2.

23. *Cork Examiner*, 21 April 1880, p. 3.

24. R.B. Forbes, *The Voyage of the Jamestown on Her Errand of Mercy* (Boston, 1847).

25. Ibid., J. Kennedy, Ballydehob, to Rev. F.F. Trench, 29 March 1847, p. 89, reprinted in *Cork Examiner*, 24 April 1880, supplement, p. 5.

26. *Cork Examiner*, 21 April 1880, p. 3.

27. Ibid., 22 April 1880, p. 3.

28. Ibid., 24 April 1880, p. 2. The banquet tickets were priced at a hefty 30 shillings each.

29. Ibid., p. 3.

30. C.J. Woods, 'Doran, Charles Guilfoyle', in James McGuire and James Quinn (eds), *Dictionary of Irish Biography* (Cambridge: Cambridge University Press, 2009), https://www.dib.ie/biography/doran-charles-guilfoyle-a2715; Owen McGee, *The IRB: The Irish Republican Brotherhood, from the Land League to Sinn Féin* (Dublin: Four Courts Press, 2005), pp. 44, 56-7.

31. Laurence M. Geary, '"The Noblest Offering that Nation Ever Made to Nation": American philanthropy and the Great Famine in Ireland', *Éire-Ireland*, vol. 48, nos 3–4, 2013, pp. 103–28.

32. *Cork Examiner*, 26 April 1880, p. 4.

33. Ibid.

34. Ibid.

35. *Freeman's Journal*, 6 May 1880, p. 5.

36. *Cork Examiner*, 27 April 1880, p. 2.

37. Ibid., 28 April 1880, p. 3, C.G. Doran to the editor, 27 April 1880. The correct quotation is 'The superfluities of the rich are the necessaries of the poor'.

38. Ibid., 30 April 1880, p. 3.

39. Colonel King-Harman, MP, William Shaw, MP, and Archbishop McCabe of Dublin were the other members of the distribution committee.

40. *Cork Examiner*, 30 April 1880, p. 3.

41. Susan Hayes Ward, *George H. Hepworth: Preacher, journalist, friend of the people. The story of his life* (New York: E.P. Dutton, 1903), p. 209. Hepworth's overblown approach to public speaking was captured in the title of a public lecture on his Irish experiences – 'The Niobe of Nations' – which he delivered on his return to New York in December 1880, *New York Herald*, 21 December 1880. Oscar Wilde was wont to use this expression when referring to Ireland, one which he – and, presumably, Hepworth also – adapted from Lord Byron, *Childe Harold's Pilgrimage* (1812–18, canto 4, verse lxxix), in which the poet calls Rome the Niobe of nations, Richard Ellmann, *Oscar Wilde* (New York: Alfred A. Knopf, 1988), p. 196.

42. *Cork Examiner*, 30 April 1880, p. 3.

43. Christopher Fitz-Simon, *'Buffoonery and Easy Sentiment': Popular Irish plays in the decade prior to the opening of the Abbey Theatre* (Dublin: Carysfort Press, 2011), pp. 71, 80–5, 107. I am grateful to Nicholas Grene for drawing my attention to this work.

44. Cited in ibid., p. 108.

45. *Cork Examiner*, 13 April 1880, p. 2.

46. Fitz-Simon, *'Buffoonery and Easy Sentiment'*, pp. 76–80 for an analysis of *The Gommoch*.

47. *Cork Examiner*, 23 April 1880, p. 1.

48. Ibid., 24 April 1880, p. 2.

49. Ibid., 5 May 1880, p. 2; *Freeman's Journal*, 5 May 1880, pp. 4–6. The American journalist James Redpath, who was not an admirer of the lord mayor, claimed that Gray

had spent £700 on the ball, 'not to honour America but to procure a knighthood', though he did not offer any evidence to support his contention: *Catholic Sentinel*, 1 July 1880, p. 5, Redpath to the editor, 21 June 1880.

50. 'Letter from the Secretary of the Navy', p. 6, Potter to Thompson, 9 May 1880.

51. *Cork Examiner*, 4 May 1880, p. 2.

52. Ibid., 5 May 1880, p. 2.

53. Ibid., 11 May 1880, p. 2.

54. 'Letter from the Secretary of the Navy', p. 7, Potter to Thompson, 12 June 1880.

55. Relief of Distress on the West Coast of Ireland, HC 1880 [c. 2671], lxii. 195, Captain George Digby Morant to Rear-Admiral R.V. Hamilton, Queenstown, 4 August 1880, p. 1; *Freeman's Journal*, 6 April 1880, p. 4, 'The Duchess of Marlborough's Relief Fund'. For details of the relief squadron gunboats see Timothy Collins, 'HMS "Valorous": Her contribution to Galway maritime history', *Journal of the Galway Archaeological and Historical Society*, vol. 49, 1997, pp. 122–42, at pp. 132–3. The commander of the squadron was the same Prince Alfred who had been shot and wounded by an insane would-be Irish assassin in Sydney in March 1868, see Chapter 3, n. 70.

56. Annual Report of the Local Government Board for Ireland, Being the Eighth Report Under 'The Local Government Board (Ireland) Act', 35 & 36 Vic., c. 69, HC 1880 [c. 2603, c. 2603-1], xxviii. 1, 39, pp. 134–8.

57. *Cork Examiner*, 24 April 1880, p. 2.

58. Ibid., 26 April 1880, p. 4.

59. *The Irish Crisis of 1879–80*, p. 49. For a jaundiced view of relief distribution, relief measures generally and their application, see Henry Robinson, *Memories: Wise and otherwise* (London: Cassell, 1923), pp. 13–27. Robinson was employed as a temporary Poor Law inspector in November 1879. Shortly afterwards he was appointed vice-president of the Local Government Board, thus commencing a long and influential career in Irish local government: Annual Report of the Local Government Board for Ireland, Being the Eighth Report Under 'The Local Government Board (Ireland) Act', 35 & 36 Vic., c. 69, pp. 11, 36.

60. *Illustrated London News*, 24 April 1880, cited in Collins, 'HMS "Valorous"', pp. 135–6.

61. James Berry, Mynish, Carna, to his sister Mary Berry in America, 1 June 1880, author's copy, courtesy of Catherine Jennings, Carna; Catherine Jennings, 'Tuke … the Quaker Philanthropist and the Free Emigration Scheme in Connemara, 1882', in *Mr Tuke's Fund: Connemara emigration in the 1880s. Ireland's forgotten famine* (Clifden: Clifden Heritage, 2012), p. 37.

62. *Tablet*, 29 May 1880, p. 687, Grealy to James Nugent, 19 May 1880.

63. James Berry to Mary Berry, 1 June 1880, author's copy.

64. *Catholic Sentinel*, 1 July 1880, p. 5, Redpath to the editor, 21 June 1880; James Redpath, 'The Famine in Ireland. Reply to the lord mayor's appeal', National Library of Ireland, John Devoy Papers, Ms 18011/2/1.

65. Relief of Distress on the West Coast of Ireland, pp. 1–3. An abstract of Captain Morant's report appeared in *The Times*, 28 August 1880.

66. Relief of Distress on the West Coast of Ireland, pp. 4-6.

67. *The Irish Crisis of 1879–80*, pp. 50–1, 252–3.

68. Ibid., p. 72.

69. Virginia Crossman, '"With the Experience of 1846 and 1847 Before Them": The politics of emergency relief, 1879–84', in Peter Gray (ed.), *Victoria's Ireland? Irishness and Britishness, 1837–1901* (Dublin: Four Courts Press, 2004), pp. 179–81; idem, *Politics, Pauperism and Power in Late Nineteenth-century Ireland* (Manchester and New York: Manchester University Press, 2006), pp. 114–16.

70. T.W. Moody, *Davitt and Irish Revolution 1846–82* (Oxford: Clarendon Press, 1981), pp. 331–4.

## Chapter 6: Secret Societies and the Land War in Late Nineteenth-century Ireland

1. See especially Maureen Wall, 'The Whiteboys', in T. Desmond Williams (ed.), *Secret Societies in Ireland* (Dublin: Gill & Macmillan, 1973), pp. 13–25; James S. Donnelly, Jr, 'The Whiteboy Movement, 1761–5', *Irish Historical Studies*, vol. 21, no. 81, March 1978, pp. 20–54; idem, 'Irish Agrarian Rebellion: The Whiteboys of 1769–76', *Proceedings of the Royal Irish Academy. Section C: Archaeology, Celtic studies, history, linguistics, literature*, vol. 83c, 1983, pp. 293–331.

2. Donnelly, 'Irish Agrarian Rebellion', p. 293. There is a rich literature on Irish agrarian secret societies. See, inter alia, Joseph Lee, 'The Ribbonmen', in Williams (ed.), *Secret Societies in Ireland*, pp. 26–35; James S. Donnelly, Jr, 'The Rightboy Movement, 1785–8', *Studia Hibernica*, vols 17–18, 1977–8, pp. 120–202; Samuel Clark and James S. Donnelly, Jr (eds), *Irish Peasants: Violence and political unrest, 1780–1914* (Madison: University of Wisconsin Press, 1983); James S. Donnelly, Jr, *Captain Rock: The Irish agrarian rebellion of 1821–1824* (Madison: University of Wisconsin Press, 2009); M.R. Beames, *Peasants and Power: The Whiteboy movements and their control in pre-Famine Ireland* (Brighton and New York: Harvester Press, 1983); Patrick J. Corish (ed.), *Radicals, Rebels, Establishments* (Belfast: Appletree Press, 1985); A.C. Murray, 'Agrarian Violence and Nationalism in Nineteenth-century Ireland: The myth of Ribbonism', *Irish Economic and Social History*, vol. 13, 1986, pp. 56–73; C.H.E. Philpin (ed.), *Nationalism and Popular Protest in Ireland* (Cambridge: Cambridge University Press, 1987); Maura Cronin,

*Agrarian Protest in Ireland, 1750–1960*, Studies in Irish Economic and Social History, vol. 11 (Dundalk, 2012). For a listing and assessment of more recent publications on Irish rural protest and collective action see Kyle Hughes and Donald M. MacRaild, *Ribbon Societies in Nineteenth-century Ireland and Its Diaspora: The persistence of tradition* (Liverpool: Liverpool University Press, 2018), pp. 1–17.

3. 15 & 16 Geo. 3, c. 21, 'An Act to Prevent and Punish Tumultuous Risings of Persons Within This Kingdom, and for Other Purposes Therein Mentioned', 4 April 1776; cited in Donnelly, 'Irish Agrarian Rebellion', pp. 328–9.

4. 1 & 2 Will. 4, c. 44, 'An Act to Amend an Act Passed in the Parliament of Ireland, in the Fifteenth and Sixteenth Years of the Reign of His Majesty King George the Third, Intituled "An Act to Prevent and Punish Tumultuous Risings of Persons Within This Kingdom, and for Other Purposes Therein Mentioned"', 15 October 1831. See, generally, Virginia Crossman, 'Emergency Legislation and Agrarian Disorder in Ireland, 1821–41', *Irish Historical Studies*, vol. 27, no. 108, November 1991, pp. 309–23; idem, *Politics, Law and Order in Nineteenth-century Ireland* (Dublin: Gill & Macmillan, 1996). There is a useful abstract of this legislation in Appendix F of this volume, 'Select List of Statutes Relating to the Preservation or Restoration of Order in Ireland, 1776–1923'.

5. For agrarian outrages see W.E. Vaughan, *Landlords and Tenants in Mid-Victorian Ireland* (Oxford: Clarendon Press, 1994), pp. 138–76. See also Ciara Breathnach and Laurence M. Geary, 'Crime and Punishment: Whiteboyism and the law in late nineteenth-century Ireland', in Kyle Hughes and Donald M. MacRaild (eds), *Crime, Violence and the Irish in the Nineteenth Century* (Liverpool: Liverpool University Press, 2017), pp. 149–72.

6. Cronin, *Agrarian Protest in Ireland*, p. 14.

7. Outrages (Ireland). Return of outrages reported to the Royal Irish Constabulary office in each month of the year 1880 and 1881, and in the month of January 1882, HC 1882 (7), lv. 615, pp. 2–3.

8. W.E. Vaughan, *Murder Trials in Ireland, 1836–1914* (Dublin: Four Courts Press, 2009), pp. 86–90.

9. *Cork Examiner*, 7 December 1881; *Cork Constitution*, 7 December 1881. The agrarian crime statistics cited by Justice Fitzgerald and those recorded in official publications differ significantly, 1,061 and 601 respectively, though the constabulary were responsible for both sets of figures. The discrepancy may hinge on definition and interpretation of agrarian crime and outrages, and while it raises questions and concerns about the reliability and use of official returns, it does not invalidate Fitzgerald's basic contention, that agrarian agitation was deeply entrenched and its incidence in 1881 substantially higher than in the previous year. See Agrarian Offences (Counties) (Ireland). Return of the number of agrarian offences in each county in Ireland reported to the constabulary office in each month of the year 1881, distinguishing offences against the person, offences against property, and offences against the public peace, with summary for

each county, for the year, HC 1882 (8) lv. 1. For Justice J.D. FitzGerald see Sinéad Agnew, 'FitzGerald, John David, Baron FitzGerald of Kilmarnock (1816–1889), judge', *Oxford Dictionary of National Biography*, 23 September 2004, https://www.oxforddnb.com/view/10.1093/ref:odnb/9780198614128.001.0001/odnb-9780198614128-e-9569

10. Terence Dooley, 'Irish Land Questions, 1879–1923', in Thomas Bartlett (ed.), *The Cambridge History of Ireland. Volume IV: 1880 to the Present* (Cambridge: Cambridge University Press, 2018), pp. 117–44, at p. 127; William J. Smyth, 'Agrarian Crimes and Evictions', in John Crowley, Donal Ó Drisceoil and Mike Murphy (eds), *Atlas of the Irish Revolution* (Cork: Cork University Press, 2017), pp. 39–41, at p. 40.

11. NAI, CSORP/1883/15390. This is the overarching reference number for a series of files, all relating to the Daniel Connell case; they are 32054; misc 1707.1911; 53300; 15354; 1666; 36517; the current reference is 1666, 'Report of Outrage', 8 August 1881. See also James S. Donnelly, Jr, *The Land and the People of Nineteenth-century Cork: The rural economy and the land question* (London and Boston: Routledge & Kegan Paul, 1975), p. 285.

12. *West Cork Eagle*, 4 January 1882; *Cork Constitution*, 24 January 1882; NAI, CSORP/1883/15390 (32054), 'Royal Irish Republic, Fenian Brother-Hood, Moonlights'.

13. Hegarty was elected to the Millstreet board of Poor Law guardians for the first time in 1877, for the electoral division of Drishane. He gave evidence to the Irish Poor Law Union and Lunacy Inquiry Commission which sat at Millstreet on 10 May 1878: Poor Law Union and Lunacy Inquiry Commission (Ireland). Report and evidence with appendices, HC 1878-9 [c. 2239], xxxi. 1, pp. 42–4. He also appeared before the Special Commission on Parnellism and Crime, on 30 November 1888: Special Commission Act, 1888. Reprint of the shorthand notes of the speeches, proceedings, and evidence taken before the commissioners appointed under the above-named act (London, 1890), vol. 2, pp. 597–619.

14. NAI, INL carton 10, 'Outrage Reports, Cork, 1880–8', Cork WR, 'Persecution of Mr Jeremiah Hegarty, JP, of Millstreet, by the Land League and National League, in consequence of his refusing to join the movement. The persecution is carried on by outrage to his person, and to the persons and property of those who neglected the teaching of the Leaguers; by intimidation, criminal conspiracy, and general lawlessness and terrorism'; *Cork Examiner*, 23, 24, 29 December 1880.

15. *Cork Examiner*, 25 March 1881.

16. Michael Davitt, *The Fall of Feudalism in Ireland or the Story of the Land League Revolution* (London and New York: Harper & Brothers, 1904), p. 165.

17. *Cork Examiner*, 25 March 1881.

18. Special Commission Act, 1888, vol. 2, pp. 598–9. The document was dated 3 September 1882, but Hegarty testified before the Special Commission on Parnellism

and Crime that it was first posted, along with other boycotting notices, in December 1880, vol. 2, pp. 597–619. Threatening notices were often illustrated with rifles, revolvers and coffins for added effect. One Millstreet notice was signed 'Rory C. Moonlight, Buckshot and Bullets'; another, 'A True Gentleman, Captain Moonlight', NAI, INL carton 10, 'Outrage Reports, Cork, 1880–8', Cork WR.

19. T.W. Moody, *Davitt and Irish Revolution 1846–82* (Oxford: Clarendon Press, 1981), pp. 418–19.

20. Donnelly, *The Land and the People of Nineteenth-century Cork*, pp. 284–5; Donnacha Seán Lucey, *Land, Popular Politics and Agrarian Violence in Ireland: The case of County Kerry, 1872–86* (Dublin: UCD Press, 2011), p. 71. According to the RIC, Canon Griffin was obnoxious because of his 'antipathy to the Land League', NAI, INL carton 10, 'Outrage Reports, Cork, 1880–8', Cork WR.

21. *Cork Examiner*, 28, 29 March 1881.

22. Ibid., 30 August 1881.

23. Ibid.; Donnelly, *The Land and the People of Nineteenth-century Cork*, pp. 284–5. For Colthurst's marriage, at St Fin Barre's Cathedral, Cork on 27 August, see *Kerry Evening Post*, 31 August 1881.

24. *Cork Examiner*, 31 August 1881.

25. Ibid.

26. NAI, INL carton 10, 'Outrage Reports, Cork, 1880–8', Cork WR. The *Oxford English Dictionary* defines buckshot as 'A coarse kind of shot, larger than swan-shot, used in shooting deer or other large game'.

27. NAI, CSORP/1883/15390 (1666); NAI, INL carton 10, 'Outrage Reports, Cork, 1880–8', Cork WR; *West Cork Eagle*, 4 January 1882; *Cork Examiner*, 4 January 1882; Georgina O'Brien (ed.), *The Reminiscences of the Right Hon. Lord O'Brien (of Kilfenora) Lord Chief Justice of Ireland* (London: Edward Arnold, 1916), p. 33.

28. See, generally, Donald E. Jordan. Jr, 'The Irish National League and the "Unwritten Law": Rural protest and nation-building in Ireland 1882–1890', *Past and Present*, vol. 158, February 1998, pp. 146–71.

29. NAI, CSORP/1883/15390 (1666); NAI, INL carton 10, 'Outrage Reports, Cork, 1880–8', Cork WR; *Cork Constitution*, 24 January 1882. There are discrepancies in names and spelling in the police and newspaper accounts of the documents found in Connell's possession. Historians have drawn attention to the brutality associated with clandestine combinations. See, for example, Hughes and MacRaild, *Ribbon Societies in Nineteenth-century Ireland and Its Diaspora*, p. 93; R.V. Comerford, 'Ireland 1850–70', in W.E. Vaughan (ed.), *A New History of Ireland. Vol. 5: Ireland under the Union, I: 1801–1870* (Oxford: Clarendon Press, 1989), pp. 372–95, at p. 390.

30. *West Cork Eagle*, 4 January 1882.

31. Cronin, *Agrarian Protest in Ireland*, pp. 14–15.

32. *West Cork Eagle*, 31 December 1881.

33. *Cork Constitution*, 24 January 1882.

34. See, for example, NAI, CO 904/183, MFA 54/107, 'Register of Informants'. The register relates to the late 1880s and early 1890s, and lists the informants' aliases, locations, the quality of the information supplied to the police, and payments received in 1889. Anthony Philbin, one of the accused in the notorious Maamtrasna murders in August 1882, turned queen's evidence for the same reason as Connell, to secure his own discharge. Margaret Kelleher, *The Maamtrasna Murders: Language, life and death in nineteenth-century Ireland* (Dublin: UCD Press, 2018), pp. 77–8.

35. Cronin, *Agrarian Protest in Ireland*, p. 15.

36. *Cork Examiner*, 11 January 1882; Donnelly, *The Land and the People of Nineteenth-century Cork*, p. 286.

37. Nocturnal Attacks (Ireland). Return giving the names and occupations of all persons arrested for or convicted of having taken part in nocturnal attacks between the months of June 1880 and June 1882, HC 1882 (403) lv. 609. For age, occupation and social profiles of members of west Donegal Ribbon lodges in the mid-1850s see Breandán Mac Suibhne, *The End of Outrage: Post-Famine adjustment in rural Ireland* (Oxford: Oxford University Press, 2017), pp. 42–5.

38. *Cork Examiner*, 11 January 1882.

39. Ibid., 14 February 1882. Her name was also given as Hanorah or Hannah Riordan, while her own version was Hannagh Reardion. She was maintained in lodgings in Cork before her transfer, on 20 February 1882, to a secure facility at Ballybough, Dublin, where she remained for at least seven months. William Verling Gregg, crown solicitor for Cork, described Reardon as 'nervous and excitable', and Sub-Inspector Alexander Heard, Clontarf RIC, Dublin, pronounced her 'a most excitable person', one who squabbled continually with other police witnesses: NAI, CSORP/1882/34685; CSORP/1883/15390 (misc 1707.1911).

40. *Cork Examiner*, 11, 16, 28 January, 1, 14 February, 28 March, 19 April 1882; NAI, CSORP/1883 15390 (misc 1707.1911), Starkie to G.E. Hillier, Inspector General (IG), RIC, 11 April 1882.

41. 11 & 12 Vic., c. 12, 'An Act for the Better Security of the Crown and Government of the United Kingdom', 22 April 1848.

42. NAI, CBS B Files/B134, Secret Societies Memorandum, 12 August–4 October 1882, members of the Moonlight society in Cork West Riding.

43. Hansard's Parliamentary Debates (hereafter HC Deb), 24 January 1881, 3rd series, vol. 257, cc. 1225–7; T. Wemyss Reid, *Life of the Right Honourable William Edward Forster*, 2 vols (London: Chapman & Hall, 1888), vol. 2, pp. 263–6, Forster to W.E. Gladstone, prime minister, 8 November 1880; Reid, *Forster*, vol. 2, pp. 293–7.

44. 44 Vic., c. 4, 'An Act for the Better Protection of Person and Property in Ireland, 1881' (Protection of Person and Property (Ireland) Act), 2 March 1881; Frank Rynne, 'Arrests Made Under the Protection of Person and Property Act, March 1881–July 1882', in John Crowley, Donal Ó Drisceoil and Mike Murphy (eds), *Atlas of the Irish Revolution* (Cork: Cork University Press, 2017), pp. 56–9. For an analysis of the occupational profile of suspects, see Samuel Clark, *Social Origins of the Irish Land War* (Princeton, NJ: Princeton University Press, 1979), pp. 267–72.

45. Resident or stipendiary magistrates were paid public officials who worked with the police force in the administration of law and order.

46. NAI 3/714/3, Protection of Person and Property (Ireland) Act, 1881, John and Cornelius Creedon, arrest warrants 49 and 50; NAI, CBS B Files/B134, Secret Societies Memorandum, 12 August–4 October 1882. John Creedon and O'Sullivan were named in the memorandum as leading members of the Moonlight society in Cork West Riding; *United Ireland*, supplement, 10 September 1881, 'Our Legion of Honour: A record of the victims of the Coercion Act of 1881'.

47. William L. Feingold, *The Revolt of the Tenantry: The transformation of local government in Ireland 1872–1886* (Boston: North-Eastern University Press, 1984); William L. Feingold, 'Land League Power: The Tralee Poor Law election of 1881', in Clark and Donnelly (eds), *Irish Peasants*, pp. 285–310.

48. NAI, 3/714/3, Protection of Person and Property (Ireland) Act, 1881, Andrew Connor, arrest warrant 136; John Mahony, arrest warrant 141.

49. NAI, CSORP/1883/15390 (misc 1707.1911), Starkie to IG, 11, 19 April 1882.

50. NAI, CSORP/1883/15390 (53300), Starkie to IG, 26 January 1882. Connell had other convictions, including two for illegal fishing and one for assault, for which he served a prison term in 1881; CSORP/1883/15390 (misc 1707.1911), Connell's prison record, which accompanied a petition to the lord lieutenant, 26 May 1882.

51. NAI, CSORP/1883/15390 (53300), Starkie to IG, 26 January 1882. In January 1882, an informer at Kilmallock, County Limerick, provided the local police with a copy of the Irish Republican Brotherhood oath, the wording of which was more specific than that sworn by Connell at Millstreet: 'In the presence of God I [name] do solemnly swear that I will do my utmost to establish the national independence of Ireland, and that I will bear true allegiance to the Supreme Council of the Irish Republican Brotherhood and government of the Irish Republican Brotherhood, and implicitly obey the constitution of the Irish Republican Brotherhood and all my superior officers, and that I will preserve inviolable the secrets of the organisation': NAI, CSORP/1883/15390 (53300).

52. *Cork Constitution*, 28 March 1882; *Cork Examiner*, 28 March 1882.

53. *Cork Examiner*, 1 August 1882, Cork summer assizes.

54. NAI, CSORP/1883/15390 (53300), Starkie to IG, 26 January 1882.

55. See, inter alia, Paul Bew, *Land and the National Question in Ireland, 1858–82* (Dublin: Gill & Macmillan, 1978), pp. 145-51; Tom Garvin, *The Evolution of Irish Nationalist Politics* (Dublin: Gill & Macmillan, 1981), pp. 73-8; Lucey, *Land, Popular Politics and Agrarian Violence in Ireland*, Chapter 4.

56. NAI, CSORP/1883/15390 (53300), Starkie to IG, 26 January, 7 February 1882. Jeremiah was arrested for an attack on the house of his namesake Frank Riordan, and robbery of firearms, on 13 January 1882. He was one of a large group of Millstreet prisoners who were returned for trial, charged with treason-felony, at the 1882 Cork spring assizes. On the crown's application, the judge postponed the trial, and the prisoners were held over, to appear at the summer assizes, NAI, CSORP/1883/15390 (misc 1707.1911), Starkie to IG, 29 March 1882. For similar links in parts of County Kerry, see Lucey, *Land, Popular Politics and Agrarian Violence in Ireland*, pp. 104-5.

57. NAI, CSORP/1883/15390 (53300; misc 1707.1911), Starkie to IG, 26 January, 22 February 1882; *Cork Constitution*, 1 August 1882.

58. NAI, CBS B Files/B97, Superintendent John Mallon, G Division, Dublin Metropolitan Police (DMP), to chief commissioner, DMP, 20 June 1882. According to Paul Bew the sum involved was £1,000, not £10,000 as Mallon claimed: Bew, *Land and the National Question in Ireland*, p. 201. For Mallon, see Jim Herlihy, *The Dublin Metropolitan Police: A short history and genealogical guide* (Dublin: Four Courts Press, 2001), pp. 137-47.

59. NAI, CSORP/1883/15390 (32054; 53300), Starkie to IG, 26 January, 7 February 1882; Mallon to chief commissioner, DMP, 15 February 1882; *Cork Constitution*, 1 August 1882.

60. NAI, CSORP/1883/15390 (53300), Mallon to chief commissioner, DMP, 15 February 1882.

61. C.P. Crane, *Memories of a Resident Magistrate, 1880-1920* (Edinburgh: T&A Constable, 1938), pp. 63-4.

62. For the association between music and nationalist politics see Richard Parfitt, '"Oh, What Matter, when for Erin Dear We Fall": Music and Irish nationalism, 1848-1913', *Irish Studies Review*, vol. 23, no. 4, 2015, pp. 480-94.

63. Crane, *Memories of a Resident Magistrate*, p. 82.

64. T.W. Moody and Richard Hawkins (eds), *Florence Arnold-Forster's Irish Journal* (Oxford: Clarendon Press, 1988), pp. 66-7.

65. NAI, CSORP/1883/15390 (53300), Starkie to IG, 26 January 1882.

66. HC Deb, 16 February 1882, 3rd series, vol. 266, cc. 808-21; 4 April 1882, vol. 268, cc. 693-8. See Charles Townshend, *Political Violence in Ireland: Government and resistance since 1848* (Oxford: Clarendon Press, 1983), pp. 148-57.

67. HC Deb, 4 April 1882, 3rd series, vol. 268, cc. 701–6. Previously, Ireland's leading nationalist daily newspaper had contended editorially that 'the government made the primal mistake in arresting men whose influence best restrained the desperate and the violent', *Freeman's Journal*, 7 March 1882, p. 4.

68. NAI, CSORP/1883/15390 (53300), Starkie to IG, 26 January, 7 February 1882.

69. Ibid., Starkie to IG, 7 February 1882.

70. Ibid., Starkie to IG, 26 January, 9 March, 24 April 1882.

71. NAI, CBS B Files/B134, Secret Societies Memorandum, 12 August–4 October 1882; Mac Suibhne, *The End of Outrage*, pp. 129–31.

72. *Cork Constitution*, 24 January 1882; NAI, CSORP/1883/15390 (53300), Starkie to IG, 26 January 1882.

73. *Cork Constitution*, 24 January 1882.

74. *Cork Examiner*, 2 August 1882.

75. Ibid., 12 January 1883; *Cork Constitution*, 12 January 1883.

76. O'Brien (ed.), *The Reminiscences of the Right Hon. Lord O'Brien*, p. 34.

77. Fitzgerald and William Nicholas Keogh, justice of the common pleas, constituted the special commission that sat in both Dublin and Cork between late November 1865 and early February of the following year to try forty-one Fenian prisoners, including much of the leadership. See Richard A. Keogh, '"Why, It's Like a '98 Trial": The Irish judiciary and the Fenian trials, 1865–1866', in Hughes and MacRaild (eds), *Crime, Violence and the Irish in the Nineteenth Century*, pp. 131–48.

78. *Cork Constitution*, 24 January 1882; *Cork Examiner*, 24 January 1882.

79. Moody and Hawkins (eds), *Florence Arnold-Forster's Irish Journal*, p. 362.

80. Kelleher, *The Maamtrasna Murders*.

81. NAI, CSORP/1882/3631, Plunkett to Thomas H. Burke, under-secretary, Dublin Castle, 21 January 1882. Thomas Oliver Westenra Plunkett (1838–89), second son of Thomas Plunkett, 12th Baron Louth, resident magistrate since 1866. The under-secretary at Dublin Castle oversaw the British civil administration in Ireland.

82. For the role and responsibilities of the special resident magistrates see Townshend, *Political Violence in Ireland*, pp. 138–47, 174–5. Two months after the appointment of the SRMs, Chief Secretary Forster thought that Plunkett was the most successful of the six, comparing him favourably to Clifford Lloyd, his colleague in neighbouring County Limerick, whose energy and initiative did not sufficiently compensate for his impulsiveness, inconsistency and tactlessness: Moody and Hawkins (eds), *Florence Arnold-Forster's Irish Journal*, p. 382. For Lloyd's assessment of the SRM system see Clifford Lloyd, *Ireland Under the Land League: A narrative of personal experience* (Edinburgh and London: William Blackwood, 1892), pp. 227–49.

83. HC Deb, 27 July 1882, 3rd series, vol. 272, cc. 1983-91.

84. *Cork Examiner*, 1, 2, 3 August 1882.

85. Ibid., 8, 13 January 1883.

86. Ibid., 12 January 1883.

87. NAI, CSORP/1882/26633, Gregg to T.H. Burke, 31 March 1882. The file contains a printed list of the names, locations and occupations of the 210 members of the jury panel assembled for the 1882 County Cork spring assizes. Gregg had aired similar concerns about the integrity of Cork jurors following the 1880 winter assizes: 'I have no doubt that fear operated on some and sympathy with a large number. I cannot say that there was actual intimidation', NAI, CO 904/182, MFA 54/107, pp. 128-30, Gregg to Burke, 24 December 1880. For crown solicitors and counsel see Vaughan, *Murder Trials in Ireland*, pp. 90-102; for juror intimidation in political and agrarian trials in the 1880s see Niamh Howlin, *Juries in Ireland: Lay persons and the law in the long nineteenth century* (Dublin: Four Courts Press, 2017), pp. 157-65.

88. *Cork Constitution*, 24 January 1882, statements by Peter O'Brien, QC, and Justice Fitzgerald. The latter was consistent in his interpretation of the law, having written an opinion on the question of uncorroborated evidence as far back as mid-1856, when he was attorney general for Ireland: Mac Suibhne, *The End of Outrage*, pp. 142-5. On this topic see also Stephen Ball (ed.), *A Policeman's Ireland: Recollections of Samuel Waters, RIC* (Cork: Cork University Press, 1999), pp. 13-14, 96, n. 35; Padraic Kennedy, '"The Indispensable Informer": Daniel O'Sullivan Goula and the Phoenix Society, 1858-9', *Éire-Ireland*, vol. 45, nos 3-4, 2010, pp. 147-83, at p. 148, n. 4; p. 175.

89. *Cork Examiner*, 12 January 1883.

90. Ibid.

91. NAI, CSORP/1883/15390 (misc 1707.1911), Starkie to IG, 29 April 1882.

92. NAI, CBS B Files/B47, Fenian suspects in Cork: file submitted to Colonel Brackenbury, assistant under-secretary, Dublin Castle, 11 June 1882; CBS B Files/B134, Secret Societies Memorandum, 12 August-4 October 1882.

93. NAI, INL carton 10, Outrage Reports, Cork, 1880-8: Cork City, information supplied by James T. Geelan, gatekeeper at Cork County jail.

94. *Cork Examiner*, 14 February 1882. For an interrogation of aspects of women's involvement with agrarian agitation in the 1880s, including assisting imprisoned suspects and activists, see Heather Laird, 'Decentring the Irish Land War: Women, politics and the private sphere', in Fergus Campbell and Tony Varley (eds), *Land Questions in Modern Ireland* (Manchester and New York: Manchester University Press, 2013), pp. 175-93.

95. See, for instance, Richard Hawkins, 'Government Versus Secret Societies: The Parnell era', in Williams (ed.), *Secret Societies in Ireland*, pp. 100-12, at pp. 107-8;

Patrick O'Farrell, *The Irish in Australia* (Sydney: New South Wales University Press, 1986), p. 51.

96. NAI, CSORP/1883/15390 (misc 1707.1911).

97. Paul Bew, 'A Vision to the Dispossessed? Popular piety and revolutionary politics in the Irish Land War, 1879-82', in Judith Devlin and Ronan Fanning (eds), *Religion and Rebellion: Papers read before the 22nd Irish conference of historians, held at University College Dublin, 18–22 May 1995 (Historical studies XX)* (Dublin: UCD Press, 1997), pp. 137-51, at p. 149.

98. NAI, CSORP/1883/15390 (misc 1707.1911), Connell to the lord lieutenant, 26 May 1882; CSORP/1883/15390 (32054), 'Royal Irish Republic, Fenian Brother-Hood, Moonlights'.

99. In his prison record sheet, which was attached to his petition to the lord lieutenant, 26 May 1882, Connell was described as eighteen years of age when arrested in the previous December, NAI, CSORP/1883/15390 (32054).

100. McCarthy subsequently identified and testified against members of the raiding party, and Jeremiah and James Twohig were partly convicted on his evidence, *Cork Constitution*, 24 January 1882.

101. NAI, CSORP/1883/15390 (misc 1707.191), Starkie to IG, 29 March 1882.

102. NAI, CSORP/1883/15390 (32054), 'Royal Irish Republic, Fenian Brother-Hood, Moonlights'. Connell's parents and his five siblings were secretly despatched to Canada in November 1882, and a sum of £50 was provided to pay for their fares and travel essentials, and to afford them some money on their arrival in Quebec. The family sailed from Queenstown on the *Novascotian* on Sunday, 19 November 1882, NAI, CSORP/1882/44570, Head Constable Michael O'Connor, Millstreet, to Captain Plunkett, 14, 16, 22 November 1882.

103. Donnelly, *Captain Rock*, pp. 110-13; Beames, *Peasants and Power*, pp. 98-101. For the European dimension, see Hughes and MacRaild, *Ribbon Societies in Nineteenth-century Ireland and Its Diaspora*, p. 18, n. 64.

104. National Library of Ireland, Ms. 43,083/7, Considine Papers.

105. Ibid.

106. Reid, *Life of the Right Honourable William Edward Forster*, vol. 2, pp. 377-8, Forster to Gladstone, 11 December 1881.

107. NAI, CSORP/1883/15390 (53300), Starkie to IG, 26 January 1882.

108. Ibid. See, generally, Owen McGee, *The IRB: The Irish Republican Brotherhood, from the Land League to Sinn Féin* (Dublin: Four Courts Press, 2005), pp. 86-7.

109. NAI, CBS B Files/B27, Alan Bell, Athenry RIC, to IG, 16 June 1882.

110. Office of assistant under-secretary for police and crime, under the command of Henry Brackenbury, a career soldier; he was replaced shortly afterwards by Edward George Jenkinson, who held the office from July 1882 until January 1887. See Townshend, *Political Violence in Ireland*, pp. 167–80. For the reverberations of the Phoenix Park murders see Matthew Kelly, 'Radical Nationalisms, 1882–1916', in Thomas Bartlett (ed.), *The Cambridge History of Ireland. Volume IV: 1880 to the Present* (Cambridge: Cambridge University Press, 2018), pp. 33–61, at pp. 38–9.

111. NAI, CBS B Files/B134, Secret Societies Memorandum, 12 August–4 October 1882. For the activities of agrarian secret societies in Castleisland and other disturbed parts of County Kerry, see Lucey, *Land, Popular Politics and Agrarian Violence in Ireland*, particularly Chapter 4: 'The Land League, Fenianism and Agrarian Violence'.

112. Davitt, *The Fall of Feudalism in Ireland*, pp. 40–3. See also Tom Garvin, 'Defenders, Ribbonmen and Others: Underground political networks in pre-Famine Ireland', in Philpin (ed.), *Nationalism and Popular Protest in Ireland*, pp. 219–44; Garvin, *The Evolution of Irish Nationalist Politics*, p. 39; Donnelly, *Captain Rock*, pp. 97–103; Mac Suibhne, *The End of Outrage*, pp. 40–1, 60–1, 167; Hughes and MacRaild, *Ribbon Societies in Nineteenth-century Ireland and Its Diaspora*, Chapter 8: 'Ribbonmen, Fenians, and Hibernians: Clashes and convergences from the 1870s'.

113. Hughes and MacRaild, *Ribbon Societies in Nineteenth-century Ireland and Its Diaspora*, pp. 268–9; Oliver MacDonagh, 'Ambiguity in Nationalism: The case of Ireland', in Ciaran Brady (ed.), *Interpreting Irish History: The debate on historical revisionism* (Dublin: Irish Academic Press, 1994), pp. 105–21.

114. Lucey, *Land, Popular Politics and Agrarian Violence in Ireland*, Chapter 4; Frank Rynne, 'Permanent Revolutionaries: The IRB and the Land War in west Cork', in Fearghal McGarry and James McConnel (eds), *The Black Hand of Republicanism: Fenianism in modern Ireland* (Dublin: Irish Academic Press, 2009), pp. 55–71.

115. NAI, CSORP/1883/15390 (53300), Starkie to IG, 26 January, 9 March, 24 April 1882; *Cork Examiner*, 12 January 1883.

116. *Cork Examiner*, 2 August 1882.

117. NAI, CSORP/1883/15390 (53300), Starkie to IG, 26 January 1882.

118. *Cork Constitution*, 2 August 1882.

119. NAI, CSORP/1883/15390 (32054). Sub-Inspector Heard, Clontarf RIC, estimated Connell's travelling expenses as follows: passage from London to Sydney, £15 15s.; ship's kit, £1 10s.; fare to London, £1 3s.; expenses on journey and in London, £1 10s.; suit of clothes £2 14s. 6d.; trunk, 8s.; cab fare from Raheny, 2s.

120. NAI, CSORP/1883/15390 (36517), Sub-Inspector Heard, Clontarf RIC to IG, 4 July 1883.

121. Breandán Mac Suibhne was more successful in tracing his subject, Patrick McGlynn, the west County Donegal schoolmaster and Ribbon informer whom the Irish authorities relocated to the Australian colony of Victoria in August 1857, *The End of Outrage*, pp. 215–19; Breandán Mac Suibhne and Jonathan Wooding, 'Hunting Down an Informer', *The Irish Times*, 16 June 2018, Ticket, pp. 25–7.

## Chapter 7: Moonlighting and Playwriting

1. Fiona Brennan, *George Fitzmaurice: 'Wild in his own way'. Biography of an Abbey playwright* (Dublin: Carysfort Press, 2007), p. xxiii.

2. See, for instance, Howard K. Slaughter, *The Plays of George Fitzmaurice: Folk plays* (Dublin: Dolmen Press, 1969), p. vii: 'Fitzmaurice's plays have been all but forgotten'.

3. Nicholas Grene and Chris Morash (eds), *The Oxford Handbook of Modern Irish Theatre* (Oxford: Oxford University Press, 2016), p. 313.

4. *The Irish Times*, 19 November 2016.

5. O'Toole, 'Foreword', in Brennan, *George Fitzmaurice*, p. xxiii.

6. Brennan, *George Fitzmaurice*, pp. 1–5.

7. *Cork Constitution*, 12 December 1881; *Cork Examiner*, 12 December 1881. The witness' name appears in different sources as Lennane, Lenane, Linnane. I have opted for the former. Courts of petty sessions were district courts, presided over by magistrates, and dealt with minor offences.

8. *Kerry Sentinel*, 2 December 1881; *Cork Constitution*, 12 December 1881; *Cork Examiner*, 12 December 1881; NAI, CSORP/1882/8333, 'Outrage' report compiled by John Cruise, county inspector, RIC, 29 November 1881. Massy had been one of the magistrates present at the Listowel petty sessions on 27 August 1881, *Kerry Evening Post*, 31 August 1881.

9. NAI, CSORP/1882/8333, Massy to the under-secretary, 27 November 1881, and Cruise's 'Outrage' report.

10. *Cork Constitution*, 12 December 1881; *Cork Examiner*, 12 December 1881.

11. Ibid.; *Kerry Sentinel*, 2 December 1881.

12. *Kerry Sentinel*, 29 November 1881.

13. *Cork Constitution*, 12 December 1881; *Cork Examiner*, 12 December 1881.

14. Ibid.

15. *Cork Constitution*, 12, 13 December 1881; *Cork Examiner*, 12, 13 December 1881. Similar alibis were provided by the families of the men accused of the gruesome Maamtrasna murders in the following year, Margaret Kelleher, *The Maamtrasna Murders: Language, life and death in nineteenth-century Ireland* (Dublin: UCD Press, 2018), pp. 67–71.

16. *Cork Constitution*, 12 December 1881; *Cork Examiner*, 12 December 1881.

17. *Cork Constitution*, 13 December 1881; *Cork Examiner*, 13 December 1881.

18. Ibid.

19. *Cork Constitution*, 13, 14 December 1881; *Cork Examiner*, 13, 14 December 1881.

20. NAI, CSORP/1882/8333, Massy to the under-secretary, 14 December 1881.

21. Ibid., 27 November, 20 December 1881.

22. Ibid., 14, 20 December 1881.

23. *Cork Examiner*, 26 January 1882.

24. Ibid., 14 December 1881, *Cork Constitution*, 14 December 1881.

25. For an analysis of the clemency appeals process see Ciara Breathnach and Laurence M. Geary, 'Crime and Punishment: Whiteboyism and the law in late nineteenth-century Ireland', in Kyle Hughes and Donald M. MacRaild (eds), *Crime, Violence and the Irish in the Nineteenth Century* (Liverpool: Liverpool University Press, 2017), pp. 165–70. For the clemency appeals submitted on behalf of the men who were convicted and imprisoned for the Maamtrasna murders see Kelleher, *The Maamtrasna Murders*, pp. 175–81.

26. NAI, GPB/PEN/1883/43: Daniel Galvin; GPB/PEN/1885/75: Bartholomew Nolan; GPB/PEN/1886/98: Michael Galvin; GPB/PEN/1886/99: Cornelius McAuliffe; GPB/PEN/1886/100: James Quinlan; GPB/PEN/1886/101: Maurice Molony; GPB/PEN/1889/82: Patrick Cronin. There are some discrepancies in Nolan's prison file; his age is given as forty-two, and he is described as the father of five children. Other sources state that he was forty-four years old and had eight children. For the physical and mental health fluctuations of the Scrahan seven while in prison see Breathnach and Geary, 'Crime and Punishment', pp. 161–70.

27. Sinéad Agnew, 'FitzGerald, John David, Baron FitzGerald of Kilmarnock (1816–1889), judge', *Oxford Dictionary of National Biography* (Oxford: Oxford University Press, 2004). https://www.oxforddnb.com/view/10.1093/ref:odnb/9780198614128.001.0001/odnb-9780198614128-e-9569

28. NAI, CSO/CRF/1882/N3. The Criminal Reference Files (CRFs) at the National Archives of Ireland are cited by year, the prisoner's initial (in this case N for Nolan), and the correspondence number. The CRF for each man sentenced to imprisonment at the Munster winter assizes in 1881 for agrarian outrages is contained within CSO/CRF/1888/C71, the file relating to Patrick Cronin, the longest serving of the prisoners.

29. NAI, CSO/CRF/1883/G9.

30. *Kerry Evening Post*, 11, 15, 22 July 1885; HC Deb, 13 July 1885, 3rd series, vol. 299, c. 420. See also NAI, CSO/CRF/1885/N6, briefing note prepared by the under-secretary.

31. HC Deb, 16 February 1882, 3rd series, vol. 266, cc. 808–21; 4 April 1882, vol. 268, cc. 693–8; 31 May 1886, vol. 306, c. 498; NAI, CSO/CRF/1886/Misc1574, briefing note by the crown's legal advisor on Richard Lalor's parliamentary question; Lalor was MP for Queen's County (Laois).

32. NAI, CSO/CRF/1885/C25; CSO/CRF/1886/C49; CSO/CRF/1887/C1; CSO/CRF/1885/Misc1356; CRF/PEN/189/82; HC Deb, 22 September 1886, 3rd series, vol. 309, cc. 1252–3.

33. Fitzgerald, ODNB.

34. NAI, CSO/CRF/1885/Misc148.

35. Cork Examiner, 12 December 1881.

36. Ibid., 14 December 1881; Cork Constitution, 14 December 1881. For Nolan's fragile mental health see Breathnach and Geary, 'Crime and Punishment', pp. 167–9.

37. NAI, CSO/CRF/1886/N3; CSO/CRF/1882/Mc23.

38. Ibid., CSO/CRF/1883/Misc1084.

39. Ibid., CSO/CRF/1886/C49.

40. Ibid.; CSO/CRF/1883/Misc1084.

41. Ibid.

42. NAI, CSO/CRF/1884/Misc1250; CSO/CRF/1883/Misc1084.

43. NAI, CSO/CRF/1885/Misc1482; CSO/CRF/1885/Misc1356.

44. NAI, CSO/CRF/1885/Misc1482.

45. NAI, CRF/PEN/1886/99.

46. Breathnach and Geary, 'Crime and Punishment', pp. 162, 164–5, 167.

47. George Fitzmaurice, The Moonlighter, in George Fitzmaurice, Five Plays (London and Dublin: Maunsel & Co., 1914), p. 79.

48. Ibid., pp. 72–4. For minor differences in the wording see Richard Parfitt, '"Oh, What Matter, when for Erin Dear We Fall": Music and Irish nationalism, 1848–1913', Irish Studies Review, vol. 23, no. 4, 2015, pp. 480–94, at pp. 485–6.

49. Fitzmaurice, The Moonlighter, p. 80.

50. Ibid., p. 87.

51. Ibid., pp. 96–7.

52. Ibid., pp. 106–7.

53. Ibid., p. 134.

# BIBLIOGRAPHY

## Unpublished Primary Sources

**Dublin City Library & Archive, 138–44 Pearse Street, Dublin 2**

'Mansion House Fund for the Relief of Distress in Ireland 1880'

**Dublin Diocesan Archives**

Papers of Edward McCabe, Archbishop of Dublin 1879–85

**National Archives of Ireland**

3/714/3, Protection of Person and Property (Ireland) Act, 1881 (arrest warrants)

CBS B Files/B27, Alan Bell, Athenry RIC, County Galway, to Inspector General, 16 June 1882

CBS B Files/B47, Fenian suspects in Cork, 11 June 1882

CBS B Files/B97, Superintendent John Mallon, G Division, Dublin Metropolitan Police, to chief commissioner, 20 June 1882

CBS B Files/B134, Secret Societies Memorandum, 12 August–4 October 1882

CO 904/183, MFA 54/107, 'Register of Informants'

CSO/CRF/1888/C71 (The criminal reference file for each man sentenced to imprisonment at the Munster winter assizes in 1881 for agrarian outrages)

Chief Secretary's Office, Registered Papers (CSORP)

CSORP/1883/15390 (Daniel Connell/Royal Irish Republic secret society)

INL carton 10, 'Outrage Reports, Cork, 1880-8'

**National Library of Ireland**

Ms. 43,083/7, Considine Papers

Ms. 18011/2, John Devoy Papers (James Redpath)

## Published Primary Sources

Hansard's Parliamentary Debates, 3rd series

## Legislation

15 & 16 Geo. 3, c. 21, 'An Act to Prevent and Punish Tumultuous Risings of Persons Within This Kingdom, and for Other Purposes Therein Mentioned', 4 April 1776

1 & 2 Will. 4, c. 44, 'An Act to Amend an Act Passed in the Parliament of Ireland, in the Fifteenth and Sixteenth Years of the Reign of His Majesty King George the Third, Intituled "An Act to Prevent and Punish Tumultuous Risings of Persons Within This Kingdom, and for Other Purposes Therein Mentioned"', 15 October 1831

11 & 12 Vic., c. 12, 'An Act for the Better Security of the Crown and Government of the United Kingdom', 22 April 1848

43 Vic., c. 4, 'An Act to Render Valid Certain Proceedings Taken for the Relief of Distress in Ireland, and to Make Further Provision for Such Relief; and for Other Purposes', 15 March 1880

44 Vic., c. 4, 'An Act for the Better Protection of Person and Property in Ireland, 1881' (Protection of Person and Property (Ireland) Act), 2 March 1881

## Newspapers and Periodicals

**Ireland**
Connaught Telegraph
Cork Constitution
Cork Examiner
Dublin Evening Mail
Freeman's Journal
Irish Ecclesiastical Gazette
Kerry Evening Post
Kerry Sentinel
Nation
The Irish Times
United Ireland
Weekly Irish Times
West Cork Eagle and County Advertiser

**Australia**
Advocate
Age
Ararat and Pleasant Creek Advertiser
Argus
Australian Sketcher
Ballarat Courier

*Bendigo Advertiser*
*Border Post*
*Brisbane Courier*
*Bulletin*
*Echo*
*Express and Telegraph*
*Freeman's Journal*
*Gippsland Times*
*Jewish Herald*
*Kyneton Guardian*
*Maitland Mercury*
*Melbourne Punch*
*Mercury*
*Newcastle Morning Herald and Miners' Advocate*
*South Australian Advertiser*
*South Australian Chronicle and Weekly Mail*
*South Australian Register*
*Tasmanian Mail*
*Warwick Argus*

### Britain
*Daily Telegraph*
*Illustrated London News*
*Lancet*
*Medical Press and Circular* (formerly *Dublin Medical Press*)
*Standard*
*Tablet*
*Times*

### Canada
*Irish Canadian*

### New Zealand
*Grey River Argus*
*New Zealand Tablet*
*North Otago Times*
*Saturday Advertiser*
*Southland Times*

### United States
*Ave Maria: A journal devoted to the honor of the Blessed Virgin*
*Catholic Sentinel*
*New York Herald*

*New York Times*
*New York Tribune*
*Pilot*

## Parliamentary Papers

Poor Law Union and Lunacy Inquiry Commission (Ireland). Report and evidence with appendices, HC 1878-9 [c. 2239], xxxi. 1

Annual Report of the Local Government Board for Ireland, Being the Eighth Report Under 'The Local Government Board (Ireland) Act', 35 & 36 Vic., c. 69, HC 1880 [c. 2603, c. 2603-1], xxviii. 1, 39

Report from the Local Government Board to His Grace the Lord Lieutenant, 28 October 1879; Correspondence Relative to Measures for the Relief of Distress in Ireland, 1879-1880, HC 1880 [c. 2483, c. 2506], lxii. 157, 187

Local Government Board (Ireland). Further reports, dated respectively 9 and 15 July 1880, made to the Local Government Board in Ireland by Dr C.J. Nixon, temporary medical inspector, relative to an outbreak of fever in the Swineford [sic] union, County Mayo, HC 1880 (277) (277-1), lxii. 271

Relief of Distress on the West Coast of Ireland, HC 1880 [c. 2671], lxii. 195

Annual Report of the Local Government Board for Ireland, Being the Ninth Report Under 'The Local Government Board (Ireland) Act', 35 & 36 Vic., c. 69, HC 1881 [c. 2926, c. 2926-1], xlvii. 269, 305

Relief Funds (Ireland). Report of the joint committee selected from the committees of the duchess of Marlborough relief fund and the Dublin Mansion House fund for relief of distress in Ireland, to administer the sum of 100,000 dollars voted by the parliament of the domain of Canada towards the relief of distress in Ireland, HC 1881 (326), lxxv. 859

Outrages (Ireland). Return of outrages reported to the Royal Irish Constabulary office in each month of the year 1880 and 1881, and in the month of January 1882, HC 1882 (7), lv. 615

Agrarian Offences (Counties) (Ireland). Return of the number of agrarian offences in each county in Ireland reported to the constabulary office in each month of the year 1881, distinguishing offences against the person, offences against property, and offences against the public peace, with summary for each county, for the year, HC 1882 (8), lv. 1

Agricultural Statistics of Ireland, 1885, HC 1886 [c. 4802], lxxi. 1

# Published Works

Akenson, Donald Harman, *Half the World from Home: Perspectives on the Irish in New Zealand 1860–1950* (Wellington: Victoria University Press, 1990)

*Australian Dictionary of Biography* (Canberra: National Centre of Biography, Australian National University)

Ball, Stephen (ed.), *A Policeman's Ireland: Recollections of Samuel Waters, RIC* (Cork: Cork University Press, 1999)

Barr, Colin, *Ireland's Empire: The Roman Catholic Church in the English-speaking world, 1829–1914* (Cambridge: Cambridge University Press, 2019)

—, '"Imperium in Imperio": Irish episcopal imperialism in the nineteenth century', *English Historical Review*, vol. 502, 2008, pp. 611–50

Bartlett, Thomas (ed.), *The Cambridge History of Ireland. Volume IV: 1880 to the Present* (Cambridge: Cambridge University Press, 2018)

Beames, M.R., *Peasants and Power: The Whiteboy movements and their control in pre-Famine Ireland* (Brighton and New York: Harvester Press, 1983)

Bew, Paul, *Land and the National Question in Ireland, 1858–82* (Dublin: Gill & Macmillan, 1978)

—, *Enigma: A new life of Charles Stewart Parnell* (Dublin: Gill & Macmillan, 2011)

—, 'A Vision to the Dispossessed? Popular piety and revolutionary politics in the Irish Land War, 1879–82', in Judith Devlin and Ronan Fanning (eds), *Religion and Rebellion: Papers read before the 22nd Irish conference of historians, held at University College Dublin, 18–22 May 1995* (Historical studies XX) (Dublin: UCD Press, 1997), pp. 137–51

Bowen, Desmond, *Souperism: Myth or reality?* (Cork: Mercier Press, 1970)

—, *The Protestant Crusade in Ireland, 1800–1870: A study of Protestant–Catholic relations between the Act of Union and Disestablishment* (Dublin: Gill & Macmillan, 1978)

Brady, Ciaran (ed.), *Interpreting Irish History: The debate on historical revisionism* (Dublin: Irish Academic Press, 1994)

Branach, Niall R., 'Edward Nangle and the Achill Island Mission', *History Ireland*, vol. 8, no. 3, 2000, pp. 35–8

Breathnach, Ciara, 'Irish Catholic Identity in 1870s Otago, New Zealand', *Immigrants & Minorities*, vol. 31, no. 1, 2013, pp. 1–26

— and Laurence M. Geary, 'Crime and Punishment: Whiteboyism and the law in late nineteenth-century Ireland', in Kyle Hughes and Donald M. MacRaild (eds), *Crime, Violence and the Irish in the Nineteenth Century* (Liverpool: Liverpool University Press, 2017), pp. 149–72

Brennan, Fiona, *George Fitzmaurice: 'Wild in his own way'. Biography of an Abbey playwright* (Dublin: Carysfort Press, 2007)

Buckley. Anthony D., '"On the Club": Friendly societies in Ireland', *Irish Economic and Social History*, vol. 14, 1987, pp. 39–58

Callanan, Frank, *T.M. Healy* (Cork: Cork University Press, 1996)

Campbell, Fergus and Tony Varley (eds), *Land Questions in Modern Ireland* (Manchester: Manchester University Press, 2013)

Campbell, Malcolm, *Ireland's New Worlds: Immigrants, politics, and society in the United States and Australia, 1815–1922* (Madison: University of Wisconsin Press, 2008)

Clare, Sister Mary Francis, *The Apparition at Knock, with the Depositions of the Witnesses Examined by the Ecclesiastical Commission Appointed by His Grace the Archbishop of Tuam; and the Conversion of a Young Protestant Lady by a Visit of the Blessed Virgin* (London: Burns & Oates, 1880)

——, *The Nun of Kenmare: An autobiography* (Boston: Ticknor & Company, 1889)

Clark, C.M.H. (ed.), *Select Documents in Australian History, 1851–1900* (Sydney: Angus & Robertson, 1955)

Clark, Samuel, *Social Origins of the Irish Land War* (Princeton, NJ: Princeton University Press, 1979)

——, and James S. Donnelly, Jr (eds), *Irish Peasants: Violence and political unrest, 1780–1914* (Manchester: Manchester University Press, 1983)

——, 'Strange Bedfellows? The Land League alliances', in Fergus Campbell and Tony Varley (eds), *Land Questions in Modern Ireland* (Manchester: Manchester University Press, 2013), pp. 87–116

Collins, Timothy, 'HMS "Valorous"': Her contribution to Galway maritime history', *Journal of the Galway Archaeological and Historical Society*, vol. 49, 1997, pp. 122–42

Comerford, R.V., 'Ireland 1850–70', in W.E. Vaughan (ed.), *A New History of Ireland. Volume 5: Ireland under the Union, I: 1801–1870* (Oxford: Clarendon Press, 1989), pp. 372–95

——, 'The Land War and the Politics of Distress, 1877–82', in W.E. Vaughan (ed.), *A New History of Ireland. Volume 6: Ireland under the Union, II: 1870–1921* (Oxford: Clarendon Press, 1996), pp. 26–52

Corish, Patrick J. (ed.), *Radicals, Rebels, Establishments* (Belfast: Appletree Press, 1985)

Cousins, Mel, *Poor Relief in Ireland, 1851–1914* (Oxford: Peter Lang, 2011)

Cox, Catherine and Maria Luddy (eds), *Cultures of Care in Irish Medical History, 1750–1970* (London: Palgrave Macmillan, 2010)

Crane, C.P., *Memories of a Resident Magistrate, 1880–1920* (Edinburgh: T&A Constable, 1938)

Crawford, E. Margaret, 'Indian Meal and Pellagra in Nineteenth-century Ireland', in J.M. Goldstrom, and L.A. Clarkson (eds), *Irish Population, Economy, and Society: Essays in honour of the late K.H. Connell* (Oxford: Clarendon Press, 1981), pp. 113–33

Cronin, Maura, *Agrarian Protest in Ireland, 1750–1960*, Studies in Irish Economic and Social History, vol. 11 (Dundalk, 2012)

Crossman, Virginia, 'Emergency Legislation and Agrarian Disorder in Ireland, 1821–41', *Irish Historical Studies*, vol. 27, no. 108, November 1991, pp. 309–23

—, '"With the Experience of 1846 and 1847 Before Them": The politics of emergency relief, 1879–84', in Peter Gray (ed.), *Victoria's Ireland? Irishness and Britishness, 1837–1901* (Dublin: Four Courts Press, 2004), pp. 167–81

—, *Politics, Pauperism and Power in Late Nineteenth-century Ireland* (Manchester and New York: Manchester University Press, 2006)

— and Peter Gray (eds), *Poverty and Welfare in Ireland, 1838–1948* (Dublin: Irish Academic Press, 2011)

—, 'Writing for Relief in Late Nineteenth-century Dublin: Personal applications to the Mansion House Fund in 1880', *Cultural and Social History*, vol. 14, no. 5, 2017, pp. 583–98

Crowley, John, Donal Ó Drisceoil and Mike Murphy (eds), *Atlas of the Irish Revolution* (Cork: Cork University Press, 2017)

Curti, Merle, *American Philanthropy Abroad* (New Brunswick, NJ: Rutgers University Press, 1963)

Curtis, Jr, L. Perry, *Apes and Angels: The Irishman in Victorian caricature* (Newton Abbot: David & Charles, 1971)

—, 'On Class and Class Conflict in the Land War', *Irish Economic and Social History*, vol. 8, 1981, pp. 86–94

—, 'Landlord Responses to the Irish Land War, 1879–87', *Éire-Ireland*, vol. 38, nos 3–4, Fall/Winter 2003, pp. 134–88

Dare, Robert (ed.), *Food, Power and Community* (Adelaide: Wakefield Press, 1999)

Davitt, Michael, *The Fall of Feudalism in Ireland or the Story of the Land League Revolution* (London and New York: Harper & Brothers, 1904)

de Nie, Michael, *The Eternal Paddy: Irish identity and the British press, 1798–1882* (Madison: University of Wisconsin Press, 2004)

Devlin, Judith and Ronan Fanning (eds), *Religion and Rebellion: Papers read before the 22nd Irish conference of historians, held at University College Dublin, 18–22 May 1995 (Historical studies XX)* (Dublin: UCD Press, 1997)

*Distress in Ireland: Extracts from correspondence published by the Central Relief Committee of the Society of Friends, no. 1* (Dublin, 1847)

Donnelly, Jr, James S., *The Land and the People of Nineteenth-century Cork: The rural economy and the land question* (London and Boston: Routledge & Kegan Paul, 1975)

——, 'The Rightboy Movement, 1785-8', *Studia Hibernica*, vols 17-18, 1977-8, pp. 120-202

——, 'The Whiteboy Movement, 1761-5', *Irish Historical Studies*, vol. 21, no. 81, March 1978, pp. 20-54

——, 'Irish Agrarian Rebellion: The Whiteboys of 1769-76', *Proceedings of the Royal Irish Academy. Section C: Archaeology, Celtic studies, history, linguistics, literature*, vol. 83c, 1983, pp. 293-331

——, 'The Marian Shrine of Knock: The first decade', *Éire-Ireland*, vol. 28, no. 2, 1993, pp. 54-99

——, *Captain Rock: The Irish agrarian rebellion of 1821-1824* (Madison: University of Wisconsin Press, 2009)

Dooley, Terence, 'Irish Land Questions, 1879-1923', in Thomas Bartlett (ed.), *The Cambridge History of Ireland*. Volume IV: 1880 to the Present (Cambridge: Cambridge University Press, 2018), pp. 117-44

Edwards, R. Dudley and T. Desmond Williams (eds), *The Great Famine: Studies in Irish history, 1845-52* (Dublin: Browne & Nolan, 1956)

Fahy, M. de Lourdes, 'Mother M. Aloysius Doyle (1820-1908)', *Journal of the Galway Archaeological and Historical Society*, vol. 36, 1977-8, pp. 70-7

Feingold, William L., *The Revolt of the Tenantry: The transformation of local government in Ireland 1872-1886* (Boston: North-Eastern University Press, 1984)

——, 'Land League Power: The Tralee Poor Law election of 1881', in Samuel Clark and James S. Donnelly, Jr (eds), *Irish Peasants: Violence and political unrest, 1780-1914* (Manchester: Manchester University Press, 1983), pp. 285-310

'FitzGerald, John David, Baron FitzGerald of Kilmarnock (1816-89)', rev. Sinéad Agnew, *Oxford Dictionary of National Biography* (Oxford: Oxford University Press, 2004), https://www.oxforddnb.com/view/10.1093/ref:odnb/9780198614128.001.0001/odnb-9780198614128-e-9569

Fitzmaurice, George, *The Moonlighter*, in George Fitzmaurice, *Five Plays* (London and Dublin: Maunsell & Co., 1914)

Fitzpatrick, David, 'Class, Family and Rural Unrest in Nineteenth-century Ireland', in P.J. Drudy (ed.), *Irish Studies, 2. Ireland: Land, politics and people* (Cambridge: Cambridge University Press, 1982), pp. 37-75

Fitz-Simon, Christopher, *'Buffoonery and Easy Sentiment': Popular Irish plays in the decade prior to the opening of the Abbey Theatre* (Dublin: Carysfort Press, 2011)

Fodey, Joe, 'The Creation of the Irish National Foresters Benefit Society, 1877', *History Ireland*, vol. 27, no. 2, March–April 2019, pp. 24–6

Forbes, R.B., *The Voyage of the Jamestown on Her Errand of Mercy* (Boston: Eastburn Press, 1847)

Foster, R.F., *Charles Stewart Parnell: The man and his family* (Hassocks, Sussex: Harvester Press, 1976, 1979)

——, 'To the Northern Counties Station: Lord Randolph Churchill and the prelude to the orange card', in F.S.L. Lyons and R.A.J. Hawkins (eds), *Ireland Under the Union: Varieties of tension. Essays in honour of T.W. Moody* (Oxford: Clarendon Press, 1980), pp. 237–87

Garvin, Tom, *The Evolution of Irish Nationalist Politics* (Dublin: Gill & Macmillan, 1981)

——, 'Defenders, Ribbonmen and Others: Underground political networks in pre-Famine Ireland', in C.H.E. Philpin (ed.), *Nationalism and Popular Protest in Ireland* (Cambridge: Cambridge University Press, 1987), pp. 219–44

Geary, Laurence M., 'The Australasian Response to the Irish Crisis, 1879–80', in Oliver MacDonagh and W.F. Mandle (eds), *Irish-Australian Studies: Papers delivered at the fifth Irish-Australian conference* (Canberra: ANU Press, 1989), pp. 99–126

——, 'What People Died of During the Famine', in Cormac Ó Gráda (ed.), *Famine 150. Commemorative lecture series* (Dublin: Teagasc/UCD, 1997), pp. 95–111

——, 'A Psychological and Sociological Analysis of the Great Famine in Ireland', in Robert Dare (ed.), *Food, Power and Community* (Adelaide: Wakefield Press, 1999), pp. 181–92

——, '"The Whole Country Was in Motion": Mendicancy and vagrancy in pre-Famine Ireland', in Jacqueline Hill and Colm Lennon (eds), *Luxury and Austerity: Historical studies XXI* (Dublin: UCD Press, 1999), pp. 121–36

——, *Medicine and Charity in Ireland, 1718–1851* (Dublin: UCD Press, 2004)

——, 'The Medical Profession, Health Care and the Poor Law in Nineteenth-century Ireland', in Virginia Crossman and Peter Gray (eds), *Poverty and Welfare in Ireland, 1838–1948* (Dublin: Irish Academic Press, 2011), pp. 189–206

——, 'The Noblest Offering that Nation Ever Made to Nation': American philanthropy and the Great Famine in Ireland', *Éire-Ireland*, vol. 48, nos 3–4, 2013, pp. 103–28

Gilley, Sheridan, 'The Roman Catholic Church and the Nineteenth-century Irish Diaspora', *Journal of Ecclesiastical History*, vol. 35, no. 2, 1984, pp. 188–207

Goldstrom, J.M. and L.A. Clarkson (eds), *Irish Population, Economy, and Society: Essays in honour of the late K.H. Connell* (Oxford: Clarendon Press, 1981)

Gray, Peter (ed.), *Victoria's Ireland? Irishness and Britishness, 1837–1901* (Dublin: Four Courts Press, 2004)

Green, James J., 'American Catholics and the Irish Land League, 1879–1882', *Catholic Historical Review*, vol. 35, no. 1, April 1949, pp. 19–42

Grene, Nicholas and Chris Morash (eds), *The Oxford Handbook of Modern Irish Theatre* (Oxford: Oxford University Press, 2016)

Harden, Victoria A., 'Typhus, Epidemic', in Kenneth F. Kiple (ed.), *The Cambridge World History of Human Disease* (Cambridge: Cambridge University Press, 1993), pp. 1080–4

Hardy, Anne, 'Relapsing Fever', in Kenneth F. Kiple (ed.), *The Cambridge World History of Human Disease* (Cambridge: Cambridge University Press, 1993), pp. 967–70

Hawkins, Richard, 'Government Versus Secret Societies: The Parnell era', in T. Desmond Williams (ed.), *Secret Societies in Ireland* (Dublin: Gill & Macmillan, 1973), pp. 100–12

Healy, T.M., *Letters and Leaders of My Day*, 2 vols (London: Thornton Butterworth, 1928)

Herlihy, Jim, *The Dublin Metropolitan Police: A short history and genealogical guide* (Dublin: Four Courts Press, 2001)

Hill, Jacqueline and Colm Lennon (eds), *Luxury and Austerity: Historical studies XXI* (Dublin: UCD Press, 1999)

Howlin, Niamh, *Juries in Ireland: Lay persons and the law in the long nineteenth century* (Dublin: Four Courts Press, 2017)

Hughes, Kyle and Donald M. MacRaild (eds), *Crime, Violence and the Irish in the Nineteenth Century* (Liverpool: Liverpool University Press, 2017)

——, *Ribbon Societies in Nineteenth-century Ireland and Its Diaspora: The persistence of tradition* (Liverpool: Liverpool University Press, 2018)

Hynes, Eugene, *Knock: The Virgin's apparition in nineteenth-century Ireland* (Cork: Cork University Press, 2008)

Iltis, Judith, 'Chisholm, Caroline (1808–1877)', *Australian Dictionary of Biography* http://adb.anu.edu.au/biography/chisholm-caroline-1894/text2231

James, Stephanie, 'Distress in Ireland 1879–80: The activation of the South Australian community', in Philip Payton and Andrekos Varnava (eds), *Australia, Migration and Empire: Immigrants in a globalised world* (Basingstoke: Palgrave Macmillan, 2019), pp. 119–50

Janis, Ely M., *A Greater Ireland: The Land League and transatlantic nationalism in Gilded Age America* (Madison: University of Wisconsin Press, 2015)

——, 'Petticoat Revolutionaries: Gender, ethnic nationalism, and the Irish Ladies' Land League in the United States', *Journal of American Ethnic History*, vol. 27, no. 2, 2008, pp. 5–27

Jennings, Catherine, 'Tuke ... the Quaker Philanthropist and the Free Emigration Scheme in Connemara, 1882', in *Mr Tuke's Fund: Connemara emigration in the 1880s. Ireland's forgotten famine* (Clifden: Clifden Heritage, 2012)

Jordan, Jr, Donald E., *Land and Popular Politics in Ireland: County Mayo from the plantation to the Land War* (Cambridge: Cambridge University Press, 1982)

——, 'The Irish National League and the "Unwritten Law": Rural protest and nation-building in Ireland 1882–1890', *Past and Present*, vol. 158, February 1998, pp. 146–71

Kelleher, Margaret, *The Maamtrasna Murders: Language, life and death in nineteenth-century Ireland* (Dublin: UCD Press, 2018)

Kelley, Tom and Linde Lunney, 'Nangle, Edward Walter', in James McGuire and James Quinn (eds), *Dictionary of Irish Biography* (Cambridge: Cambridge University Press, 2009), https://www.dib.ie/biography/nangle-edward-walter-a6133

Kelly, Matthew, 'Radical Nationalisms, 1882–1916', in Bartlett (ed.), *The Cambridge History of Ireland*, vol. IV, pp. 33–61

Kennedy, Padraic, '"The Indispensable Informer": Daniel O'Sullivan Goula and the Phoenix Society, 1858-9', *Éire-Ireland*, vol. 45, nos 3–4, 2010, pp. 147–83

Keogh, Richard A., '"Why, It's Like a '98 Trial": The Irish judiciary and the Fenian trials, 1865–1866', in Hughes and MacRaild (eds), *Crime, Violence and the Irish in the Nineteenth Century*, pp. 131–48

Kinealy, Christine, *Charity and the Great Hunger in Ireland: The kindness of strangers* (London: Bloomsbury, 2013)

—— and Gerard Moran (eds), *The History of the Irish Famine*: 'Fallen leaves of humanity'. *Famine in Ireland before and after the Great Famine* (Abingdon, Oxon: Routledge, 2018)

Kiple, Kenneth F. (ed.), *The Cambridge World History of Human Disease* (Cambridge: Cambridge University Press, 1993)

Laird, Heather, 'Decentring the Irish Land War: Women, politics and the private sphere', in Campbell and Varley (eds), *Land Questions in Modern Ireland*, pp. 175–93

Laracy, Hugh, 'Moran, Patrick', Dictionary of New Zealand Biography, first published in 1993. Te Ara - The Encyclopedia of New Zealand, https://teara.govt.nz/en/biographies/2m55/moran-patrick

Lee, Joseph, 'The Ribbonmen', in Williams (ed.), *Secret Societies in Ireland*, pp. 26–35

Lloyd, Clifford, *Ireland Under the Land League: A narrative of personal experience* (Edinburgh and London: William Blackwood, 1892)

Lucey, Donnacha Seán, *Land, Popular Politics and Agrarian Violence in Ireland: The case of County Kerry, 1872–86* (Dublin: UCD Press, 2011)

——, 'Power, Politics and Poor Relief During the Irish Land War, 1879–82', *Irish Historical Studies*, vol. 37, November 2011, pp. 584–98

Luddy, Maria, *Women and Philanthropy in Nineteenth-century Ireland* (Cambridge: Cambridge University Press, 1995)

—— (ed.), *The Nun of Kenmare: An autobiography* (London: Routledge/Thoemmes Press, 1998)

Lyons, F.S.L., *John Dillon: A biography* (Chicago: Chicago University Press, 1968)

——, *Charles Stewart Parnell* (London: Collins, 1977)

—— and R.A.J. Hawkins (eds), *Ireland Under the Union: Varieties of tension. Essays in honour of T.W. Moody* (Oxford: Clarendon Press, 1980)

MacArthur, William P., 'Medical History of the Famine', in Edwards and Williams (eds), *The Great Famine*, pp. 263–315

Mac Curtain, Margaret, 'Cusack, Margaret Anne [name in religion Mary Francis Clare, called the Nun of Kenmare] (1829–1899)', *Oxford Dictionary of National Biography* (Oxford: Oxford University Press, 2004), https://www.oxforddnb.com/view/10.1093/ref:odnb/9780198614128.001.0001/odnb-9780198614128-e-45792

MacDonagh, Oliver and W.F. Mandle (eds), *Irish-Australian Studies: Papers delivered at the fifth Irish-Australian conference* (Canberra: ANU Press, 1989)

MacDonagh, Oliver, 'Ambiguity in Nationalism: The case of Ireland', in Brady (ed.), *Interpreting Irish History*, pp. 105–21

Mac Suibhne, Breandán, *The End of Outrage: Post-Famine adjustment in rural Ireland* (Oxford: Oxford University Press, 2017)

—— and Jonathan Wooding, 'Hunting Down an Informer', *The Irish Times*, 16 June 2018, Ticket, pp. 25–7

Magray, Mary Peckham, *The Transforming Power of the Nuns: Women, religion, and cultural change in Ireland, 1750–1900* (New York and Oxford: Oxford University Press, 1998)

McCarthy, Philomena, *The Nun of Kenmare: The true facts* (Kenmare: St Clare's Convent, 1989)

McCartney, Donal and Pauric Travers, *The Ivy Leaf: The Parnells remembered* (Dublin: UCD Press, 2006)

McGarry, Fearghal and James McConnell (eds), *The Black Hand of Republicanism: Fenianism in modern Ireland* (Dublin: Irish Academic Press, 2009)

McGeachie, James, 'Science, Politics and the Irish Literary Revival: Reassessing "Dr Sigerson" as polymath and public intellectual', in Cox and Luddy (eds), *Cultures of Care in Irish Medical History*, pp. 113–40

McGee, Owen, *The IRB: The Irish Republican Brotherhood, from the Land League to Sinn Féin* (Dublin: Four Courts Press, 2005)

McGowan, Mark, 'Boyle, Patrick', in *Dictionary of Canadian Biography*, vol. 13, University of Toronto/Université Laval, 2003, http://www.biographi.ca/en/bio/boyle_patrick_13E.html

McGuire, James and James Quinn (eds), *Dictionary of Irish Biography* (Cambridge: Cambridge University Press, 2009)

McL. Coté, Jane, *Fanny and Anna Parnell: Ireland's patriot sisters* (Houndmills: Macmillan, 1991)

Moffitt, Miriam, *Soupers and Jumpers: The Protestant mission in Connemara, 1848–1937* (Dublin: Nonsuch, 2008)

——, *Society for Irish Church Missions to the Roman Catholics* (Manchester and New York: Manchester University Press, 2010)

Molloy, Kevin, 'Victorians, Historians and Irish History: A reading of the *New Zealand Tablet*, 1873–1903', in Patterson (ed.), *The Irish in New Zealand*, pp. 153–70

Moody, T.W., *Davitt and Irish Revolution, 1846–82* (Oxford: Oxford University Press, 1994)

—— and Richard Hawkins (eds), *Florence Arnold-Forster's Irish Journal* (Oxford: Clarendon Press, 1988)

[Moore, Thomas], *Memoirs of Captain Rock, the Celebrated Irish Chieftain, with Some Account of His Ancestors, Written by Himself* (London: Longman, Hurst, Rees, Orme, Browne & Green, 1824)

Moore, Thomas, *Memoirs of Captain Rock, the Celebrated Irish Chieftain, with Some Account of His Ancestors, Written by Himself*, edited and introduced by Emer Nolan, with annotations by Seamus Deane (Dublin: Field Day, 2008)

Moran, Gerard, 'Famine and the Land War: Relief and distress in Mayo, 1879-1881', *Cathair na Mart: Journal of the Westport Historical Society*, vol. 5, no. 1, 1985, pp. 54–66; vol. 6, no. 1, 1986, pp. 111–27

——, '"Near Famine": The crisis in the west of Ireland, 1879–82', *Irish Studies Review*, vol. 5, no. 18, Spring 1997, pp. 14–21

——, '"Near Famine": The Roman Catholic Church and the subsistence crisis of 1879–82', *Studia Hibernica*, vol. 32, 2002–3, pp. 155–77

Murray, A.C., 'Agrarian Violence and Nationalism in Nineteenth-century Ireland: The myth of Ribbonism', *Irish Economic and Social History*, vol. 13, 1986, pp. 56–73

O'Brien, Georgina (ed.), *The Reminiscences of the Right Hon. Lord O'Brien (of Kilfenora) Lord Chief Justice of Ireland* (London: Edward Arnold, 1916)

[O'Brien, William], *Christmas on the Galtees: An inquiry into the conditions of the tenantry of Mr Nathaniel Buckley, by the special correspondent of the Freeman's Journal* (Dublin: The Central Tenants' Defence Association, 1878)

O'Brien, William and Desmond Ryan (eds), *Devoy's Post Bag, 1871–1928*, vol. 1 (Dublin: Fallon, 1948)

O'Farrell, Patrick, *The Irish in Australia* (Sydney: New South Wales University Press, 1986)

Ó Gráda, Cormac (ed.), *Famine 150. Commemorative lecture series* (Dublin: Teagasc/ UCD, 1997)

Ó Tuathaigh, Gearóid, 'Irish Land Questions in the State of the Union', in Campbell and Varley (eds), *Land Questions in Modern Ireland*, pp. 3–24

—, 'Introduction: Ireland 1800-2016: Negotiating sovereignty and freedom', in Thomas Bartlett (ed.), *The Cambridge History of Ireland. Volume IV: 1880 to the Present* (Cambridge: Cambridge University Press, 2018), pp. 1–29

Palmer, Norman Dunbar, *The Irish Land League Crisis* (New Haven: Yale University Press, 1940)

Parfitt, Richard, '"Oh, What Matter, when for Erin Dear We Fall?": Music and Irish nationalism, 1848-1913', *Irish Studies Review*, vol. 23, no. 4, 2015, pp. 480–94

Parnell, C.S., 'The Irish Land Question', *North American Review*, vol. CXXX, no. 1, April 1880, pp. 388-406

Parnell, Fanny, *The Hovels of Ireland* (New York: Thomas Kelly, 1880)

Patterson, Brad (ed.), *The Irish in New Zealand: Historical contexts and perspectives* (Wellington: Stout Research Centre for New Zealand Studies, Victoria University of Wellington, 2002)

Payton, Philip and Andrekos Varnava (eds), *Australia, Migration and Empire: Immigrants in a globalised world* (Basingstoke: Palgrave Macmillan, 2019)

Philpin, C.H.E. (ed.), *Nationalism and Popular Protest in Ireland* (Cambridge: Cambridge University Press, 1987)

Póirtéir, Cathal (ed.), *The Great Irish Famine* (Cork: Mercier Press, 1995)

Pomfret, John E., *The Struggle for Land in Ireland, 1800-1923* (Princeton: Princeton University Press, 1930)

Post, John D., *Food Shortage, Climatic Variability, and Epidemic Disease in Pre-Industrial Europe: The mortality peak in the early 1740s* (Ithaca and London: Cornell University Press, 1985)

Redpath, James, *Talks about Ireland* (New York: P.J. Kenedy, 1881)

Reid, T. Wemyss, *Life of the Right Honourable William Edward Forster*, 2 vols (London: Chapman & Hall, 1888)

*Report of the Central Committee for Relief of Distress in Ireland, with Appendices* (Dublin: Browne & Nolan, 1864)

Robins, Joseph, *The Miasma: Epidemic and panic in nineteenth-century Ireland* (Dublin: Institute of Public Administration, 1995)

Robinson, Henry, *Memories: Wise and otherwise* (London and New York: Cassell, 1923)

Robinson, Solveig C., 'Fullerton [née Leveson-Gower], Lady Georgiana Charlotte (1812–85)', *Oxford Dictionary of National Biography*, https://www.oxforddnb.com/view/10.1093/ref:odnb/9780198614128.001.0001/odnb-9780198614128-e-10242

Roddy, Sarah, 'Spiritual Imperialism and the Mission of the Irish Race: The Catholic Church and emigration from nineteenth-century Ireland', *Irish Historical Studies*, vol. 38, no. 152, November 2013, pp. 600–19

Rynne, Frank, 'Permanent Revolutionaries: The IRB and the Land War in west Cork', in Fearghal McGarry and James McConnell (eds), *The Black Hand of Republicanism: Fenianism in modern Ireland* (Dublin: Irish Academic Press, 2009), pp. 55–71

——, 'Arrests Made Under the Protection of Person and Property Act, March 1881–July 1882', in John Crowley, Donal Ó Drisceoil and Mike Murphy (eds), *Atlas of the Irish Revolution* (Cork: Cork University Press, 2017), pp. 56–9

Slaughter, Howard K., *The Plays of George Fitzmaurice: Folk plays* (Dublin: Dolmen Press, 1969)

Smyth, William J., 'Conflict, Reaction and Control in Nineteenth-century Ireland: The archaeology of revolution', in John Crowley, Donal Ó Drisceoil and Mike Murphy (eds), *Atlas of the Irish Revolution* (Cork: Cork University Press, 2017), pp. 21–55

Solow, Barbara L., *The Land Question and the Irish Economy, 1870–1903* (Cambridge, MA: Harvard University Press, 1971)

*The Irish Crisis of 1879–80. Proceedings of the Dublin Mansion House Relief Committee, 1880* (Dublin: Browne & Nolan, 1881)

Townshend, Charles, *Political Violence in Ireland: Government and resistance since 1848* (Oxford: Clarendon Press, 1983)

Tuke, James H., *Irish Distress and Its Remedies: The land question. A visit to Donegal and Connaught in the spring of 1880* (London: W. Ridgway, 1880)

Vaughan, W.E. (ed.), *A New History of Ireland. Volume 5: Ireland under the Union, I: 1801–1870* (Oxford: Clarendon Press, 1989)

——, *Landlords and Tenants in Mid-Victorian Ireland* (Oxford: Clarendon Press, 1994)

—— (ed.), *A New History of Ireland. Volume 6: Ireland under the Union, II: 1870–1921* (Oxford: Clarendon Press, 1996)

——, *Murder Trials in Ireland, 1836–1914* (Dublin: Four Courts Press, 2009)

Wall, Maureen, 'The Whiteboys', in Williams (ed.), *Secret Societies in Ireland*, pp. 13–25.

Ward, Susan Hayes, *George H. Hepworth: Preacher, journalist, friend of the people. The story of his life* (New York: E.P. Dutton, 1903)

Warwick-Haller, Sally, *William O'Brien and the Irish Land War* (Dublin: Irish Academic Press, 1990)

Whelan, Irene, 'The Stigma of Souperism', in Cathal Póirtéir (ed.), *The Great Irish Famine* (Cork: Mercier Press, 1995), pp. 135–54

White, John, 'The Cusack Papers: New evidence on the Knock apparition', *History Ireland*, vol. 4, no. 4, 1996, pp. 39–44

Williams, T. Desmond (ed.), *Secret Societies in Ireland* (Dublin: Gill & Macmillan, 1973)

Woods, C.J., 'Doran, Charles Guilfoyle', in McGuire and Quinn (eds), *Dictionary of Irish Biography*, https://www.dib.ie/biography/doran-charles-guilfoyle-a2715

# INDEX

Illustrations are indicated by page numbers in bold.